Planning with Complexity

University of Liverpool

Planning, public policy, and administration are increasingly challenged by complexity, fragmentation, uncertainty, and global processes. Traditional approaches do not provide solutions to wicked problems. These challenges are stimulating alternative theory and practices around the world.

Integrating existing theories and research from case studies, the authors argue that collaborative decision-making is a powerful method for getting beyond division and conflict to craft policy solutions and generate capacity for long term sustainability. They outline a new theory of collaborative rationality to help make sense of the new practices. They inquire in detail how collaborative rationality works, the theories that inform it, and the potential and pitfalls of democracy in the twenty-first century.

This scholar–practitioner author team, each with over 30 years of experience, has produced a reader-friendly guide that reflects a unique synergy between theory and practice. This book is essential reading for students, educators, scholars, and reflective practitioners in the fields of urban planning, public policy, political science, and public administration. It provides insights that can move both practice and scholarship to the new level required to meet the challenges of an age of complexity and help ensure democratic, effective, and just public decisions.

Judith E. Innes is Professor in the Department of City and Regional Planning at the University of California, Berkeley, USA.

David E. Booher is Senior Policy Advisor and Adjunct Professor at the Center for Collaborative Policy, California State University, Sacramento, USA.

Planning with Complexity

An introduction to collaborative
rationality for public policy

Judith E. Innes and David E. Booher

Routledge
Taylor & Francis Group

LONDON AND NEW YORK

First published 2010
by Routledge
2 Park Square, Milton Park, Abingdon, Oxon OX14 4RN

Simultaneously published in the USA and Canada
by Routledge
270 Madison Avenue, New York, NY 10016, USA

Routledge is an imprint of the Taylor & Francis Group, an informa business

© 2010 Judith E. Innes and David E. Booher

Typeset in Univers by
Keystroke, Tettenhall, Wolverhampton
Printed by
Edwards Brothers, Inc.

British Library Cataloguing in Publication Data
A catalogue record for this book is available from the British Library

Library of Congress Cataloging-in-Publication Data
Innes, Judith Eleanor.
    Planning with complexity / Judith E. Innes and David E. Booher. — 1st ed.
       p. cm.
    Includes bibliographical references.
    1. Community development, Urban. 2. Political planning. 3. Social participation.
    I. Booher, David E. II. Title.
    HN49.C6I536 2009
    307.1′416—dc22   2009022752

ISBN10: 0–415–77931–6 (hbk)
ISBN10: 0–415–77932–4 (pbk)
ISBN10: 0–203–86430–1 (ebk)

ISBN13: 978–0–415–77931–9 (hbk)
ISBN13: 978–0–415–77932–6 (pbk)
ISBN13: 978–0–203–86430–2 (ebk)

Contents

Preface

The book you have in your hand culminates a journey that began over forty years ago (though time may show it is merely a way station). The journey mirrors developments in planning and policy making during that time – the effort to integrate theory and practice, the search for more effective ways to conduct policy, and the growing role of collaboration. This journey began in 1967 when author Innes was a student at MIT in Urban Studies and Planning. She took a class from Jack Howard, the respected founder of the department and planning consultant for the Boston Redevelopment Authority. In that capacity he had advised the city to tear down the urban village in Boston's West End which inspired another colleague, Herbert Gans to write a book (Gans 1962) that discredited the redevelopment idea. Howard's course offered a list of "best practices" for land use planning, which he compiled into large notebooks for students. At the end of the class he told students that he had given them the best that he knew about practice but, he added with tears in his eyes, his generation of planners had failed. He hoped that ours would do better. At that moment Innes decided that it would be her project to find a new mode of practice. She tossed out the notebook and began her search.

At about the same time, Booher was a student at the University of Tennessee, involved as an activist in the civil rights movement, as well as in the free speech and anti-Vietnam war movements. He helped start the University of Tennessee chapter of the American Civil Liberties Union and served as its president. During this time he found himself negotiating among university administrators and other student activists to prevent violent confrontations during free speech activities. This was the beginning of his evolution through many professional roles to his current one as designer and facilitator of collaborative processes. Throughout his career he has sought to understand his experiences and the frustrating challenges of trying to get something accomplished.

Innes' intellectual journey began before MIT, when she was a legislative assistant to a Congressman, optimistically hoping to help him make good decisions. What she soon discovered was that although staff could provide him with the best information the nation had to offer, when it came to voting, he called on trusted cronies. Vast amounts of information gathered dust, while legislators felt they did not have the information that would help them decide. This experience led her to enroll in MIT's program, where she thought she would learn how to inform policy and planning more effectively. She began by taking rigorous quantitative methods courses, but discovered these methods could not be applied to the urban social problems that interested her because there were no agreed on understandings of the issues, much less measures of key phenomena. Therefore she focused her dissertation on the history and use of several national level indicators that appeared to be influential. What she learned was that the few indicators that directly influenced policy had been developed collaboratively by the major policy players. Moreover, policy was made de facto as part of the deliberation over measurement concepts (de Neufville 1975). These findings challenged assumptions that had been an integral part of her graduate education and she began to search for a new way of framing and understanding how planning and policy processes actually proceed.

At the University of California she delved into this task in her teaching, exploring a variety of perspectives on knowledge and multiple research methodologies, as well as on organizational behavior and the emergent field of implementation. One of her early papers brought these topics together. She and her co-author (de Neufville and Christensen 1980) contended that the then popular idea of optimizing, or finding the one best solution, did not work because the conditions of certainty required did not apply for most policy problems. The problems were wicked ones with multiple and conflicting goals and surrounded by technological uncertainty. Trying to apply the then popular optimizing ideal led to premature closure on solutions and the institutionalization of arbitrary rules and procedures. The optimizing framework entailed false assumptions of certainty and static contexts.

Innes' alternative strategy was to seek out qualitative understandings of whether and how programs worked. This led her to study how and whether new state growth management programs in the 1980s were and were not working. What she found was that, regardless of whether the program was built on regulatory bureaucracy, judicial decision making, or traditional planning, some form of collaborative dialogue was necessary for implementation (Innes 1992a). These findings led her to seek out collaborative policy making dialogues as a research focus. She led a study commissioned by the California Legislature (Innes et al. 1994) examining 13 cases using consensus building as a strategy to manage growth. The report concluded that consensus building had emerged as an important method of deliberation which had produced agreements, innovations and social, political and intellectual capital among previously warring stakeholders (Gruber 1994).

At about the same time she observed that others in planning and public policy were also studying practice and focusing on deliberation and communication. It seemed a timely moment to declare the emergence of the new paradigm in planning thought that she had been looking for since MIT. She wrote an article for the *Journal of Planning Education and Research* in the hope that the declaration itself would focus attention on this cluster of scholarship, encourage discussion, and further the development of this stream of thought. This article argued that the emergent paradigm relied on grounded theorizing using qualitative, interpretive analysis of what planners do, rather than on logical deductive quantitative analysis (Innes 1995). This perspective, she argued, saw planning as an interactive, communicative activity and offered critical reflections on the practices it documented. This article has been more widely cited than any of her other work, both by those who agreed and those who disagreed. A debate had begun. Fourteen years later, after extensive additional case study research, she was ready to write this book.

Booher has been a reflective practitioner over the years, paying attention to how his strategies worked and why and continuing to remain abreast of the relevant world of ideas. After graduating from the University of Tennessee he continued to believe that social movements were important to changing policy, but decided to seek a more sustainable approach to a career. He put this idea into motion first by obtaining master's degrees in political science and planning, and then by working as a planner for the Tennessee State Planning Office. In this role he again experienced the potential for collaboration when he organized stakeholder processes to address several controversial planning issues. But during the 1970s there was no clear practice model for collaboration in planning. Soon he decided, just as Innes had, that public policy change did not flow from the expert advice provided to decision makers. He concluded that effectiveness in policy making depended on skillful navigation of politics.

He moved to California, where he saw cutting edge planning issues emerging, and built a career as a policy consultant and lobbyist. During this time he helped shape many planning laws relating to housing, formal plans, infrastructure, environmental impact analysis, and fiscal policy. By the mid 1980s he was rethinking this approach as well because he was increasingly frustrated with the adversarial approach to policy making which so often resulted in impasse. At best the approach tinkered at the edges of critical planning issues and, at worst, resulted in bad policy decisions. Despite numerous laws, California was unable to address such problems as planning and financing infrastructure, an unworkable general plan framework, dysfunctional fiscal policy, and unsustainable management of the water supply – all of which were central to the challenge of managing growth in this diverse and changing state.

At about this time Booher read two books which changed his professional direction: *Getting to Yes* and *Breaking the Impasse* (Fisher and Ury 1981; Susskind and Cruikshank 1987). He recalled his early experiences with collaboration in Tennessee and began to experiment with interest-based, mutual gains negotiation and consensus building in his legislative consulting role. He began trying to get stakeholders together to address some of the legislative issues that were controversial, rather than using traditional lobbying approaches to push through specific proposals. He was encouraged by the results because stalemates were broken and creative legislation was crafted that had not been conceived before. When a stalemate emerged in the legislature in 1988, with 59 competing legislative proposals for state growth management programs on the table, he suggested convening a consensus project that would engage the many conflicting stakeholder groups. It would try to reach an agreement on legislation, and it would report to the legislative leadership. Everyone agreed to try this, and, with funding from the Hewlett Foundation and other private parties, the Growth Management Consensus Project (GMCP) got underway. From this experience he learned a great deal about the potential and pitfalls of collaboration.

Innes and Booher's paths first crossed when she interviewed him for her study of the GMCP (Innes 1994a). They began to develop shared understandings of collaborative policy making as she continued to follow other collaborative projects led by Susan Sherry, Director of the newly created California Center for Public Dispute Resolution at California State University Sacramento.[1] Booher left politics to work full time on collaboration as a practitioner, researcher, and teacher at the Center. Innes came with a sociological perspective and he with a political perspective, and we shared an interest in learning how to create effective change. Together we helped each other understand what happened and why and shared theory, ideas and practices we had learned along the course of our careers. This book represents a synthesis, or perhaps more accurately, a synergy of our thinking, practice, and research such that the combination is much greater than its parts.

We have not traveled this journey alone, but in the company of many other scholars and practitioners whose creative work has continually informed our thinking. These include the community of so-called communicative planning theorists[2] and of the deliberative policy analysis and public administration scholars.[3] Though most started from different places and followed unique paths, many have been through learning processes and evolution similar to ours. A 1996 panel at the joint meetings of the Association of Collegiate Schools of Planning and the Association of European Schools of Planning in Toronto demonstrated this vividly. Four planning scholars, each starting from a different disciplinary background – Patsy Healey, John Forester, John Bryson, and Judith Innes – plotted out their intellectual journeys showing how they all ultimately converged. This convergence we believe has occurred because many scholars and professionals have become disillusioned about the adequacy of the traditional model for advising officials in contemporary times and frustrated with rigid, one-size-fits-all bureaucratic procedures and public officials so buffeted by multiple constituencies that they are unable or unwilling to take strong action. Many professionals, in our observation, have begun to search for new ways of thinking, gathering evidence, and deciding, turning their attention particularly to communication and deliberation among citizens, stakeholders, and professionals. Collaborative practices today are spreading and evolving along with theory, as the potential players learn more about how they work and how they can improve the outcomes of planning and policy. We offer this book as a contribution to this evolution.

Change will be hard and slow in coming. The biggest obstacle to change is the powerful mental model that grips professionals and scholars in policy fields. The assumption is that their job is to "fix" problems and meet goals. They need to find answers and to sell them to decision makers. But the approach we lay out in this book is about creating and implementing new forms of deliberation among many players seeking to get better together and about developing public and private actions that improve our situation and make our societies more resilient. Because the world is so complex and changing, problems will never be "fixed," though they may be reframed, new actions may be undertaken, new players may be empowered, and new purposes identified and pursued. For the policy professional the mode of operating we put forward is difficult to grasp, much less to carry out. It means letting go of the hope to be a leader in finding the "right" solutions and making sure they happen. It means providing collaborative leadership for change in which many others will play a part. Our readers should not look for easy answers or prescriptions in this book. What they will find here are reflections on many aspects of collaborative decision making that we hope will enrich their understandings and make them more capable as they confront unique conditions, combinations of issues, and players. This book is about making new steps and ultimately moving beyond collaboration to creating new forms of practice and governance.

Notes

1   In 2000 the Center was renamed the Center for Collaborative Policy better to reflect what it was being asked to do by its public clients. In addition to helping adversaries resolve public disputes, it was helping agencies, stakeholders and the public to use collaborative processes to improve public policy outcomes.

2   There are more such theorists than we can list here, but those whose work has had most influence on our thinking over the years include Patsy Healey, John Forester, Charles Hoch, Lawrence Susskind, James Throgmorton, Howell Baum, Jean Hillier, Richard Margerum, Judith Allen, Connie Ozawa, Leonie Sandercock, Tore Sager, Thomas Harper and Stanley Stein.

3   These include for example, Maarten Hajer, Frank Fischer, Dvora Yanow, John Dryzek, Nancy Roberts and John Bryson.

Acknowledgments

This book was made possible by the contributions along the way of many others. Innes' colleague, the late Judith Gruber, conducted substantial research and did intensive interviewing on several of the projects reported here. She contributed to sharpening our thinking through many dialogues over the years. Her insights permeate the book. Susan Sherry, Executive Director of the Center for Collaborative Policy at California State University Sacramento, has shown us how collaboration can be done for some of the most important and controversial policy issues in the state. Both of us have learned from watching her at work and talking with her and the other facilitators at the Center.

Many graduate students have done research as part of our projects and their theses over the years and have contributed their insights to the design and implementation of the research. Some have written sections of the original reports. These include most notably, Sarah Connick, who worked with Innes on water management issues. Others who have had an impact on our work include Robert Thompson, P. Anthony Brinkman, Ray Laraja, Catherine Hudzik, Jane Rongerude, and Gerardo Sandoval. Philip Olmstead helped with preparation of the final manuscript. We are grateful to all of these students.

An array of international colleagues commented on papers and panel presentations and challenged us in constructive dialogue both in meetings and in journals. There are far too many to list here, but we want especially to thank Patsy Healey, Lawrence Susskind, John Forester, Alessandro Balducci, and Charles Hoch for their helpful comments on some of the papers that went into the making of this volume. Similarly we benefited from the experience and wisdom of a number of practitioners, especially the members of the California Planning Roundtable.

Martin Bierbaum of the Municipal Land Use Center of the College of New Jersey, Jay Rothman of the ARIA Group and Jill Williams of the Andrus Foundation all provided us with substantial assistance by reviewing, correcting, and commenting on case studies in which they were involved.

Thanks finally to the generations of students in Innes' CP 281 planning theory class, who struggled over these ideas and whose insights and questions have led more than anything else to her evolving understandings and convinced her of the need for this book.

Glossary of acronyms

ABAG	Association of Bay Area Governments
ADR	Alternative dispute resolution
BAASC	Bay Area Alliance for Sustainable Communities
BAC	Bay Area Council
BART	Bay Area Rapid Transit
BATNA	Best Alternative to a Negotiated Agreement
BCDC	Bay Conservation and Development Commission
BDAC	Bay Delta Advisory Committee
BOR	Bureau of Reclamation
CA	Collaborative agreement
CAS	Complex adaptive system
CBDA	California Bay Delta Authority
CC	Community Council
CCII	Community Capital Investment Initiative
CCMP	Comprehensive conservation and management plan
CCP	Center for Collaborative Policy
CEQA	California Environmental Quality Act
CHI	Community Health Initiative
COG	Council of Government
CRI	Collaborative Regional Initiatives
CTA	California Teachers Association
DAD	Decide, Announce, Defend syndrome
DAT	Data Assessment Team
DIAD	Diversity, interdependence, authentic dialogue
DWR	Department of Water Resources
EBCRC	East Bay Conversion and Reinvestment Commission
EBMUD	East Bay Municipal Utility District
EIR	Environmental impact report
EJ	Environmental justice
EPA	Environmental Protection Agency

EWA	Environmental Water Account
FACA	Federal Advisory Committee Act
FMP	Fishery Management Plan
FOSC	Friends of Sausal Creek
GMCP	Growth Management Consensus Project
ISTEA	Intermodal Surface Transportation Efficiency Act of 1991
IURD	Institute of Urban and Regional Development
JPA	Joint Powers Agreement
KSSP	People's Science Movement
MOA	Memorandum of Agreement
MOU	Memorandum of Understanding
MTC	Metropolitan Transportation Commission
NEPA	National Environmental Policy Act
NGO	Non-governmental organization
NII	Neighborhood Improvement Initiative
NMFS	National Marine Fisheries Service
NOAA	National Oceanographic and Atmospheric Administration
Ops	Operations Group
OSP	Office of State Planning
Psi	Professional social inquiry
ROD	Record of Decision
RTP	Regional transportation plan
SBC	Sierra Business Council
SC	Steering Committee
SDD	San Diego Dialogue
SFEP	San Francisco Estuary Project
SPC	State Planning Commission
TAC	Technical Advisory Committee
TEK	Traditional ecological knowledge
TRET	Technical Review and Evaluation Team
UCSD	University of California San Diego
VMT	Vehicle miles traveled

1 Thinking differently for an age of complexity

The world we have created today as a result of our thinking thus far has problems which cannot be solved by thinking the way we thought when we created them.

Attributed to Albert Einstein

Water planning as a wicked problem

At the end of the 1980s, the Sacramento region of California faced daunting water resource challenges. The population was growing rapidly, placing new demands on the water supply. As it grew, so did the economy, making additional demands on the supply. At the same time the fisheries and ecosystems of the American and Sacramento Rivers, which have their confluence in Sacramento, were threatened by periods of insufficient flows. The County of Sacramento for a variety of reasons, litigated to block expansion of the City of Sacramento's water treatment plant. An active environmental community had long fought water agencies in the region when they sought to develop new water supplies. In this context the regional groundwater table had been subject to extensive and continuing overdraft, which was causing subsidence and water quality problems that could permanently damage the aquifers' capacity to store water. In addition the various water agencies in the region were in conflict. Some served agricultural users and others municipal and industrial users. Some relied on groundwater supplies and others relied primarily on surface water. Though these supplies are part of a common pool, they are regulated according to different principles, allocated in different ways, and subject to different levels of government. Efforts to develop a regional water plan had gone nowhere in the face of mutual suspicions among key players (Connick 2006).

This situation was a classic case of a wicked problem (Rittel and Webber 1973). There was no consensus even on the definition of the problem, much less on goals to achieve. Even if experts worked on it, there would be no stopping rule, no correct answers, and no objective way to determine what would be a good decision. As Rittel and Webber point out, publics and their values have become increasingly differentiated, and we are increasingly aware of our world as an open interactive system, constantly in motion. In Sacramento the divergence in views among the actors in the region made it impossible to agree on the desirable means of policy, much less the appropriate ends. Fragmentation of decision making among the agencies prevented any of them from taking effective action. The traditional processes for addressing the problem, which relied on government experts, on the political power of legislation, or on litigation of rights and responsibilities had failed to improve the prospects for a sustainable approach to the regions' water resources. The uncertainty inherent in this complex system moreover, meant that even powerful actors and knowledgeable experts could not make predictions on which effective policy could be based. By 1992 the City and County staff advised their elected officials that legislation and litigation had not worked in addressing their challenges and was unlikely to do so. They said, "We have to try a different approach if we are to address this problem."

The approach they tried was to institute a collaborative policy dialogue among the players. The strategy worked – agreements were reached on managing and conserving the water supply for multiple purposes, actions of players were coordinated, and continuing uncertainty dealt with by continuing dialogue. The story is told in Chapter 3. Hundreds of experiments in collaborative policy making have been tried around the world when problems have become intractable. These have been met with varying degrees of success because they are unfamiliar, the organizers lack the knowledge of other's experiences, and there is no simple formula for implementing such dialogues in particular times and places. This fledgling set of practices is just beginning to be articulated and explored in education and research. This book aims to build on this work to spread and deepen the understanding of policy and planning professionals and public administrators about both the practice and theory of collaborative dialogues as a strategy for inquiry and decision about the wicked problems that dominate their work.

Such dialogues, it must be acknowledged, are at odds with the norms and practices of decision making institutions in industrialized nations. Indeed in the face of a wicked problem such as that of the Sacramento and American Rivers, the usual practice in the U.S. would be for public agencies each to come up with regulations and rules pertinent to their narrow missions. Interest groups would bring lawsuits and legislators would look for "fixes" or reorganize, perhaps setting up a "czar" whose job would be to "solve" the problem. All would be able to claim credit for doing something, but the fundamental problem would not be addressed, and conflict and paralysis would become endemic. While we believe that this dysfunctional system is well recognized as such not only by scholars, but also by reflective practitioners, our governments continue to rely on it for lack of an alternative. At this moment we believe the foundations are established for a new way of understanding and practicing public decision making.

This book is written for those who find many existing planning and policy practices inadequate and who seek to understand how collaborative approaches can work and why and where. We build on what we have learned over the past 30 years of our own scholarship and practice, as well as on the work of colleagues in urban planning, public policy, and public administration. We unpack and shine a light on emergent collaborative practices. We address some of the thorniest and most controversial issues surrounding these new practices. The book provides a framework for an understanding of the dynamics of collaborative processes, as well as a micro level look at how they work. We offer theoretical perspectives and practical principles, along with case examples. We look at the conditions under which these practices can be effective and when they should not be used. We outline the range of collaboration methods and provide an approach to assessing the value of various processes. We look at key concerns of observers, including the role of power inside and outside the processes, the role of various kinds of information, the relationship of these typically ad hoc processes to the formal institutions of government, and the implications for public participation. We explore the theoretical arguments that help to understand and assess these activities, which have largely emerged without explicit grounding in theory. Readers who are familiar with our published work will recognize many of the ideas and examples, but many others appear for the first time here. Some of the case material we draw on has not been formally published and is not widely distributed.

Context and origins of collaborative public decision making

Times have changed. Globalization, the rise of instant communications and the Internet, the movement of immigrant groups into new countries, and increasing levels of education are but a few of the changes that are transforming societies around the world. The second order effects of these changes are many. They include clashes of cultures and an accompanying loss of identity and shared values. They also include the development of a "new tribalism" in response to the changes and increasingly fragmented and contentious societies at all scales. With higher levels of education and political savvy, interests, especially in the U.S., have grown more organized and vocal, with each group focusing on its own, often narrow, interest. Government structures are typically poorly set up to deal with these challenges. Bureaucratic agencies are hierarchical in structure, routinized in their practices and each designed to fulfill a limited mission. They are unable to address the multiple goals of their constituencies, much less deal with rapid change. They cannot address the interdependencies among their missions to achieve sustainable management of natural resources. They are not set up to look at cities or regions as wholes, nor to address complex, rapidly changing problems. The courts, particularly in the U.S., play a major role in a system of adversarial legalism and make decisions where there are winners and losers and no one is satisfied. Elected officials, even those who are most intelligent and hard working, cannot begin to grasp the complexity of the world they deal with. All too often they settle into rhetoric and reactive responses to the interests that support them. The result is inappropriate or ineffective governmental action, inaction, or even paralysis, like that which caused Sacramento water planners to look for a different approach.

Attitudes and understandings among citizens, scholars, and practitioners in this context have evolved. Confidence in government in the U.S. has declined steadily

(Nye, et al. 1997). Citizens are increasingly likely to mistrust data provided by government. Traditional public participation methods in the U.S. such as public hearings too often become battles among angry citizens and events practitioners and elected officials that all dread (Innes and Booher 2005). The positivist model of knowledge had dominated education and much professional practice well into the 1980s, but today a social constructionist view has begun to take hold, along with a critical/communicative approach. The adherents to these alternative views are increasing and professional curricula are evolving. These perspectives, which will be discussed in Chapter 2, suggest that no longer is "scientifically" developed knowledge by experts regarded as the only, or even the best, form of knowledge for public decisions. Some of the conventions associated with the expert model of speaking truth to power no longer are so widely accepted. These include the formal separation of values from analysis and its corollary, the separation of policy practitioners from politics. The close association of bureaucracy with formal expertise as a major source of its legitimacy is no longer as persuasive as it was, and agencies have to look for new forms of legitimacy. Increasingly, many governmental and nongovernmental players see value in dialogue.

This interest in dialogue corresponds to a time when debate over public issues has grown more strident as multiple voices strive to be heard, rely on sound bites, formulate rigid positions and demonize the opposition. Environmental groups are a case in point. They have organized their campaigns around specific technical fixes to problems of sustainability and global warming, like smart growth or fuel efficiency. These positions become their rallying points, but fall far short of addressing the basic societal problems behind the problem, such as trade policies, cultural life style preferences, social justice, public finance, or the influence of money in politics. Moreover, they trigger equal and opposite reactions from interests like car manufacturers which stymie much of environmentalists' agendas (Shellenberger and Nordhaus 2005). Yet many groups continue to insist on their positions, blaming the failures on a "lack of political will" by the elected leadership, as if everyone accepted the correctness of the environmentalists' positions, and was simply too cowardly or craven to do the right thing. Many interests have concerns and proposals about which they feel just as passionately, but they focus on specific things they think they can influence. No one speaks for the larger picture. Many push on tactics, but few push for a strategy that recognizes the full implications for the encompassing complex social and environmental system.

Both governmental and nongovernmental players in many nations have begun experimenting with collaborative dialogue as a way to address conflict that seems irresolvable. These experiments range from public agencies pulling together stakeholders, some of whom had not been involved in decision making, for joint discussions of issues (Healey 2006; Healey 2007); to fully fledged consensus building efforts among an inclusive set of stakeholders; to design proposals for public action like that in the Water Forum. Some efforts are simply about seeking a shared identity as a starting place for change or other efforts to heal community rifts through building trust and finding shared realities. These are often nongovernmental, initiated by concerned citizens. In the U.S. an array of innovative nonprofit organizations is trying to solve problems collaboratively and build civil society in a variety of contexts, including education, neighborhood revitalization and services, economic development, and leadership development (Chrislip 2002; Putnam and Feldstein 2003). Castells chronicled this global trend of social mobilization that he called the "embryos of a new society" (Castells 1997: 362). Public agencies as well are exploring collaborative forms of public involvement beyond legally mandated forums, including visioning workshops, discussion forums, and stakeholder-based advisory committees.

Trends

Three trends in the evolution of planning and policy making are important to understand as we launch this book. First, the traditional linear methods relying primarily on formal expertise are being replaced by nonlinear socially constructed processes engaging both experts and stakeholders. In the traditional processes, at least in theory, decisions proceeded from goals provided by elected officials, to data collection, analysis, and formulation of plans and policies by experts, to implementation performed both by elected officials and bureaucrats. In the practices we see emerging, many actors – experts, stakeholders, elected officials, and the public – are engaging jointly to address planning and policy problems. Together they collect information about a situation and consider what it might mean. They may start with some general shared concerns, but collectively they do not start with specific goals. They do not operate on the assumption that there is an optimal solution. They formulate options and consider what the consequences of those options might be. In the course of this they may jointly formulate objectives, but often only midway in the process. Nor does implementation proceed in a linear way from a decision. It is always contingent and evolving, even cycling back to goals as new things are learned. In this perspective there is not a universal truth to be discovered. Instead there are facts to be explored in the effort to create a shared understanding of reality that can be a basis for action. These facts and understandings, moreover, are always subject to reexamination and revision in recognition of the tentative nature of knowledge.

In the second trend, ideas about appropriate knowledge for planning and policy are changing. In traditional practice expert "scientific" knowledge is dominant. Lay knowledge is important only as it reveals general public preferences, but it is suspect when it comes to analyzing a situation or formulating plans or policies. Increasingly, however, the public and decision makers are recognizing the limitations of science and expertise, amid growing instances of disagreement among scientists when, for example, definitive findings on benefits or dangers of medications turn out to be wrong. The use of expertise itself depends on lay knowledge, but many experts do not publicly acknowledge that their knowledge is socially constructed. In collaborative planning processes many kinds of knowledge are important in understanding problems. The successful processes we have observed included methods in which experts, lay people, and people with unique local knowledge engaged to jointly create an understanding of the challenges they faced and of the potential of the options they considered. As a result they were able to reach a shared sense of the validity and relevance of information so that they could use it in the actions they undertook.

The third trend is that new forms of reasoning are beginning to play a larger role and gain scholarly recognition and legitimacy. Rather than instrumental reasoning from ends to means relying on logical steps and objective evidence, participants in the policy processes, especially in collaborative planning, rely on a variety of other methods of making sense of issues and persuading others. While formal argumentation from premises to conclusions remains a part of deliberation, other kinds of reasoning can be more powerful in group dialogues. In these, participants use storytelling and role playing as a primary way to explain and persuade. For example, they tell stories about how they are experiencing the current situation. They play roles in anticipating how certain options might affect that situation. They then use a kind of intellectual bricolage to develop new options and strategies as they draw on their many experiences and their broader knowledge for components that can be assembled in various ways to create new approaches (Innes and Booher 1999b).

Collaborative rationality

We see in these trends the emergence of a new form of planning and policy. We call this collaborative rationality and see it as an alternative to the traditional linear model, with its emphasis on expert knowledge and reasoning based upon argumentation. This idea is grounded in the work of Habermas (1981) and his notion of communicative rationality (to be discussed in Chapter 2), as well as in the lessons practitioners and managers of collaborative processes have learned through their extensive practice.[1] While we will discuss and explain this concept throughout the book, the basics have to do with the process for deliberation. A process is collaboratively rational to the extent that all the affected interests jointly engage in face to face dialogue, bringing their various perspectives to the table to deliberate on the problems they face together. For the process to be collaboratively rational, all participants must also be fully informed and able to express their views and be listened to, whether they are powerful or not. Techniques must be used to mutually assure the legitimacy, comprehensibility, sincerity, and accuracy of what they say. Nothing can be off the table. They have to seek consensus.

These principles are conditions to be aimed at, though they can never be completely achieved. For example, it is infeasible to include every actor, but representatives of most or all basic interests can often be brought together. Likewise complete consensus may not be achieved, but as long as substantial agreement is reached among a supermajority and all efforts are made to find creative ways to satisfy all participants before reaching closure, the results can be regarded as collaboratively rational. This rationality also depends on the group having made a prior agreement on what to count as consensus. This is parallel to the scientific method, where certain data gathering and analysis procedures have to be followed for the results to be considered accurate and rational. We argue that processes which approximate collaborative rationality are legitimate and that the decisions they reach are rational, not only in the sense of being well informed and in the spirit of democracy, but also in the sense that they represent a collective form of knowing and deciding.

We do not contend that collaborative planning and policy is appropriate for all planning or policy decisions. For example, it is not needed when there is already agreement about ends and means, when cause and effect relationships are well understood, and when there is relative certainty about how the decision will play out in the system (Christensen 1985). It is not feasible when an immediate decision is needed to protect life and property.[2] It is not possible when the actors affected are not interdependent and hence have no reason to engage with one another. In situations such as these other decision processes are needed. But for the many wicked problems we face, collaborative planning is more likely to generate feasible and legitimate decisions than traditional decision making. We will summarize the argument for this claim later in this chapter, but first a short view of the current context will help provide the foundation for the argument.

Collaborative dialogues in practice

The practices and purposes of collaborative dialogues and collaborative policy making around the world are tremendously varied.[3] They have been used not only in many large scale water resource conflicts, but also, for example, in urban regeneration in Newcastle (Healey, et al. 2003), regional design in Milan, in land disputes between the Bedouin and Israelis (Susskind, pers. comm.), and in major international disputes in Tajikistan (Saunders 2001) and in Northern Ireland. Collaborative dialogues are often focused on spatial, territorial issues because so many players have differing interests in particular places or resources, which cannot be realized without some type of cooperation. Collaborative methods are also used for social service delivery coordination and planning (Bardach 1998). They may be used anywhere where there are shared interests in common resources or challenges. They may be instigated by government agencies, legislators, judges, or by nongovernmental actors; they may take place at any scale, from the organization, to the neighborhood, to the region; they may go on for weeks or years. They may start with a core group, but over time become complex, networked sets of dialogues, with wide ranging participants who may never meet face to face, but whose ideas flow through what Healey calls "relational webs" (Healey 2007), resulting in what we have called "network power" (Booher and Innes 2002).

These collaborative efforts can and often do produce significant agreements. These agreements may be the least of the consequences, however, as the processes themselves build capacity for self-management in communities, improve policy knowledge, and create innovative strategies tailor-made to the unique conditions of particular situations. They can transform intractable problems into tractable ones as participants come to see in new ways and develop new values and goals and a sense of common purpose. They build social, political and intellectual capital that can be used not only for the immediate problem, but for much more over time. They can empower previously invisible players, giving them a place at the table for the first time. They are a key part of the phenomenon of governance, which has gained attention in recent years as increasingly hierarchical government is supplemented by the activities of a shifting panoply of players linked to one another through networks (Hajer and Wagenaar 2003).

What we and others have done is to study many cases of collaboration through first hand, mostly interpretive, research.[4] Our first objective was to identify the various forms collaborations take, especially the more formal consensus building processes, to understand their dynamics, and to identify what kinds of outcomes emerged. The second objective, which we pursued iteratively with the first, was to draw on theory in a variety of fields that would help us make sense of what we were seeing and that would point in directions to help improve the practice. We have moved toward building our theory of collaborative rationality out of this material, drawing on aspects of others' theoretical insights and using them as a lens through which to interpret the cases.

We have researched or participated in dozens of collaborative and consensus building processes on a range of topics, many in resource management, particularly water, but also in transportation, growth management, and health. We interviewed hundreds of participants and observed these processes first hand over months, or even years. We reviewed the extensive case study literature. We drew heavily on all this work in developing our own theory and in illustrating our argument throughout the book. The research shows that collaborative processes can accomplish things that normally do not emerge from government as usual. These processes can be more flexible and adaptive than top down agency decision making or legislative vote trading. One major challenge is that collaborative processes coexist uneasily with formal government, as we will demonstrate in the case of CALFED in Chapter 3. In this case elected officials imposed the hierarchical tradition of accountability and oversight on a self-organizing collaborative effort, with the result that it ended much of the collaborative activity. Public officials, not surprisingly, harbor doubts about the legitimacy of any sort of public decision making other than representative government.

The importance of institutional change

When government policies fail to solve problems, the typical reaction is to try to fix the policy or to tinker at the edges of the system. Very seldom do leaders or the public question the institutions that have failed, nor do they often ask whether different kinds of practices and structures could be more effective, much less look to ways to transform the existing model of government. We are proposing in this book that it is time to step back and consider fundamental changes in governance and in our institutions. Currently there is a substantial mismatch between the institutions we rely on and the actual practices that are emerging. Our norms for government do not match the reality. Though we give lip service to the importance of expertise in public decision making, it plays a much more limited role than we pretend it does. We live in a complex, fragmented and changing world, but most of our institutions of government operate as if we could count on stability and predictability. Because it is so hard to change institutions we try to make do with what we have even though the "fit" between these and contemporary conditions is poor.

One of the main challenges is that public agencies and public officials tend to operate on the assumption that they have the prerogative and obligation to make their own autonomous decisions. They often do not talk to one another about problems, even when their activities intersect. Often regulatory agencies are secretive and do not even share information across agencies. They fear being seen as subject to political influence if they are publically forthcoming about their deliberations. This tendency, which is clearly at odds with collaboration, is linked to the dominance of instrumental rationality – the ideal of goal directed behavior guided by experts and designed to find the "right" policy. As a result we end up with the Decide, Announce, Defend syndrome (DAD), which wreaks havoc on public engagement with decision making. This syndrome in turn is grounded in a culturally embedded mechanical metaphor for policy making. We tend to see a problem as being like a machine that experts can take apart and fix, reassembling it so it is again in working order. As Lakoff and Johnson (1980) have shown, metaphors are more than literary devices. They shape the way we think about a problem and how we think about actions we can take.

In collaborative practice, by contrast, problems are treated as puzzles as participants work jointly to put pieces together to create a shared picture of the future and a strategy for getting there. This open ended approach is at odds with both bureaucratic norms and the ideal of finding the one right policy. Politicians and agency heads, moreover, tend to see collaboratively produced decisions as a threat to their power and often preempt them.

We believe that we are in a period where collaborative efforts are gradually transforming traditional institutional structures and norms. We share Giddens' view that structure provides norms and constraints on the action of agents, but that the actions of those agents can change the structure, typically gradually and perhaps invisibly in the short run. But structure is no more than the combined actions and practices of agents that persist over time and space. Structure and agency interact and evolve (Giddens 1984). The cases and examples in this book illustrate how this gradual process is taking place.

Our basic argument

There are three elements in the logic of our basic argument. First, collaborative processes that are designed and managed to generate collaborative rationality are likely to produce, not only effective options for how actors can move forward together to deal with their problems, but also individual and collective learning that will help make the community more adaptive and resilient. A central aspect of this claim is that for wicked problems there is no solution that can be shown to be optimal. Hence, the challenge is to find a way for players to jointly improve their situation rather than find the best or fairest "solution." Because causality cannot be definitively established and because the system is constantly subject to unanticipated change, the idea of a best solution is a mirage. Instead diverse actors engaged in dialogue offer a wide variety of experience, knowledge, and ideas that offer a rich terrain of options to explore.

The second element of our argument is that it very much matters *how* the collaborative process unfolds. We see much confusion in the literature on this subject. Often the word "collaboration" is used in a generic sense of just getting a group of people together to cooperate instead of trying to meet the conditions of collaborative rationality. Others see collaboration as a bargaining process that leads to compromise and lowest common denominator solutions, rather than an opportunity to discover new mutually beneficial options. Still others see collaboration as a process by which public agencies and powerful players co-opt their opposition, rather than a place where opposing views can be fully aired and taken into account. We have seen examples of what we think of as pseudo collaboration put forward in the literature, along with claims that these show that collaboration does not work. While we regard these versions of collaboration as representing the common pitfalls of poorly designed processes, we maintain that these failures do not discredit collaboratively rational processes. To comment on the adequacy of a given process it cannot be depicted by broad brush, but must be unpacked and looked at in detail to see if it meets the conditions of collaborative rationality.

The final element of our argument is that collaborative processes can lead to changes in the larger system that help make our institutions more effective and adaptive and make the system itself more resilient. These processes do not just produce immediate outcomes like agreements and joint activities, but participants' experiences with them often lead them to extend collaboration to other contexts. Participants learn more deeply about issues and other interests which they transfer to their organizations. They develop new skills. They build new networks that they use to get new sorts of things done that they could not have otherwise considered. As they extend their ambitions and activities, they discover that the norms and structures of traditional government constrain adaptation and impede resilience in response to stresses. Collaborative planning however is well adapted to dealing with a complex, changing and fragmented system. In order to do so, however, such collaboration may be manifested in a kind of shadow practice within and among formal organizations of government (Innes, et al. 2007).

Outline of the book

This book examines collaborative decision making from many angles. It builds our argument about the nature and value of this set of practices, beginning with the social theory that illuminates and helps to improve it, moving on to case examples, to reflections on actual praxis, to in-depth exploration of collaborative dialogue, to the ways in which information can be integrated and the ways conflicts in science can be resolved, to a discussion of the role of local knowledge and environmental justice, and finally to the long term implications of the emergence of collaborative decision making. Throughout we rely heavily on examples and case material.

Chapter 2 makes the case that practice needs theory and offers our conception of theory as a way of seeing informed by both social theory and grounded theorizing built on in-depth case analysis and comparison. The chapter moves from an exploration of the role of knowledge and rationality in practice, and the so-called Rational model on which planning and policy professionals have heavily relied, through alternative kinds of knowledge and rationality ultimately to an outline of our theory of what we call collaborative rationality. Along the way the chapter explores the rationality of collaboration and the core idea of emancipatory knowledge that comes of dialectic, praxis and challenging of assumptions. It looks at some of the key theorists in planning and at Dewey's conception of the community of inquiry, which presages and potentially guides collaborative planning in practice. Negotiation theory is an important foundation for collaboration. It offers a framing for our theory in complexity science illustrating how collaboration is well adapted to a complex system. Finally we offer our own theory of how collaborative dialogues can and do work, grounded in part in each of the sets of ideas we have offered. This theory, which we have labeled DIAD, is our touchstone for assessing collaborations throughout the book.

In Chapter 3 we offer six in-depth case examples of collaborative efforts which had varying degrees of success in terms of outcomes. They are chosen to be on different scales and topics using differing processes. The purpose is to offer sufficient detail about how they started and how they were managed to allow us to diagnose how and why they did or did not work. These include The Water Forum example at the beginning of the chapter, the Police–Community Relations process that followed the Cincinnati riots, the state planning process in New Jersey, the Collaborative Regional Initiative (CRI) known as the Bay Area Alliance for Sustainable Communities (BAASC), which was a voluntary effort by civic leaders to shape growth patterns, and the East Bay Conversion and Reinvestment Commission (EBCRC) which brought together regional stakeholders to influence the conversion of military bases to civilian use. We analyze each of these cases in terms of their context, how they were started, their structure and process, their first order results, implementation strategy and second and third order effects and system adaptations that resulted. Finally, we assess what processes led to these outcomes in the light of our theory.

Chapter 4 examines the praxis of collaboration – that is, the nuances of the many tasks that are involved in creating a successful collaborative process. It builds on the cases in Chapter 3 and on other examples to explore a range of practices that address key challenges in collaboration. This chapter aims to answer many of the questions that get asked in both literature and discussions of collaborative dialogues, like, as a practical matter, how to choose stakeholders and get them to the table, how to deal with diverse stakeholders, and how to use a single text negotiating document. The chapter then goes on to the praxis of creating authentic dialogue according to the principles of collaborative rationality, weaving theory and examples together to see how this can be done in a practical way. It discusses the different designs for collaborative processes from small to large groups with varying tasks. A section addresses the complex question of power in and around these processes and the chapter ends with the contradictions and paradoxes that arise as we try to develop and use collaborative processes.

In Chapter 5 we probe the nature and dynamics of dialogue, which are at the center of collaborative rationality. Dewey's concept of a community of inquiry is helpful in understanding how collaborative rationality works. Through dialogue a community of actors can inquire into their situation and what they might do together to improve it. Instead of linear decision making based upon logical argumentation in a win-lose debate, a community of inquiry engages in collective framing and reframing, creating metaphors, storytelling, role playing, and using cognitive bricolage to jointly form a picture of the problems the community faces and how it can address those problems. This dialogue can be transformative, changing the thinking of the actors and the nature of their relationships. It can lead them down a path different from any they had previously thought existed. Dialogue helps participants identify new opportunities and work out creative solutions to challenges. The chapter looks at how dialogue transforms opinion to judgment, how it can transform beliefs and values and how it can lead to innovation. It goes on to unpack the details of how policy dialogues work, looking at framing as a source of conflict, at the role of metaphors and of storytelling, at the importance of humor, at the ways that dialogue can proceed through role playing and drama, and at finding solutions through collective bricolage.

Chapter 6 explores how knowledge is and is not linked to action in practice and looks particularly at the dialogic strategies that can both improve the quality of policy information and make it an integral part of choice and action. The chapter challenges the mythology surrounding the Rational model to make the case that for knowledge to motivate action it has to be tailor-made to particular times, places, and conditions and that dialogue has to play a major role in this process. The knowledge has to be understood and trusted by those expected to act on it so they need to be part of the process of producing the knowledge. The chapter looks at the findings of research on the uses of research, which indicate that it is almost never used in the way the Rational model anticipates. It outlines the varied types of information used in legislative, planning and regulatory arenas. It looks at examples where dialogue played a key part in the design and use of research and indicators at the local and national level. Then we move to the thorny problem of conflicting science, exploring the various institutional arrangements to deal with it and then focusing on the collaborative approach, known as joint fact finding. We explore joint fact finding in a series of examples from water management to hazardous waste cleanup.

From our perspective lay and local knowledge is at least as critical as science in the making of sound planning and policy decisions. Local knowledge is more pervasive and more persuasive than scientific knowledge because it offers the detailed, situated knowledge that is crucial to effective action. In Chapter 7 we explore this theme in detail. We argue that seeking out and explicitly incorporating local and lay knowledge is essential to achieving robust and well informed policy and resilience in society. Including local knowledge is essential to assuring decisions are just because these voices are normally marginalized in planning and policy. This chapter identifies and explains at least three interrelated anxieties that interfere with integrating local knowledge into public decision making: anxieties about epistemology, difference, and uncertainty. These anxieties lead to a push for control in public agencies through procedures, agenda setting, specialized discourses, and predefined problem frames that exclude local voices. The chapter offers examples of what has gone wrong when local knowledge is ignored, drawing on potato farming in the Andes, sheep farming and radiation in the U.K., and Love Canal in the U.S. The chapter then turns to success stories where local knowledge has been integrated and produced results reflecting that knowledge. These include watershed stewardship in an urban area of California, action research by planning students in a poor Manhattan neighborhood, cooperative data gathering and analysis on environmental health issues in Brooklyn, New York and co-management of fisheries in the U.S. Finally the chapter addresses the challenges of trying to incorporate the voices of the marginalized in stakeholder collaborative dialogues, concluding that this may have to be done by proxy because of the inherent contradictions in such an effort. We offer examples where there have been serious attempts to include these voices and discuss alternative ways to incorporate their local knowledge in a policy process.

In our final chapter we move beyond collaboration to address ways in which democratic governance can become more adaptive and help to build a resilient society that not only withstands stresses and crises but that can respond creatively to these. This chapter is designed to point toward concepts, norms and actions that can be part of the new institutions and can supplement, or even supplant, the traditional government model that dominates today.

We have planned this book to be useful to students, educators, scholars, and reflective practitioners in the fields of urban planning, public policy, political science and public administration, including those who provide mediation and facilitation services for public policy. Ultimately our work is intended to provide insights that will move both practice and scholarship to a new level.[5] We hope that it will spawn dialogue and enhance society's ability to learn from this emergent and still poorly understood phenomenon of collaborative policy making. We hope that it will help to assure that collaborative processes are more just, more effective, and better informed. We hope that it will help all of us to deal with conflict and difference in a creative and productive way.

Notes

1   This approach has deep roots in the practices of conflict resolution. The William and Flora Hewlett Foundation provided millions over 20 years to support these emerging practices and research to help extend and apply them (Kovick 2005).

2   On the other hand, collaboration processes can be very effective for agencies and citizens planning for the eventuality of emergency actions. The response to Hurricane Katrina is an object lesson for how failure of public agencies to collaborate among themselves and with citizens in planning can have disastrous consequences.

3   Although we see collaborative planning emerging throughout the world and will occasionally make references to examples outside the United States, the focus of this book is on practices in the United States.

4   While parts of this research have been formally published, the complete stories of the cases along with important details can be found in working papers and monographs (Connick 2006; Connick and Innes 2003; Innes 1992a; Innes 2004; Innes and Booher 2003a; Innes, et al. 1994; Innes, et al. 2006; Innes, et al. 2007; Innes and Gruber 2001; Innes and Gruber 2005; Innes and Rongerude 2006; Innes and Sandoval 2004). Some of the key case studies by others include Forester 1999; Healey 1997; Heikkila and Gerlak 2005; Margerum 1999; Scholz and Stiftel 2005; Susskind, et al. 1999). These represent much of the basic data we rely on in this volume, along with Booher's professional experience. We also build on the ideas and theory we have developed in a dozen or more journal articles drawing on these materials, as referenced throughout the book.

5   This book will offer a deeper understanding of how collaborative planning works, but it is not a how to guide. There are many very good guides that do focus on how to carry out collaborative processes in different contexts (Bryson 2004; Carpenter and Kennedy 2001; Chrislip 2002; Kaner and Lind 2007; Sarkissian, et al. 2009; Schuman 2005; Schuman 2006; Straus 2002; Susskind and Cruikshank 1987).

2 How can theory improve practice?

Why practice needs theory

Collaborative practice has emerged from the work of practitioners and citizens. It has not been driven by theory, nor, for the most part, built on theory. Academics are playing catch up, trying to learn from the practice. The principal exception is that the theory of interest-based negotiation has been the basis for alternative dispute resolution (ADR) (Fisher, et al. 1991). This in turn has been a basic building block for broader, anticipatory dialogues and consensus building collaborations designed to preempt disputes and create plans and policies (Carpenter and Kennedy 1991; Crump and Susskind 2008; Susskind and Cruikshank 1987; Susskind, et al. 1999; Wondolleck and Yaffee 2000). These collaborative efforts have moved well beyond ADR, relying on trial and error, learning through networks of practitioners and through how to and best practice books, as well as through a growing body of documented cases (Brunner, et al. 2002; Durant, et al. 2004; Healey, et al. 2003; Susskind, et al. 1999). Many organizations promote collaborative practice through web-sites, conferences, and training[1] to the point where the practices are widespread, though far from standardized, at least in the U.S.

It has now become essential to situate these practices in relation to con-temporary social and political theory. Social theorists and practitioners have been operating quite separately until recently, but they draw their inspiration and learning from the same context. Not surprisingly practice and theory converge in many respects, and we believe that each can enhance the other. Theory provides ways of seeing how and why practices do or do not work in particular ways; it offers a critical distance that helps surface unexamined assumptions and places activities in perspective; it provides a basis for an evaluative framework; and it generates insights leading to new ideas and directions. Theory can help practitioners and academics understand why collaboration is proliferating at this moment in history, what its societal consequences are, whether it is just, how it addresses power and whether or how it is changing our institutions (Healey 1999). Theorizing collaboration can help to advance social theory itself. Theory helps us to see how to make collaboration collaboratively rational, the results of which can be viewed as both legitimate and informed.

Our conception of theory

Over the past 15 years we have been building grounded theory out of what we have learned from case study research and from the insights of other theorists. We are like the bricoleur (Levi-Strauss 1966), who puts together pieces drawn from different sources to create new needed things. We do not do experimental design or formal hypothesis testing. We do not start with a theory of society like the neo-Marxists' notion of the determinative power of the capitalist economic and political structure and then examine our evidence through such a lens. We do not take existing theory and "apply" it to empirical data. We are not developing theory about what is right and just. Rather we do in-depth interpretive research on complex examples of collaboration, trying, on the one hand, to describe the cases in their rich detail and, on the other, to identify and explain their dynamics. We do this by asking questions about what is puzzling or not readily explained by common sense and familiar theory. We search for answers both by cross-case comparisons and by developing a coherent narrative that makes sense of what we have observed. The ideas and theories briefly offered in this chapter have become the infrastructure of our thinking and underlie our theory of collaborative rationality. We believe that understanding these ideas can help our readers to develop their own reflective and creative way to build these new sets of practices.

We test our theory in an interpretive mode. It is a good theory: if it makes sense to explain complex situations in our cases and others; if when applied to a case, it allows one to see aspects that were previously invisible, or seemingly unimportant; if those involved in the case think it is on target; and if it generates new ideas, new thinking, and even debate. We agree with tests Lave and March offer for a good theory (Lave and March 1993). It has truth, beauty, and fertility. It has truth because it accounts for the evidence in a way that rings true. It has beauty because of its ultimate simplicity and because it reveals what has not been seen before. It has fertility because the ideas open up new lines of inquiry.

We begin with discussion of ways of knowing, alternative epistemologies and their associated concepts of rationality because policy professionals' knowledge is their stock in trade, along with their claims to rationality. We lay out the contrast between the positivist, instrumental rationality that has dominated these fields in recent years and the emerging interpretive and qualitative approach that is increasingly in use. Then we move to the ideas of the critical theorists, especially Jurgen Habermas, and the notion of an alternative type of rationality based on dialogue among people with diverse views and experience. Also key to our thinking is Habermas' idea of emancipatory knowledge that challenges the status quo, with all its embedded power relations. The American pragmatists, especially Dewey, have had a significant influence on planning thought. Their ideas parallel Habermas' in many respects and prefigure collaborative rationality in their conception of communities of inquiry. We note key points in negotiation theory as it is a foundation for the actual methods used in collaboratively rational processes. We introduce complexity science because it is a framing that illuminates how and why collaboration works in the ever changing contemporary world and because it is a key component in our theory of collaborative rationality. Finally we outline our theory, which we call DIAD to represent the key components of collaborative rationality: diversity, interdependence, and authentic dialogue.

Knowledge and rationality in planning and public policy

The legitimacy of public action depends significantly on the acceptability of the knowledge used for developing and justifying it. The legitimacy of professionals who assist decision makers hinges significantly in turn on their knowledge. Indeed the definition of a profession is "a calling requiring specialized knowledge and often long and intensive academic preparation" (Merriam Webster 2003). There exist multiple ways of knowing, each built on different assumptions and employing different methods, and differing in their claims about what counts as knowledge. These range from a "scientific," ostensibly objective approach, to a qualitative, interpretive approach focusing on understandings and meanings, to experiential, holistic and pragmatic approaches. Professionals and decision makers often tacitly use one or more of these ways of knowing without conscious recognition that there is a choice. Some of these are less understood or accepted than others in the planning and policy world, but each is built on a substantial philosophical foundation. Each works differently, focuses attention on different kinds of information, and each has different strengths and limitations. In collaborative decision making, knowledge is at least as central as it is in other modes of policy making, but this type of inquiry values many kinds of knowledge and sorts through them in different ways from the more conventional inquiry of the lone analyst. We will explore this topic in Chapters 6 and 7 using many examples, but here we lay out the epistemological foundations for these forms of knowledge. For collaborative decision making, understanding these foundations is particularly critical, as participants both demand and offer multiple ways of knowing which need to be respected and incorporated.

Rationality of a public decision is also critical to its acceptability, but the idea of rationality is contested and varying notions of rationality are wrapped together with different ways of knowing. What can be viewed as rational in one epistemology is not necessarily so in another. Western thought typically assigns rationality to a sort of scientific inquiry, whereas collaborative policy making relies heavily on interpretive, pragmatic and dialectical ways of knowing. Accordingly, it requires the construction of an alternative concept which we call collaborative rationality.

Positivist analysis in a political world

For most of the second half of the twentieth century both the policy literature and the practice reserved the term *rational* for a particular approach to public decision making. The idea was that public decisions should be based on objective data, logical deductive analysis and systematic comparison of alternatives. This powerful normative model is grounded in positivist epistemology (Popper 1966; Bernstein 1976), and it implies that neutral experts should gather, compile and analyze data which, in turn, decision makers should use to make public decisions. The data has to be measurable and gathered through known and tested tools like surveys. Knowledge in this model involves seeking facts and looking for laws relating variables. Behind this idea is the belief that there is an objective world out there that can be observed and measured in a consistent way by trained observers. The model also assumes the world can be broken down into analytically manageable components which can be studied separately and fixed independently, like the parts of a machine. Most analytical methods associated with this view in practice assume linear additive causal relations. Though the practitioners of these methods recognized the reality of nonlinear relations and feedback loops, for many years there were not well developed techniques to address these. Most assumed linear analyses were good enough approximations.

A social order is embodied in this so called Rational[2] model, suggesting that there should be a division of labor in public decision making. Thus elected officials set goals; with the help of experts they identify problems; experts generate alternatives; experts then evaluate these and reach conclusions about their efficacy; decision makers, on the basis of this information, decide on policies and actions; and bureaucrats implement these. In the ideal version of the model, trained experts are in the employ of decision makers who await their advice and act like scientists are supposed to, dropping their preconceived ideas in the face of new evidence (Mitroff 1974). The model is compatible with traditional bureaucracy, which needs simple, objective information to justify its actions. A symbiotic relationship of the "Rational" model with bureaucratic norms and political demands has helped to assure its institutionalization over many years. It persists today as the dominant model in the education of professionals and the accepted logic for public decision makers. It interferes, however, with the potential legitimacy of collaborative decision making with its uses of different sorts of knowledge.

The rational model works perversely in pluralist politics

Politics with deal making behind the scenes has been the normal practice in the U.S. as in many other societies, despite lip service to the Rational model. Often the political approach is cloaked in technical analyses to give it legitimacy. For example, in a study we conducted of the Metropolitan Transportation Commission (MTC), the San Francisco Bay Area's regional transportation planning agency (Innes and Gruber 2005), we found that the technical planners did extensive analyses of projects, not to decide among alternatives, but to give cover to the political leadership, which chose projects designed to spread the wealth among constituencies. This dynamic is so common that social scientists (Rein and White 1977) long ago outlined the system that produces and maintains it. They argue that, although neither experts nor politicians normally use the analytic work to make decisions, they both have reasons to act as if they do. The scientists cannot be blamed for the policies that did not use their data, while leaders avoid blame for failed policies because they were using expert advice. Agency officials may co-opt, or even explicitly control, the analyses their staff produce (Innes and Gruber 2001; Brinkman 2004). When they hire outside consultants, they do so typically from firms with known methods and orientations that will produce fairly predictable results. Consultants' livelihood can be threatened if they are known to challenge established practices or beliefs.

The positivist mental model, with its concept of breaking the system into separate parts for analysis, has endured in part in the U.S., because it fits the pluralist political system where decision making is often driven by interest groups which focus on narrowly defined problems and promote technical fixes. For example, environmental groups like the Sierra Club focused political and fund raising efforts in the 1990s around reducing auto emissions. They fixated on the idea of setting a particular standard of fuel efficiency for automobiles, but this failed due to the greater power of the auto industry (Shellenberger and Nordhaus 2005). The promotion of a fix called attention away from the larger systemic factors that produce climate change. It skipped the step of deliberation over the dynamics of change or over the practicalities of proposals. Its focus on the measurable diverted attention from the elusive yet important issues critical to the implementability of a policy. The false certainty behind the fixes and the blaming of officials for lacking political will to do the "right" thing precluded consideration of the alternatives that the Rational model calls for.

Because the positivist approach as taught in professional education does not typically incorporate the reality of politics and its many interests, there can be a big disconnect between professional analysis and getting things done in the practical world. However schools have continued to teach positivist analytic methods as the principal form of expertise, along with its idealized decision making model.[3] The policy professions will not easily let go of this model, though they know it to be unrealistic, because it has given them legitimacy and it is entrenched institutionally in education and public decision making. It is part of their identity. This reality continues to be a hindrance to collaborative policy making becoming a normal part of public decision making, rather than the exception it is today.

The rational choice school discovers collaboration is rational

Intellectual support for collaborative decision making has emerged recently from an unlikely source – political theorists of the so-called rational choice school. These scholars are grounded in positivist analysis, and their work has influenced professional practice and education in pervasive ways over the years. Such scholars have argued that cooperation is both impossible and irrational. Rational choice theory is built on the assumption that we live in a world where every man is out for himself. "Rational man" is one who makes deliberate, calculated choices designed to serve his own interests; he does not assume that anyone will cooperate or assist him. Thomas Hobbes argued that to deal with such a world we need an authoritarian government to control society, make rules and punish transgressors (Hobbes 2009). Adam Smith contributed the idea that each Rational man, working to maximize his individual welfare in an ideal market system could produce a high level of welfare for society as a whole (Smith 1776). Mancur Olson told us that collective action was only possible by a small and powerful group of interests, each with a tremendous stake in the issue (Olson 1965). Garrett Hardin contended that shared resources were doomed to overuse by selfish individuals for whom it was rational to use as much as possible for themselves without regard to others' needs, much less to the needs of the community (Hardin 1968).

Rational choice theorists often cite the prisoners' dilemma[4] to show how and why individuals would rationally choose to benefit themselves even when they harm others. In policy fields this model has been used to account for, and even legitimize, many beggar-thy-neighbor activities. It is a justification for urban redevelopment because in blighted areas no one has the incentive to be the first to improve his property. Instead government appropriates the land, demolishes the properties and sets standards for new development. Arrow demonstrates in his famous theorem (Arrow 1963) that if people can only vote for their top two candidates, their third choice could win, rather than one of the top two. All of these contentions are grounded in logical argument starting from the Rational man premise, rather than in direct observation. They all assume players work independently, do not communicate, and cannot develop a sense of collective purpose.

A significant literature has been built on these assumptions, and the premise is so pervasive in academic quarters that some scholars internalize it, even when it does not fit their experience. A case in point was a faculty seminar at UC Berkeley, evenly divided between political scientists and sociologists, where the group was discussing Putnam's book about social capital in Italian regions (Putnam 1993). The political scientists puzzled over why anyone would ever do anything that did not serve his individual interest, as Putnam claimed they did in some regions. The sociologists, whose scholarly culture is built on a different premise – that we all learn our values and preferences within our community and that it is normal, even second nature, to protect that community – were puzzled by the political scientists' questions. One sociologist who knew the individuals well asked them why they thought trust and cooperation was something that needed explaining, since each of them did many things not in their own interest, spending vast amounts of time on students, on university committees, and other activities that did not contribute to their promotions or salary increases. They were stumped at first but finally one said, "Yes I realize that, but I feel as if I am a sucker." Somehow the culture of their disciplines had turned a theoretical assumption about human nature into a norm which did not offer a way for these scholars to understand what they were doing as rational or even intelligent for that matter.

In the 1990s some rational choice theorists began to discover that under certain circumstances, cooperation could be rational even using their model. Axelrod showed experimentally that repeated prisoners' dilemma games produced cooperative behavior so long as players knew the game would continue (Axelrod 1984). The most important theorist for understanding collaboration in terms of the Rational man model is Elinor Ostrom, who developed theory about the origins and maintenance of collaborative resource management on the basis of dozens of cases of actual practice around the world

(Ostrom 1990). Starting from the notion that individuals are self-interested utility maximizers, she sought to explain why some examples of cooperative and sustainable management of common pool resources do exist. She looked at the characteristics of the resource, such as a grazing commons or water supply, the conditions the users faced, and the rules and principles they developed for collective management. She found that cooperation and trust could be explained without dropping the assumption of rational self-interest. She discovered that new institutional structures had evolved in some communities, with norms of cooperation and a shared logic supporting them. These were all voluntary efforts collectively governed. Belief in the public interest by participants was not necessary for an explanation, nor was altruism, which would be irrational. Ostrom's work has laid the theoretical groundwork for a logic of collaborative institutions for resource management.

Interpretive knowing: a foundation for collaborative dialogue

Some years ago, in conversation with a colleague at UC Berkeley, we noted the importance of moving on from the positivist model in view of its limitations in the practical world. He agreed, but said he would keep using it because there was no alternative. What was missing, we decided, was not so much other ways of making decisions, but a set of well-developed alternative procedures set on a comparable philosophical foundation that would preserve the legitimacy of the policy professions. Otherwise we would have to continue to be like the drunkard who loses his keys in the dark, but keeps looking for them under the lamppost because "the light is better." We begin our search for a new model of planning compatible with collaboration, with an exploration of how interpretive qualitative knowing or phenomenology can provide an alternative by which to understand and justify collaborative inquiry.

Phenomenology offers a more grounded form of knowledge, as well as one that can not only address the full complexity of a situation, but also explore it in a way that allows solutions to be tailor-made to unique circumstances. Phenomenologists argued (Bernstein 1976) that knowledge is about phenomena as wholes, rather than divided into components, and the goal of knowing is understanding rather than explanation. The starting place for knowing is everyday life and the understandings of ordinary people, rather than abstractions like variables. Meaning is central, and intentions and beliefs are themselves constitutive of reality, rather than reality being out there to be discovered. Whereas positivist researchers would discount meaning as purely subjective, in the interpretive mode meaning and belief are basic data. From the phenomenologists' perspective, moreover, no one can be the neutral observer required by positivist thought. Instead the observer filters knowledge and therefore must be self-conscious about her own biases and how they may affect her perceptions. The idea of intersubjectivity is central, as knowing depends on the ability to put oneself in the other's place. We have a shared humanity and to some degree can tap into each others' subjectivity. Subjectivity in this view is not just a personal experience, but it is built in a community through a social construction process. Interpretive views are in this way also consistent with collaborative dialogue, where meaning is collectively constructed.

In the interpretive account, phenomena can only be understood in context and cannot be pulled out and studied in an abstract way. The interpretive view emphasizes the uniqueness of each situation rather than its similarities to others. Its goal is to develop narratives that make sense of the complex dynamics of particular situations rather than laws to apply across multiple cases. Indeed much of collaborative dialogue is built on storytelling, as Chapter 5 illustrates. It is about wisdom and enlightenment rather than using tools to make something. Because every situation is unique we cannot pull out universal principles or simply transfer a strategy from one context to another. On the basis of interpretive knowledge, however, we can be more reflective, inventive, and sophisticated as we confront each new situation with understanding and insight.

We can theorize in the interpretive mode, but the theories are not in the form of variable-based hypotheses like a current one in planning: "the more sprawling the community the higher the percentage of obese residents, controlling for socioeconomic status."[5] Theory in the interpretive approach consists in building new constructs based on in-depth case analyses and cross-case comparisons. That is, the researcher stands back and looks at the larger picture to find an order that makes sense of what he has observed. For example, an interpretive researcher might conclude after research in several communities, that a sprawling place can develop a culture which is not only about driving, but also about a whole complex of related activities such as going to fast food places and engaging in sedentary entertainment. A place may attract people who already are inactive and wives who concentrate on cooking and housekeeping. The theory might be in the form of a story about how this culture reinforces itself as such people coexist in a sprawling environment.

Many aspects of collaborative processes mesh well with interpretive ways of knowing. They focus on particular situations rather than look for general principles; participants offer knowledge from their experience as well as from research; they challenge statements of fact and causality; and they build shared meaning around issues. Indeed collaborative dialogue is, more than anything else, a process of negotiating meanings – of problems, of evidence, of strategies, of justice or fairness, and of the nature of desirable outcomes. If meanings and values were already shared, bureaucracy could handle the issue in a routine way and experts could use established positivist principles and methodologies to solve problems. In collaborative dialogues participants listen to each other's information and to that of experts and engage in joint learning.

An alternative rationality for collaborative dialogue

While interpretive theorists made a breakthrough in helping to demonstrate how knowledge – even the presumably objective, scientific kind – is constructed through a social process, their perspective does not offer a place to stand to stake a claim on rationality, since in their view everything is relative. While some interpretive theorists suggest there is an objective reality out there, they offer no way to access it, even in theory. This way of knowing can be simply self-justifying and circular. A collaborative dialogue in this mode could result in the group jointly constructing a proposal that serves members' interests, but which is poorly informed, infeasible, or unjust and can lay no claim to rationality.

The most important perspective for understanding how collaborative dialogue can be rational comes from the Frankfurt School of critical theorists, particularly Jurgen Habermas. He lays out his theory of communicative rationality, identifying conditions under which the results of deliberations can be viewed as rational (Habermas 1981). While these conditions can never be perfectly achieved, any more than a pure scientific experiment can be implemented in the social world, we see his theory as the basis of collaborative rationality.

The Frankfurt School, which included such thinkers as Adorno, Horkheimer, and Habermas (Bernstein 1976), argued that reality is hidden under socially constructed understandings, theories, assumptions, and language. These reflect and reinforce power relationships in a society which in turn shape and distort knowledge. The "lifeworld," the world of everyday experience, is "colonized" by conceptions from these socially constructed understandings, placing us at a distance from our own reality, forcing us to see it through the lens of society. For example, we have come to understand certain mental states as "illness," and to see certain life styles as healthy. This evolution is not only created by science, it offers technology for manipulation and control. Critical theorists went further than phenomenologists, building their philosophy on challenging the hegemony of science and technology. They contended that constant change and transformation was the reality rather than the stasis that is a tacit assumption behind both positivist and interpretive ways of knowing. In their view contradictions are normal. Knowing involves exposing these, rather than attempting to rationalize them, as do experts in Berger and Luckmann's account of the social construction of reality (Berger and Luckmann 1967).

Knowledge in the Frankfurt School view is emancipatory, in that it requires getting past reified power relations and unacknowledged assumptions that distort knowledge. The knower must surface and critique all assumptions, as well as engage in critical self-reflection. Frankfurt theorists were influenced by Freud and his concept of transformation through self-reflection, which involves identifying one's own rational-izations to uncover what one has repressed.[6] Emancipatory knowledge also comes through a dialectical process. This dialectic allows knowers to grasp the many-sidedness of reality and get a sense of the whole, while being aware of contradictions. Dialectic never achieves stasis but reflects the shifting dynamics of the world, as evolving views continually confront one another. In a well managed collaborative dialogue, participants can challenge each other's assumptions and force self-reflection. They can jointly develop a nuanced understanding of a shifting reality.

Finally, emancipatory knowers engage in praxis. Praxis involves skills, intuitive knowledge, and tacit theory that come from deep and extended experience. This praxis gives would be knowers a link to a reality that cannot be fully articulated through discourse. Critical theorists contend that experience built on accumulated understanding largely bypasses language. In contrast to the neutral positivist observer, or the disinterested observer of interpretive theory who brackets his own subjectivity, this knower is deeply engaged in the world and has practical purposes for learning. But for practice and experience to amount to knowledge it must be intertwined with theorizing. Praxis makes it possible to look beyond the distortions introduced by abstract knowledge.

While Habermas contends instrumental action and rationality are important, his focus was on what he called communicative action and communicative rationality (Habermas 1981). In his view communications themselves are ways of acting in the world (Forester 1989). He contends that if communicative processes meet certain conditions, what emerges can be said to be rational – though in a very different sense than that associated with positivist thinking. The first condition is that dialogue must be face to face with all of the all differing interests. Second it must meet four speech conditions: all utterances must be comprehensible among participants; statements must be true in the positivist sense, using adequate logic and evidence; speakers must be sincere; and each must have the legitimacy to make the statements they do. They have to be able to develop sufficient intersubjective understanding to put themselves in one another's place and be mutually understood. There can be no coercion or domination by a participant, and all must be treated equally and listened to equally. Moreover, all participants must have equal access to information. Finally participants must question assumptions and take nothing for granted. Participants must be persuaded only by the force of a better argument and not by power, ignorance, or peer pressure. If these conditions can be met and the process results in agreement about the nature of a phenomenon or the desirability of an action, then the results are rational. This concept of communicative rationality serves a similar function to the scientific method for policy making, in that it is an ideal to be aimed at rather than something that can be perfectly achieved. This idea is the basis for the more practical concept of collaborative rationality which we address later in this chapter and in Chapter 4.

Applications in planning

While many scholars in professional fields make use of the ideas of Habermas, practitioners mostly remain unaware of them. Nonetheless practitioners of collaborative policy dialogues have independently invented practices which to a considerable degree mirror communicative rationality. This is not so surprising as both practice and theory have emerged from the same historical and political contexts and both address the same dilemmas. Three academics in planning and public policy were at the forefront of introducing the ideas of Habermas into these fields, showing how they could provide insights into practice – John Forester, Patsy Healey and John Dryzek.

John Forester was a pioneer in this regard, beginning with his seminal article "Critical theory and planning practice" (Forester 1980), which introduced Habermas' critical communications theory into planning. He showed, based on his observational research in a large city planning department, that planning practice is a form of communicative action through its attention-shaping effects. He argued that planning is not narrowly about developing means to particular ends, which was the predominant scholarly view at the time. He explained Habermas' speech conditions and showed how, in communicating, planners were acting on the world, not just transmitting knowledge, and showed how and when distortions in these communicative ideals affected citizens or developers. In an influential piece he argued that power was exercised in planning in great part through systematic distortions of information (Forester 1982). He made the case that a progressive planner had the responsibility for addressing these distorted communications to help equalize power among the parties.

These two articles, along with his first book (Forester 1989), influenced many planning theorists, including ourselves, as they provided an accessible way of understanding the relevance to planning practice of some of Habermas' key ideas. His work helped the field to see how centrally planning was about communication and how important the nature of that communication was to action, fairness, and the distribution of power. His later work continues its focus on planning as communicative action, moving into negotiation, mediation, and collaboration and the practices and the thinking of planners who engage in this work (Forester 1999; Forester 2009).

A second pioneer is British scholar Patsy Healey, whose influential 1992 article, "Planning through debate: the communicative turn in planning theory" argues that "the Habermasian conception of inter-subjective reasoning among diverse discourse communities, drawing on technical, moral and expressive-aesthetic ways of experiencing and understanding, can provide a direction for forms and practices of a planning behavior appropriate for societies which seek progressive ways of collectively making sense together" (Healey 1992b). She sought in her later research to find examples and look at their consequences. She also published an article looking at the micro level communicative activities of a planner's day (Healey 1992a) and another on the communicative work of plans (Healey 1996), along with a series of other books and articles focusing on how this type of discourse is central to place-making (Healey 1997; Healey 2006).

A third pioneer is political theorist John Dryzek, whose book, *Discursive Democracy*, critiqued instrumental rationality on a number of counts. Dryzek, whose focal concern is public policy making, contends that instrumental rationality destroys the "more congenial, spontaneous, egalitarian and meaningful aspects of human association" (Dryzek 1990). He says it is antidemocratic because of its potential to support social engineering in the name of rationality. It also, he argues, represses the playfulness and creativity that are necessary to freedom. Moreover, it is not effective in dealing with complex phenomena because it can only work by disaggregating them into parts. Instrumental rationality therefore makes effective and appropriate policy analysis impossible and has informed inappropriate and unfruitful social science instruments and methods. He makes a case for applying communicative rationality to deciding what desirable action is "based on a reciprocal understanding of the accepted . . . legitimate opinions and conceptual frameworks of other actors," in the absence of a shared commitment to the ultimate reasons why it is desirable. Dryzek emphasized the importance of applying Habermas' conditions to avoid compromises distorted by the "skewed distribution of power in society" and to prevent processes from falling into "hopeless pluralism" (Dryzek 1990).

Communities of inquiry

It turns out, however, that Habermas, founders of the fields of planning and public policy, and contemporary scholars, including Forester, have had their thinking significantly shaped by an earlier generation of philosophers – the American pragmatists (Hoch 1984a; Healey 2009). This school of thought, which was pushed aside by positivism and the Rational model for years, is undergoing a revival, particularly in professional fields like planning and public administration.[7] While the leading classical pragmatists (Charles Sanders Peirce, William James, John Dewey, and Jane Addams) differed in many ways in their thinking, coming as they did from entirely different backgrounds,[8] and while their thinking evolved considerably over their lifetimes, their work converged on an important and far reaching idea – that learning and knowing proceed through communities of inquiry. They believed that the process starts with a problematic situation which requires inquiry, just as do most planning and policy tasks. Participants in inquiry must start with an attitude that is scientific in the sense that it relies on working hypotheses that guide the gathering and interpretation of data and the testing of these through dialogue, experience, and experiment. In the pragmatic view nothing is ever really settled and we must constantly keep learning. Participatory democracy is part of this effort, especially as Dewey and Addams saw it. The idea of communities of inquiry was an effort to merge together scientific inquiry, praxis, joint learning, and democracy. It was the embodiment of Dewey's idea of democracy as a way of life (Dewey 1927). Because collaborative dialogue is also a version of a community of inquiry, we will take some time to explain it here. We believe that understanding pragmatists' perspectives can both inform and help to understand the rationality of these dialogues. By the same token, recent practices of collaborative policy making offer technology and methods for inquiry that Dewey did not imagine.

The classical pragmatists were autodidacts, untrammeled by scholarly "disciplines," which barely existed in the years from the Civil War through World War I, their prime years of creativity and philosophical ascendance in the U.S. They began by challenging the dominant metaphysicians who focused on the "nature of being," or ontology and the nature of reality. They did not think there was a fixed reality out there, much less that one could access it just by thinking about it. They were empiricists in the sense that they believed in the importance of searching out facts and data, while at the same time they were social constructionists who saw knowledge as an evolving social product. Indeed they were intellectual forebears of the phenomenologists who laid out the ideas of social construction of knowledge. In the early twentieth century pragmatists challenged analytic philosophers like Bertrand Russell, who focused on logic, clarity of argument, language, and the value of the natural sciences, but whose intellectual practice was largely separate from the empirical world. Indeed these analytic philosophers sired not only the positivism we have discussed above, but also logical positivism, which focused on formal logic without the necessity for verification. It evolved into the positivism that became the dominant paradigm for some professional fields and social sciences such as economics and political science (Menand 2001).

In the 1980s, with the emergence of interpretive epistemology and methods to guide research and the growth of collaborative dialogues, pragmatism was rediscovered. It provides a powerful alternative to the Rational model in its ideal of communities of inquiry. Dewey regarded ideas as tools for learning and saw the philosophical focus on how we know as a waste of time, a puzzle for the leisure classes to contemplate and meaningless if separated from the particular individuals and contexts in which knowing takes place. The pragmatists saw the universe as in progress and believed all problems were amenable to the exercise of intelligent action. They opposed hard and fast dichotomies and were often accused of imprecision as they resisted abstract thinking. They believed that the test of an idea or a practice was in its consequences and that learning involved doing and reflecting in a community. Dewey's goals in education were to develop creative intelligence in the students, including

> the ability to discern complexities of situations, imagination that is exercised in seeing new possibilities and hypotheses; willingness to learn from experience; fairness and objectivity in evaluating conflicting values and opinions; and the courage to change one's views when demanded by the consequences of our actions and the criticisms of others.
>
> (Bernstein 1971: 222)

His ideas on democracy were parallel. For him democracy was grounded in participatory inquiry that engages a full range of views. He contends that

> freedom of inquiry, toleration of diverse views, freedom of communication, the distribution of what is found out to every individual as the ultimate intellectual consumer, are involved in democratic as in scientific method.
>
> (Dewy quoted in Bernstein 1971: 223)

He goes on to say

> Democracy as compared with other ways of life is the sole way of living which believes wholeheartedly in the process of experience as end and as means; as that which is capable of generating the science which is the sole dependable authority for the direction of further experience and releases emotions, needs and desires so as to call into being the things that have not existed in the past.
>
> (Dewy quoted in Bernstein 1971: 223)

Experience, inquiry and education are at the heart of Dewey's philosophy, as they are at the heart of collaborative policy making. We explore these ideas further in Chapters 5 and 6.

Negotiation theory and alternative dispute resolution

The most directly influential theory for collaborative dialogues in practice draws on the path breaking book *Getting to Yes* (Fisher and Ury 1981). The central insights of this book have transformed negotiation around the world and created the foundation for alternative dispute resolution (ADR) and consensus building. The authors developed principles that were later to become watchwords for collaborative dialogues. These include: separate the people from the problem; focus on interests not positions; invent options for mutual gain; insist on using objective criteria; and develop your BATNA (Best Alternative to a Negotiated Agreement). If participants can treat each other civilly while disagreeing over the problem, that is an essential start for collaboration. If they can avoid taking hard and fast positions which lead to hostility and stalemate and instead reveal to each other their underlying interests, they can potentially find common ground. For example, if a neighborhood group insists on the position that a proposed building should be no more than three stories while the developer insists that he has to have eight, the negotiation is at an impasse. But if the neighbors say their interest is in protecting the nearby park from shadows and the developer says his interest is in making a profit, the negotiation can then focus on creating new designs based on meeting both parties' interests. With interests in mind instead of positions, it is possible to find solutions that are not simply compromises or tradeoffs. If other interests besides shadows and profit can be introduced, like aesthetics or traffic, the potential is even greater to create joint gain for the parties with innovative solution packages. These are the same principles that guide professionally managed collaborative decision making.

Several further contentions from Fisher and Ury became guiding principles for collaborative practice. First, they contend that to make a decision that will be accepted over time, parties should agree on objective criteria for the choice of options. Second, to negotiate effectively each party must work out what is the best it can do if there is no agreement – that is, their BATNA. Players must keep their BATNA in mind during discussion to make sure they do not agree to something they should not and to get a sense of where their limits are and when they should leave the negotiation. Players can get more leverage if they can improve their BATNA by, for example, finding a new external ally. Third, since durable agreements are deeply rooted in people's interests, both hard bargaining (insisting on one's way) or soft bargaining (giving in to avoid conflict) are equally destructive. The soft bargainer resents the other player afterwards, and the hard bargainer may not get true agreement. Thus for collaborative dialogue to produce durable conclusions, every participant must both know his or her interests and explain and stand up for them. Finally, Fisher and Ury argue that if you win at the expense of the other party you create an enemy, but if you can find a mutual gain solution, you create an ally. This insight carries over to collaborative dialogues, which build social and political capital that lasts into the future.

Interpretive knowing: a framing for collaborative planning and deliberative public policy

During the past 25 years or so theorists in policy fields also began to turn away from "armchair theorizing," which involved thinking about how to make planning processes more logical, efficient, and effective (de Neufville 1983) in the Rational model style, to a new way of thinking more conducive to understanding communication and collaboration. In planning these new theorists began building grounded theory based on what planning practitioners did in context and what planning practice was actually like (Innes 1995). A key event was an international planning theory conference held in 1988 in Turin, Italy, which brought together British, Italian, and American theorists. This set the foundation for an international community of scholars who were looking at practice through various theoretical lenses. The new planning theorists sought to understand planning in phenomenological and critical theory traditions, rather than to develop laws or principles of how to do planning to get particular outcomes. The research involved extensive observations of practice, interviews with practitioners, and storytelling. It shone light on practice and raised questions. Part of this sense making involved drawing on theorists such as Habermas and Foucault for insight. Debates and discussions began to take place in the meetings of the Association of Collegiate Schools of Planning and the Association of European Schools of Planning and in the growing numbers of planning journals. The edited volume *Explorations in Planning Theory* (Mandelbaum, et al. 1996) collected key papers from the first joint conference of these two associations in 1992 in Oxford. A networked set of scholars across the U.S., Europe, and beyond have developed an approach to planning grounded in the idea of communicative action.[9]

A parallel movement, inspired by interpretive epistemology, has emerged in the fields of public policy, public administration, and political science. The scholars label their theories "post-positivist." They pay attention to discourse, to the relationship of citizens and experts, to deliberation, and to a variety of other topics which they investigate through interpretive methods (Fischer 2003; Hajer and Wagenaar 2003; Yanow 2000). They set up a group on Theory, Policy and Society as part of the American Political Science meetings[10] and held sessions, organized an annual conference in Europe on interpretive method in policy studies, and began to build an international intellectual community. Unlike planning however, this movement has thus far remained a minority voice in these fields which, more than planning, have been dominated by a positivist methodological credo.

The movements converged in 1993 in a co-edited book called *The Argumentative Turn* (Fischer and Forester 1993) which included articles by key thinkers and researchers across public policy and planning. Authors in this book emphasized discourse, framing, and narrative as well as policy argumentation. It quickly became a widely used text in both fields. A second book ten years later, edited by one of the authors in the first book, continued the tradition, combining planning and public policy theorists (Hajer and Wagenaar 2003).

Complexity science

While each school of thought discussed so far has played a part in the emergence of the praxis of collaborative policy making, none offers a developed framework for understanding how collaboration plays a part in a complex, changing and uncertain world. For this we turn to the contemporary paradigm of complexity science. Many of our colleagues, unfamiliar with this rich body of ideas and theory, dismiss it as unnecessary. After all, we already know the world is complex. What else is there to say? Complexity science however is a lens which provides illuminating, even transformative, ways of understanding what is going on in the world. It offers an alternative to the machine model to guide our thinking and practice. Complexity science focuses on the larger dynamic system in which actions take place and suggests a holistic and interactive approach to societal issues − one that is highly compatible with collaborative policy making. Indeed it could be argued that, if the world mirrors what complexity science sees, this kind of interactive, inclusive policy making is essential.

In our view developments in complexity science will be seen in the not too distant future to have caused a revolution in thinking that affected every branch of knowledge. Though it remains outside the mainstream in the social sciences, it is being picked up rapidly as understanding spreads. Science author James Gleick (Gleick 1987), in his popular account of this emerging science, notes that passionate advocates contend that twentieth-century science will be remembered for just three things: relativity, quantum mechanics and chaos. Chaos, they contend has become the century's third great revolution in the physical sciences. Like the first two revolutions chaos cuts away at the tenets of Newton's physics. As one physicist put it "Relativity eliminated the Newtonian illusion of absolute space and time; quantum theory eliminated the Newtonian dream of a controllable measurement process; and chaos eliminates the LaPlacian fantasy of deterministic predictability" (Gleick 1987). Of the three the revolution in chaos applies to the universe we see and touch, to objects at the human scale. Everyday experience and real pictures of the world have become legitimate targets for inquiry. There has long been a feeling, not always expressed openly, that physics has strayed too far from human intuition about the world.

Research in chaos and complexity originated with physical scientists working to understand behaviors in phenomena that could not be understood through the linear mathematics of physics grounded in the Newtonian model of the universe.[11] When studying these phenomena at first, scientists avoided nonlinear equations because they were difficult to solve, instead using approximate linear equations. The systems were nonlinear, however, so that inputs were not necessarily proportionate to outputs and the usual approach of breaking the system into components for study and then reassembling them did not predict accurately. One of the early pioneers of complexity science, the meteorologist Lorenz (1993), discovered that even a minor alteration in a model for the behavior of weather would make a dramatic and rapid difference in weather predictions. This extreme responsiveness to small actions is one of the hallmarks of a complex adaptive system (CAS), and it is often referred to as the "butterfly effect." The image is of a butterfly flapping its wings in the Amazon affecting the weather in the state of North Dakota.

The development of high-speed computers in the 1970s gave scientists new techniques and mathematics that they could use to solve nonlinear equations. These revealed surprising patterns showing an underlying order in seeming chaos. When a nonlinear equation is solved, instead of a formula, the result is a pattern and visual description of the system's complex dynamics. Ilya Prigogine turned to nonlinear mathematics to investigate how living systems are able to maintain their life processes under conditions of non-equilibrium. This work resulted in his theory of dissipative structures (Prigogine and Stenger 1984), in which there is a combination of structure and flow. For example, in a rapidly moving river, a standing wave structure is maintained while molecules of water stream through it. This work was published at the same time as Giddens' on the structuration of society (Giddens 1984) making much the same point – that agents enact structure while structure constrains them, and both evolve together through time and space. Prigogine and Stenger also showed that when the flow of energy increases, the system may experience instability, at which point it can transition into a new state with new forms of order that can be seen through computer models. A major economic crisis like that of 2008–9 could result in a new social and economic order as our complex societies find ways to adapt, with or without intervention.

These evocative ideas about systems are difficult to introduce into policy making because Newtonian physics has had such a deep impact on our way of thinking about the world. Policy science and management and the Rational model developed with concepts of Newtonian physics as the foundational metaphor. The tacit framing is that a policy is analogous to a machine. If it is not working, we can break it down into its parts, figure out what is broken, fix it, and put it back together with the problem corrected. Policy making is linear, and we can work through a step by step process starting from goals, to analysis, formulation, and implementation and come out with the desired result. It is an input/output system, where we can examine each of the inputs and predict the impact on the system. Components of a system interact with each other in a way that produces predictable end states. If we knew enough about the parts, we could predict the behavior of the system. But complexity thinking denies this metaphor, leaving us with a much more uncertain and elusive image of reality.

The rich set of ideas generated by complexity theorists offers fertile ground for innovation in approaches to policy and to the "out of the box" thinking we need at this point in history. Complexity science converges with the critical theorists' focus on the dialectical nature of knowledge, as it does with the dynamic of Giddens' structuration theory (Giddens 1984). Indeed it emphasizes the interactive and evolving nature of the social world rather than reifying simplicity and stability that do not exist. While complexity science was at first known as chaos theory, over the years it has become clear that a complex system demonstrates patterns of behavior. These do not allow precise prediction of specific events or outcomes of interventions, but they do focus attention on the system rather than simply its parts. Complex systems, under certain conditions, can be complex adaptive systems (CAS), self-organizing and perhaps moving to higher levels of system performance. Thus an ecosystem after a fire can reemerge as a more bio-diverse and dynamic environment. As professionals we can encourage policies that are designed to encourage self-organization, system wide learning and adaptiveness.

Scholars have outlined five features of CAS in particular that can be helpful in applying the ideas to planning and policy (Cilliers 2005; Portugali 2008; Stacey 2001; Tsoukas 2005). It is most productive to focus on the interactions and relationships rather than the system as a whole, which is probably impossible to grasp. As we do this we need to keep the following in mind. First, the system is made up of very large numbers of individual agents connected through multiple networks. Second, these agents interact dynamically, exchanging information and energy according to localized heuristics. Even if specific agents only interact with a few others, the effects propagate through the system. As a result the system has a memory that is not located at a specific place, but is distributed throughout the system. Third, the interactions are nonlinear, iterative, recursive, and self-referential with many direct and indirect feedback loops. Fourth, the

Table 2.1 Features of complex adaptive systems

Feature	Summary description
Agents	The system comprises large numbers of individual agents connected through multiple networks.
Interactions	The agents interact dynamically, exchanging information and energy based upon heuristics that organize the interactions locally. Even if specific agents only interact with a few others, the effects propagate through the system. As a result the system has a memory that is not located at a specific place, but is distributed throughout the system.
Nonlinearity	The interactions are nonlinear, iterative, recursive, and self-referential. There are many direct and indirect feedback loops.
System behavior	The system is open, the behavior of the system is determined by the interactions, not the components, and the behavior of the system cannot be understood by looking at the components. It can only be understood by looking at the interactions. Coherent and novel patterns of order emerge.
Robustness and adaptation	The system displays both the capacity to maintain its viability and the capacity to evolve. With sufficient diversity the heuristics will evolve, the agents will adapt to each other, and the system can reorganize its internal structure without the intervention of an outside agent.

Source: Cilliers 2005; Stacey 2001; Tsoukas 2005.

system is open to its environment, and its behavior is determined by the interactions (Schelling 1978; Stacey 2001). Fifth, the system displays both the capacity to maintain its viability and the capacity to evolve. With sufficient internal diversity, the heuristics for action will evolve, the agents will adapt to each other, and the system can reorganize its internal structure without the intervention of an outside agent.

A large and growing literature already explores the implications of CAS thinking for the private sector.[12] Futurist Alvin Toffler anticipated the CAS approach to business: "Instead of being routine and predictable, the corporate environment has grown increasingly unstable, accelerative, and revolutionary . . . The adaptive corporation, therefore, needs a new kind of leadership. It needs managers of adaptation equipped with a whole set of new, nonlinear skills" (Toffler 1984). More recently a literature has emerged, focusing on business case studies that offer lessons from CAS on product design (Chiva-Gomez 2004), innovation (Rose-Anderssen, et al. 2005), organizational development (van Eijnatten and van Galen 2005), successful computer businesses (Brown and Eisenhardt 1998; Eisenhardt and Tabrizi 1995), and business process and strategy (Rose-Anderssen, et al. 2005).

Although one could comment in the same way about unpredictability and instability in the public sector, there have been few comparable studies on government or public policy. Notable exceptions include case studies on modeling urban and regional dynamics (Allen and Allen 1997; Epstein and Axtell 1996), on urban regeneration (Moobela 2005), and on health services (Kernick 2005). In our research we use CAS thinking to theorize about the central aspects of collaborative planning, diversity, interdependence, and interaction (Booher and Innes 2002). We concluded, for example, that traditional approaches to evaluating public programs did not make sense for collaborative planning and developed an evaluation framework based upon CAS (Ambruster 2008; Connick and Innes 2003; Innes and Booher 1999a). We have also suggested the potential of CAS for metropolitan development (Innes and Booher 1999c) and for the development and use of indicators for sustainable communities (Innes and Booher 2000).

Complexity thinking suggests that as policy professionals we need to operate at the system scale rather than focus piecemeal on individual fixes. To do so we need the insights of critical theory, pragmatism, communicative planning and deliberative policy analysis. The insights of complexity science added to these suggest that we need to build dispersed intelligence, linked together through networks and dialogue among diverse players, searching out many types of knowledge, if we are to have a hope of operating effectively in our complex, uncertain and constantly changing world.

Collaborative policy processes are complex adaptive systems

If we look at collaborative processes through the lens of CAS we can find ways to make these processes more effective. They should be self-organizing, with diverse agents, many interactions, and nonlinear dynamics as they evolve if they are to be creative and adaptive. As in complexity theory, inclusion of all agents is required for coherent and novel patterns of action to emerge. The Law of Excess Diversity in complexity says that a system must reflect the diversity of the environment if it is to be robust and adaptative. "For a system to survive as a coherent entity over the medium and long term, it must have a number of internal states *greater* than those considered requisite to deal with the outside world" (Allen 2001). The inclusion of all interests and perspectives is also a condition for communicative rationality and for Dewey's idea of social intelligence. Thus there is a substantial convergence of complexity thinking with the theories we have outlined above.

Collaborative policy processes have many parallels with complex systems. They can range in size from a handful of participants to hundreds organized in a network of interlocking committees and task forces, each working on different aspects of the situation. Such structure allows communication among groups and permits ideas and actions to propagate through the system. Rather than following the linear path of the Rational model, this type of policy making may jump back and forth as formulation of a tentative solution leads to new questions that may alter the goals and require new analysis. Likewise, early steps of implementation may lead to changed understandings that result in the revisiting of all of the steps. Participants come to see their work as grounded in the contingency that Dewey argues is integral to social intelligence – that is, they recognize that nothing is permanently settled and that they must keep up their inquiry and testing of their ideas. During the interactions, negative feedback from the environment may discourage proposed approaches or positive feedback may encourage deeper focus on one or more approaches in a way parallel to the patterns in CAS. Collaborative policy making also resembles CAS in that it is sensitive to initial conditions. For example, the apparently minor decision to exclude a particular stakeholder may dramatically change how the system evolves over time, whereas a major factor like lack of trust may not make much difference. These nonlinear features often put collaborative processes in tension with conventional public decision making so sometimes stakeholders must operate informally around the less flexible bureaucracy to allow the collaborative process to function in its natural, nonlinear ways despite conflicting formal practices.[13]

Collaborative processes are resilient in the sense that they can absorb radical change in the environment and still maintain their integrity like a standing wave. For example, we have observed many processes shaken by divisive media reports or by changes in the political environment. Participants were able to regroup, adjust, and continue their work. Collaborative processes create new knowledge and unanticipated policies and practices. They can result in changes in the values, goals, shared understandings, and underlying attitudes of the participants. Such changes in turn enhance the capacity of both individuals and the group as a whole to approach action in contingent ways, recognizing that the world might not turn out to be as they imagine it. These processes help participants prepare to move in an alternative direction if they need to.

The DIAD (diversity, interdependence, authentic dialogue) theory of collaborative rationality

We have developed a theory (diagrammed in Fig. 2.1) to help explore what collaborative policy making can accomplish and under what conditions (Innes and Booher 2003a). It is both a descriptive and a normative theory – descriptive of successful collaborative processes and normative in that it provides a model for the design and implementation of collaborative processes that can produce significant outcomes. This theory borrows substantially from ideas we have outlined above, and it is informed by the findings of our research projects, as well as observations based on our practice. From our early work we learned that many of the most valued outcomes of collaborations were of the systemic variety – that is, they not only produced specific outcomes, but they also affected the system by changing attitudes, relationships, and capabilities of players. These collaborative processes were constantly evolving and adapting. So we frame our understanding of collaborative processes within the concept of complex adaptive systems.

The conditions for collaborative rationality

Three conditions are critical to whether a collaborative process can be collaboratively rational, productive of socially valuable outcomes, and adaptive to the opportunities and challenges of its unique and changing context. These conditions include full diversity of interests among participants, interdependence of the participants, who cannot get their interests met independently, and engagement of all in a face to face authentic dialogue meeting Habermas' basic speech conditions. We contend that both theory and practice demonstrate that if such players engage around a meaningful shared task under

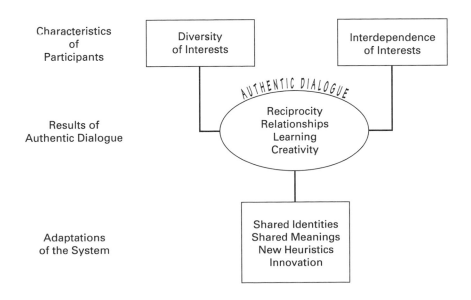

Figure 2.1 **DIAD network dynamics**

these conditions, the dialogue can produce innovations that lead to an adaptive policy system in a context of complexity and uncertainty.

The condition of diversity implies that a collaboratively rational process must include not only agents who have power because they are "deal makers" or "deal breakers," but also those who have needed information or could be affected by outcomes of the process. This condition is consistent with Habermas' idea of communicative rationality in its requirement for inclusion of all perspectives. There must be many values, interests, perspectives, skills, and types and sources of knowledge in the process for robust ideas to develop and for the system to build a capacity to adapt over time.[14] A social system needs this variety, just as an ecological system needs biodiversity. If one strategy or idea does not work, other possibilities float around in the dialogue that can be explored or combined to produce new approaches.[15] In practice it is not uncommon for powerful agents to exclude some affected interests or perspectives, but when this happens, the results of the dialogue are likely to be infeasible, uninformed or unjust. While such processes may be called collaborative by some, they are not collaboratively rational. Keeping this distinction in mind is critical to preventing the misuse and misrepresentation of what we regard as pseudo collaboration, which can co-opt players and deceive the public into thinking a proposal has taken into account a wide set of perspectives.

The condition of interdependence holds that agents must depend to a significant degree on the other agents in a reciprocal way. That is, each has something others want. This condition helps assure that participants will maintain the interest and energy to engage with each other throughout the process and have the incentive to reach agreement. Negotiation theory tells us that interdependence among interests is key to moving past zero sum games to creative mutual gain agreements. This interdependence means that, on the one hand, players cannot achieve their objectives alone and on the other that, given their diversity, the likelihood is that some players will value certain results more than others. Therefore as a group they may be able to put together a package that will provide for players to get more of what they value most without necessarily reducing the value that accrues to others. Interdependence makes this dynamic possible, though not guaranteed, and it keeps people at the table.

Complexity science views agents as linked together in a loosely integrated network, where interdependence is the nature of things. Like the butterfly in Brazil and the weather in North Dakota we are all interdependent in more or less obvious ways. As noted above, both Ostrom and Axelrod demonstrate that instrumentally rational, self-interested players cooperate when they are interdependent and need each other to accomplish their purposes (Axelrod 1984; Ostrom 1990). Where agents are not interdependent, DIAD theory suggests the process cannot be collaboratively rational, nor can it produce high quality outcomes.

The third condition, authentic dialogue, requires that the agents must engage with each other on a shared task in a deliberation that closely adheres to Habermas' ideal speech conditions. That is, the deliberations must be characterized by engagement among agents so that they can mutually assure that their claims are legitimate, accurate, comprehensible, and sincere. The deliberations must be inclusive of all major interests and knowledge. They cannot be dominated by those with power outside the process, and all must have equal access to all the relevant information and an equal ability to speak and be listened to. In authentic dialogue all participants can challenge any assumptions or any assertions. Nothing is taken for granted, and nothing is off the table. Deliberations take a natural course without constraints or direction by external control. Authentic dialogue is consistent with a phenomenological view of knowledge in that it relies on what participants know from their everyday life and not just on specialized, scientific expertise. It jointly constructs knowledge through interaction and joint learning in pragmatist style. Authentic dialogue also reflects the idea from complexity science that interactions among agents are the most important points of inquiry for understanding system behavior.

Many examples of processes that are called "collaboration" fail to meet the conditions of authentic dialogue. They may not be self-organizing but controlled by their conveners to preclude specific topics. They may become solely exercises in bargaining and tradeoffs (although bargaining itself can be one form of exchange in collaborative rationality). Or they may not maintain ideal speech conditions, either because they do not have the expertise to do this, or because outside pressures such as political posturing (strategic communication) or media attention lead to distortions in the necessary speech conditions.

Results and system adaptations

If these three conditions are met, four key results typically emerge in the dynamics of interaction. First, the agents discover the reciprocal nature of their interests. Instead of solely competing, agents become aware that meeting their own interests can come from working with the reciprocal interests of others. They can begin to explore opportunities for joint approaches that address multiple interests. Agents may then be able to articulate the interests of other agents with their own. Agents can come to recognize that their own interests cannot be achieved without the needs of other agents being met, and search for options with mutual and joint gains.

Second, the stakeholders also develop new relationships which often survive the conclusion of the collaborative process. Often they have had prior relationships with the other stakeholders, but these may have been defined by their conflicts. Authentic dialogue can change the nature of their relationship as participants gain new understandings of their counterparts. They come to recognize the fundamental human concerns and experiences they all share. They gain new appreciation of what it is like to "walk in the shoes" of the other person. They often build new professional working relationships in the process. They may find they share recreational or vocational interests as well. It is not uncommon for trust to be engendered in this new relationship, and in our experience it is not unusual for friendships to develop among formerly adversarial agents.

Third, both single loop and double loop learning emerge from collaboratively rational dialogue as agents discover both new means to achieve their interests and come to reexamine and reframe the interests they previously held (Argyris 1993). As illustrated in Figure 2.1 agents not only learn from each other about new actions and strategies they can explore to meet their goal, they also may rethink their initial goals and interests in the policy issue. A case in point occurred when environmentalists and developers came to realize in one process engaged in by Booher that preventing or encouraging housing development was less important than certainty regarding when and how development would be allowed.

Finally DIAD theory says that collaborative rationality can lead to second and third order effects, which we call adaptations to the system because they transcend the agreements and the process itself. Participants start to develop shared meanings, for example of the water resource they share, so that they are no longer like a set of blind men with an elephant with each defining the water resource differently, e.g. a drinking water supply, habitat for fish; or an entitlement worth money. Instead they come to see it more holistically as resource for a region that plays a part in its overall welfare and on which all are dependent. In the process of this discovery they often develop shared identities, as for example both users and protectors of the water resource. As they work together they also develop new heuristics for how to collectively and individually address water quality or supply problems. They do not have to work out from scratch how to proceed every time an issue arises.[16]

These shared heuristics for engaging with each other (for example, listening, challenging assumptions, and seeking mutual gains) can carry over into future interactions beyond the collaborative process. As individuals they learn ways to deal with their local issues that are consistent with the sustainability of the system without having to wait for direction from some hierarchical authority (Innes and Booher 1999c). Finally over time they may be able to turn the creative ideas invented in the dialogue into actual innovations. A real innovation requires a conversation with its environment so that it can become part of it (Rogers 1962). A new idea has to mesh with the context and the motivations of the players for it to become an innovation in practice. As Giddens' structuration theory suggests, though participants are influenced by the structure (norms and institutional arrangements) in which they are embedded, their new heuristics and norms can gradually alter this structure. As complexity science suggests, these evolving heuristics can enhance the adaptiveness and sustainability of the system.

Conclusion

In this chapter we have worked through the various schools of thought that provide ways to understand and improve collaborative practice and better address the wicked problems that surround us. We see theory and practice converging in many respects and hope in this book to help build the bridges that we need. Many social theories of the past 100 years or more have fed into the development of the practice and theory collaborative policy making, communicative planning and deliberative policy analysis. Phenomenology and the acceptance of the idea that we socially construct knowledge, along with the emergence of the critical theorists' ideas about the dialectical nature of knowing, the importance of praxis and the need to challenge assumptions provide important underpinnings for conducting and justifying collaborative practice. These both owe a profound debt to American pragmatism as a forebear of these. Pragmatism has additionally played a direct role in shaping the thinking of the founders of American planning. Today even the theorists of instrumental rationality have found that collaboration can be in an individual's self-interest. The growth of negotiation theory and practice has provided the foundation for collaborative policy making in recent years.

We look forward to the evolution of collaboration through the lens of complexity science. This provides a new metaphor to help us see the task of policy making to replace the machine metaphor we have so long taken for granted. Complexity thinking points in the direction of paying attention to systems as a whole rather than components and offers us ways to assure greater adaptiveness and creativity in a world of constant change and even crisis.

Finally, we offered here our DIAD theory of the features needed for a collaboratively rational process. We explored what we have found to be outcomes of processes that meet the conditions for collaborative rationality. This theory will be a theme throughout the book, particularly in the next chapter, where we offer six case studies of ostensibly collaborative policy making and assess them in terms of our theory.

Notes

1   See for example the Center for Collaborative Policy (www.csus.edu/ccp/), Policy Consensus Initiative (www.policyconsensus.org), and the Consensus Building Institute (www.cbuilding.org).

2   We capitalize Rational to distinguish the specialized version associated with positivist professional practice from the more generic meaning of rational.

3   They do this despite the fact that surveys show that quantitative skills rank very low in importance for practicing planners, well behind oral and written skills and negotiation.

4   This is the dilemma of two prisoners kept in separate cells who face the problem of deciding whether to confess or not. If one confesses and the other does not, the former will benefit at the expense of the other. If neither confesses, they both benefit, but not as much.

5   In the last few years there has been in the U.S. a growth of interest in finding specific measurable relationship between development patterns and human health and considerable funding for research on this.

6   Organization and planning theorist Donald Schon also explored this in his classic volume *The Reflective Practitioner*, Schon, D. A. (1983). *The Reflective Practitioner: How Professionals Think in Action*, New York: Basic Books.

7   This revival involve Bernstein's perspectives (Bernstein 1971) and Menand's intellectual history of nineteenth and early twentieth century American philosophers including Peirce, James, and Dewey (Menand 2001) as well as the work of Rorty (Murphy and Rorty 1990). Planning scholar Charles Hoch has devoted a series of articles to illustrating how pragmatism does and should shape planning thought (Hoch 1984a, 1984b, 1996, 2002, 2007). British scholar Patsy Healey recently "discovered" American pragmatism, which had little attention in Europe, and wrote a useful overview, reflecting her strong sense that these ideas paralleled her own and helped to illuminate and deepen her

understandings (Healey 2009). Public administration scholar Patricia Shields has used pragmatism to help rethink her field (Shields 2003, 2004).

8   Peirce was a mathematician; James trained as a medical doctor and became a psychologist; Dewey was a transcendentalist philosopher, and Jane Addams a social worker.

9   See the chapter by Patsy Healey in Larry Vale and Bish Sanyal's *History of Planning Ideas* (Healey, forthcoming).

10   www.cddc.vt.edu/tps/www.essex.ac.uk/ECpR/standinggroups/perspectives/index.htm

11   For an introduction and overview of complexity science, we suggest the following: Holland 1995; Kauffman 1995; Kelly 1994; Waldrop 1992.

12   Allen 2001; Axelrod and Cohen 2000; Bar-Yam, et al. 2004; Capra 1996; Cilliers 2005; McKelvey 2001; Richardson 2002; Stacey 1996; Stacey 2001; Tsoukas 2005.

13   See the CALFED case in Chapter 3 and the article by Innes, et al. (2007). "Informality as a planning strategy: collaborative water management in the CALFED Bay-Delta Program," *Journal of the American Planning Association* 73(2): 195–210.

14   Hong and Page have demonstrated that randomly selected, diverse groups perform better than groups made up of the highest performers Hong, L. and Page, S. (2001), "Problem solving by heterogeneous agents," *Journal of Economic Theory* 97(1): 123–63.

15   This is a metaphor for what happens to unused ideas. They get tossed into a garbage can, where they remain until someone looking for new approaches searches through it, Cohen, et al. (1972), "A garbage can model of organizational choice."

16   In a sense the agents using these heuristics represent a boundary community of practice that bridges the separate communities of practice the agents come from. Wenger argues that "Its enterprise is to deal with boundaries and sustain a connection between a number of other practices by addressing conflicts, reconciling perspectives, and finding resolutions" (Wenger 1998: 114). In Wenger's framing, traditional policy processes can be conceived of as multiple communities of practice that involve mutual engagement in a joint enterprise with a shared repertoire. The distinction between these traditional communities of practice and collaborative communities of practice are the shared heuristics based on authentic dialogue and the condition that all affected agents are engaged, not just the usual suspects.

3 Stories from the field

Why collaborations should not be regarded as black boxes

Too often scholars and practitioners think of collaborative processes more or less as black boxes. They seldom inquire into the dynamics of actual deliberations, the structure of the processes, who the participants are, or the methods by which conclusions are reached. But all these things matter because they make the difference between an authentic collaboration and a process that co-opts, manipulates, or simply does not reflect a genuine agreement, much less a societally beneficial conclusion. An inauthentic collaboration may produce little or nothing and simply be a waste of time and money; it may be window dressing for decisions already made; or it may be a lowest common denominator agreement or even a cooptation process.[1] Alternatively, commentators may pass judgment on collaboration as a decision method based on one or two processes they know about. In depth interpretive inquiry into actual collaborations is essential if we are to advance either practice or theory. Otherwise practitioners will design collaborative processes that are doomed to fail, and theoreticians will draw conclusions about collaboration based on a stylized, armchair version of the practice.

This chapter is designed to help fill this gap in our understanding. Many case studies of collaboration have been published (Brunner, et al. 2002; Chisholm 1989; Koontz 2004; Mandarano 2005; Owen, et al. 2008; Scholz and Stiftel 2005; Susskind, et al. 1999; Thomas 2003), but such case studies do not often provide the detail on process and context that would allow an assessment of how and why they did or did not work. In this chapter we offer stories of six public decision processes that were ostensibly collaborative, unpacking and laying out for each the nature of the discussion, the internal dynamics, and the process design. At one end the examples range from highly collaborative, productive processes that come close to meeting the main conditions we laid out in the DIAD theory and that reflect "best practices" of professionally facilitated processes. Further along the continuum we outline somewhat less collaborative and professional efforts that nonetheless had important outcomes and then move to mixed processes that had some collaborative components, but fell short of collaborative rationality to a considerable degree. These processes differ in scale from state, to regional, to local. They differ in content between issues, types of participants, process design, and dialogue management. All of them, except Cincinnati, are cases we know well through in-depth, on-site research, including interviewing and observation or through participation ourselves. In the Cincinnati case ample video coverage offered some direct observation which we supplemented with evaluation reports and discussions with the mediator.

While each case is unique, we frame these stories in terms of six common features for comparison: a) their context; b) how they started; c) their structure and process; d) first order results; e) implementation strategy; and f) second and third order effects, which we term system adaptations. We follow each case with an analysis of the degree to which it was collaboratively rational. We then look for correspondence with our DIAD theory to help us "see" what went on through this lens and point to reasons for comparative success and failure.

Our first two cases are of collaborative dialogues that largely followed the principles of our DIAD theory and had significant beneficial outcomes, including instigating institutional change. One concerns a contentious regional resource management issue, another an urban race relations conflict. The third case, involving the development of a state growth management plan, was an early experiment in consensus building which followed some, but not all, key principles of collaborative rationality. It has evolved over

Table 3.1 Summary of case studies

Case	Policy Issue	Location	Initiator	Process
Sacramento Water Forum	Regional water planning	Sacramento Region	Local government	Stakeholder negotiation
Cincinnati Community Police Relations Collaborative	Race relations and public safety	City of Cincinnati	Federal court	Community engagement collaborative
New Jersey State Plan Process	State comprehensive planning	New Jersey	State government	Cross acceptance advisory committee
CALFED	State water planning	California	Federal and state agencies	Interagency collaboration with stakeholder advisory committees
BAASC	Growth management	San Francisco bay region	Advocacy groups	Coalition building and advocacy
EBCRC	Military base conversions	San Francisco bay region	U.S. Congressman	Stakeholder advisory committee

more than 20 years, and many lessons emerge from the experience. We follow these with a case on statewide water management in California that had powerful and important results, though some aspects did not meet the conditions of authentic dialogue. This process fell short of hopes, primarily because of the loss of funding and high level support after changes in government. We follow these with two cases that were ostensibly collaborative, a voluntary association of civic leaders working on regional sustainability and smart growth and an effort to assist the San Francisco Bay Area to recover economically from a series of major military base closures. Both involved high level stakeholders in ongoing meetings over several years, but when we examine their dynamics, we find they fell far short of collaborative rationality. Though they had some agreements and some outcomes, they failed in a variety of ways that can be attributed to their design and structure and to the nature of their interactions. Neither achieved the quality of outcomes or the second and third order effects that the others did. Table 3.1 offers a summary of the cases.

Collaborative rationality in action: The Sacramento Area Water Forum[2]

Among the many cases we have studied, the Sacramento Area Water Forum is one that comes close to meeting the ideal of collaborative rationality and producing the kinds of outcomes we outline in our DIAD theory. While its success was substantially dependent on factors such as significant funding, high level support, and patience from key players that may not always be forthcoming, this story does offer an exemplar of what can be accomplished, and how, under nearly ideal conditions. In that sense it is a test of the theory of collaborative rationality.

Context

The Sacramento Area Water Forum was a consensus seeking collaboration among multiple parties with interests in the water resources and ecological health of the lower American River in northern California. It did not arise out of any specific dispute or crisis, but it emerged in a region with a history of conflict with regard to water and where several previous attempts at regional water planning had been unsuccessful. The American River basin has a long history of legal wrangling over water supplies and the health of the river. In a landmark case, a water purveyor from outside the region – the East Bay Municipal Utility District (EBMUD) – sought in the 1970s to obtain American River water. The County joined environmental organizations in a lawsuit against EBMUD which was not to be decided till almost 20 years later. The court established minimum flow levels that would have to be met before EBMUD could divert water. This was one of the key issues that provided the incentive for the stakeholders to participate. In the language of negotiation theory, this court decision changed the BATNA of many players for whom the best alternative was no longer going it alone. Other conflicts were also part of the picture. Sacramento County, which has an extensive park system along the river, had established itself as a protector of the river and had battled expansion of the City of Sacramento's water treatment plant. Similarly, Sacramento-based environmentalists had challenged a number of other water districts seeking to develop new water supplies. Flood control, dam building and growth were all issues in the region.

Getting started

The City and County of Sacramento joined in initiating the process. Staff read up on consensus building and decided this could be the way to proceed, given that both legislation and litigation had failed to resolve issues. Other water purveyors supported the idea of developing a new regional plan through this process. Staff did an assessment and identified stakeholders in four categories of interests: water; development and business; environment; and the larger public. All participants represented public or private agencies, nonprofits, or advocacy organizations. Groups were asked to name their own representatives and get their boards to approve. Beginning in 1993, individuals representing 15 stakeholder organizations worked to develop an agreement on water management in the Lower American River region. In the course of the process, additional stakeholders were brought in, and several other agencies that were not official members of the Forum participated in developing some elements of the agreement.

The stakeholders brought to the table diverse opinions and, in some cases, histories of conflict and hostility. Even within caucuses of like interests, there were often bitter differences like those between urban and agricultural water purveyors or between water-oriented environmentalists and land use-oriented ones more accommodating of growth. They could work together, however, because they recognized the interdependence of their interests. In the context of regional water-supply issues, each of the parties had something it needed or wanted from the other. The City was flush with surface water rights, but was blocked on the expansion of its water treatment plant by lawsuits from the County and environmentalists. The County, which was primarily dependent on groundwater, needed access to new surface water to meet growing demands. Developers were interested in getting supplemental surface water supplies as the County General Plan required for new growth. The regional groundwater table had been subject to continuing overdraft, which increased pumping costs, and caused subsidence and water quality problems, potentially harming the aquifers' ability to provide drinking water. Nearly every purveyor in the region had plans for new projects it hoped to build to meet the demands of the growing region, most of which would be required to go through a California Environmental Quality Act (CEQA) or National Environmental Policy Act (NEPA) environmental review process, and/or a State Water Resources Control Board hearing. Environmental groups would likely oppose any new projects. Taxpayer, neighborhood, and business groups were concerned about increasing costs, the reliability of future supplies, and assuring that public funds were spent on the things for which they had been raised. In short, all had reasons to be at the table and stay there. It was a promising setting for reciprocity as the players valued different things and to varying degrees.

Structure and process

The dialogue process, which we observed over several years, was dynamic and intense.[3] Susan Sherry of the California Center for Public Dispute Resolution at California State University Sacramento,[4] who had considerable experience in growth management issues, facilitated.[5] Sacramento County provided key staff, and a range of consultants was hired to do studies and analyses as needed during the process. Stakeholders consensually agreed to all staff and consultants.

Sherry began with a conflict assessment to see if the conditions were favorable for a consensus-based process and to identify the range of interests involved. She found that, although the staff had not done a formal conflict assessment, the stakeholders they had identified were the ones she too believed needed to be included and that the caucuses that they had identified were, for the most part, well grouped according to the stakeholders' interests. In her assessment, she sought to bring to the table "those who are directly affected by the issue, those who could make change happen, and those who could block change." Some of the participants had prior experience with collaborative processes, which would help later on. Some, particularly environmental groups, were reluctant to participate as they were more experienced with adversarial procedures, and they worried that this process would divert their energies. They agreed to join once they had sent a letter to the group asserting their right to leave the process at any time. All players of course had this right, but they wanted it on paper. Several important players chose not to officially participate as stakeholders, but they attended many meetings and participated in the discussion. These included the U.S. Bureau of Reclamation, which supplied water to many of the purveyors through Central Valley project contracts, and EBMUD, which could not get its water entitlement unless the issues in the Lower American River were addressed.

Staff[6] took on many tasks throughout the process. They, along with the facilitator, planned meetings, strategized, anticipated issues, engaged in shuttle diplomacy, drafted documents, discussed the interests and personalities, and made sure that details did not fall through the cracks. Staff often drew out the process longer than participants might have, just to make sure all had a clear understanding of exactly what it was to which they were committing their organizations.

Although staff members were in theory neutral and agreed to by the group, early on it became clear that some were suspected of being aligned with particular interests because of their backgrounds. Staff members were assigned to issues in their areas of expertise, as well as to managing communications with particular caucuses. The water purveyors felt most comfortable with the engineer who had extensive experience with water planning for the region. Environmentalists felt more comfortable with the individual who had formerly worked for environmental causes, although he had also worked for several water agencies. At one point, many purveyors were distrustful of him, considering him to be "more green than blue." In our conversations with staff, however, they said they viewed it as their responsibility to see whatever issue the group was working on from a variety of perspectives, to identify what interests might be at stake, and to assure that all the Water Forum stakeholders were aware of theirs and others' interests. One staff member reported her surprise when, despite many years working for a water purveyor, she became adept at identifying and articulating the interests of the neighborhood organizations. Across the board, the staff maintained a high level of self-awareness in regard to their professional biases and sought to manage them. As time went on the stakeholders developed a deep level of trust in staff expertise and balance.

The Water Forum process entailed five overlapping phases – planning, organization, education, negotiation and resolution of issues, and implementation. The planning and organization phases began when city and county staff started bringing key parties together to explore their interest in participating. The organization phase entailed many steps often neglected in collaborative processes, including training in interest-based negotiation and procedural tasks such as defining ground rules, establishing meeting schedules, conducting deal-breaker analyses, and developing communications strategies to the stakeholder boards and the larger public. The organization phase blended into the education phase, in which stakeholders met to review information regarding water-supply issues and the Lower American River, and educated one another about their perspectives on the issues. Toward the end of the education phase the separate caucuses developed statements of their interests (as opposed to positions), and identified the list of issues requiring resolution. At the beginning of the negotiation phase, the interests that the parties had identified became decision making criteria for the resolution of issues. These became the basis for a single text negotiating document. The single text method is often used by facilitators to track agreements as they move through the process and to show what the emerging package of ideas is. It is an evolving document, and anything in it can be changed as the negotiations develop and surface new issues or point the way to unforeseen opportunities.

The Forum had an overarching Working Group involving all stakeholders, along with teams of stakeholders tasked with addressing particular substantive issues – the Surface Water Team, the Groundwater Team, the Demand Conservation Team, and the Habitat Management Team. Each team had members from each caucus so teams were diverse and representative. It was within these teams that the bulk of the negotiations took place and detailed agreements were developed. As teams developed agreements, they presented them to the Working Group, which might accept them or send them back for more work. The group called on experts frequently to gather data, do modeling, or analyze issues as they emerged. Water management is a highly technical arena with many uncertainties – a complex interactive system with many moving parts, including snowfall and rain, various human activities and demands, as well as fishery needs and habitat concerns. This potential minefield for conflict became a place where civil discussion could take place around the analyses because the entire group not only had agreed to the choice of experts, but also stakeholders had ample opportunity to challenge the experts, as well as to delve into the methods they used and their implications.

Expertise as handled in this process brought robust information along with predictions about conditions and consequences of alternative strategies and in doing so helped to build trust among the stakeholders.

Throughout the process, some stakeholders were simultaneously operating in other arenas – lobbying for new legislation and bringing lawsuits, often against the interests of other stakeholders. Ms. Sherry insisted on full disclosure of these activities and reminded the group frequently that they were "living in two worlds" and they should "check their guns at the door." While these activities sometimes caused anger in Forum meetings, on the whole, participants accepted that each had to operate in a variety of ways to serve the interest of their constituencies. The collaborative task would be to make the agreements at the table more attractive than the side deals or adversarial procedures that all were able to engage in. The back and forth of these activities was a further source of pressure to reach agreement.

It is instructive to see how the Forum worked through complex conflicts to reach agreement. In some cases it would become clear that a particular issue was insoluble, a "sticking point." The facilitator handled these by acknowledging the problem and then moving on to other things. For example, although all the individuals around the table, speaking for their agencies and themselves, agreed that for demand con-servation purposes all customers should have water meters so they could regulate their usage, the Charter of the City of Sacramento would have to have a voter approved amend-ment if meters were to be required. Polls made clear this would not be approved. Environmentalists had been adamant on this point, but realized they had to back off. The group found alternative approaches that would move toward more water metering.

Groundwater was also a problematic topic as users had different kinds of rights. The group approached this by beginning with criteria for the solution, as is recom-mended in *Getting to Yes* (Fisher, et al. 1991) and in texts on consensus building. It is easier to decide on criteria than on specific solutions, and the criteria make it easier to identify which solutions will be acceptable. They developed four criteria based on two fundamental principles – fairness and the ability of the water purveyors to maintain their autonomy as water districts. The four criteria were that any acceptable solution should

1   allow current users to continue to exercise their rights;

2   recognize that both exercised and unexercised overlying rights are vested rights in the sense that they pass from owner to owner with the sale of the land;

3   provide that similarly situated present and future groundwater users will be treated the same; and

4   create certainty for all current and future users by ensuring that the basin is maintained at its sustainable yield. (Connick 2003)

This became the framework for a productive discussion. The group ultimately created a groundwater management plan and signed a Joint Powers Agreement (JPA)[7] among the pertinent stakeholders to assure it would be implemented.

Once the Forum had a draft agreement, stakeholders brought it to the boards of the groups they represented. This was a critical step to assure that the agencies and advocacy groups would be prepared to implement it. Members of all caucuses joined in the presentations to make clear why certain things were included. Then the stakeholders met and the facilitator asked them to tell stories about the reactions. Many of them had to do with the time and money required, but others were about specific substantive issues. The group brainstormed and worked out ways to deal with these. They continued to strengthen mutual assurances by working on what they called "caveats" and "quid pro quos." They articulated what each stakeholder got and gave so that if a stakeholder was not getting something he was entitled to by the agreement, he would not have to hold to the rest of the agreement. Caveats were "what if?" statements that identified changed conditions that might require adaptation. In some cases they developed strategies for dealing with these and in some cases they assigned the issue to the Successor Effort. This was a process they referred to as making two worlds into one. They made it an obligation to support all elements of the agreement including those not directly relevant to them, unless they were not getting their own interests met.

First order results

After six years of collaborative dialogue and an expenditure of nearly $10 million, more than 41 entities developed, including jurisdictions, agencies and stakeholder groups, who were committed to carrying out a plan for regional water management for the next 30 years. These parties worked collaboratively among themselves, within their own stakeholder organizations, and in the wider community to develop the 400-page Water Forum Agreement, which they entered into by signing a Memorandum of Understanding in the spring of 2000.[8] This was a comprehensive package of linked actions designed to provide a "safe and reliable water supply for the region's economic health and planned development" and "preserve the fishery, wildlife, recreational and aesthetic values of the Lower American River." Its provisions included increasing surface water diversions; reducing diversions during dry years; assuring a water flow regime that more closely matched the needs of fish; monitoring and restoring fish habitat; improving recreation opportunities; conserving water; and managing groundwater and surface water in an integrated manner. The agreement also created a successor collaborative effort responsible for overseeing and monitoring its implementation or even altering the plan as needed to deal with unanticipated situations. In addition to these formal outcomes articulated in the written agreement, the Water Forum has had other important results, including new and productive working relationships among former foes, the development of a stronger culture of collaboration within the Sacramento region that spreads beyond the water arena to such issues as transportation and land use, and the creation of spinoff organizations and agreements.

The Forum's dialogues produced innovative ways of solving problems and sometimes entirely new ways of framing issues and objectives. Much of what the group did applied new norms and began to create new practices. One of the innovations was triggered by new information which emerged late in the process, endangering the tentative agreement. Water releases from Folsom dam for the fish were going to be too warm because the water purveyors were taking from the cold water pool near the bottom of the reservoir. Moreover, two of the key species, salmon and steelhead, which spawned at different times, also required different water temperatures. The Forum came up with the idea of installing a new temperature control device that would allow purveyors to take the warm water from the top and allow cold water releases for the fish. It could adapt to changing weather and water conditions, as well as to fish needs and timing of their spawning period. It is testimony to the political capital and trust stakeholders had developed among themselves, and to the shared understanding they had of the issues, that they as a group were able to lobby Congress (including the Sacramento area's anti-environmentalist congressman) and get the funding to install the device.

Many of the ideas the Water Forum came up with in their complex and detailed negotiations (in consensus building it is often said that the "devil is in the details," but it is also the case that creativity can emerge from the details) involved ways of setting up flexible and adaptive systems. For example, instead of a one-rule-fits-all for purveyors, the agreement had individual plans for purveyors because one might have mostly ground-water and another surface water. These supplies fluctuate in differing ways, though all supplies are linked. As one stakeholder said "We have different straws but they are all dipping into the same water." Not far into the process the purveyors discovered that, although they had what they thought were inalienable legal rights to particular water sources, a new court ruling, referred to as the Hodge flow decision,[9] meant they would not necessarily be allowed to exercise those rights. The group would have to develop a strategy to maximize the amount available and protect them all to the greatest degree possible. They would have to cooperate. Finally the group came up with an innovative, policy-oriented approach to the American River flow (rather than a rigid rule-based standard) that called for people to pull together in conference in dry years to talk and figure out what to do. This was called the Successor Effort[10] to make clear it was not a new layer of government, but a stakeholder group that would continue the collaboration as needed.

Implementation

The resolution phase (Carpenter and Kennedy 2001) was the longest and had many subparts. Once participants had come to agreement on fundamental issues, there ensued a long process of ironing out the details that arose as the parties came to understand the full implications of their commitments in the agreement – that is, to understand what would be needed to move from having an agreement in concept to actually living it. Although implementation is often thought of as actions taken after a plan is adopted, in the Water Forum implementation began as soon as the group was able to develop agreements on early steps. Most of the stakeholders were the implementers themselves, but agreeing on what ought to be done was not enough. The stakeholders needed assurances that each would do his part. At first purveyors felt they should only have to deal with things they were directly responsible for, like environmental damage caused by their project, but soon they began to realize the benefits to all of habitat mitigation, for example, which would make many things they all wanted easier. Purveyors agreed to contribute to a habitat mitigation fund, thus giving assurances to the environmentalists. Getting workable assurances was particularly problematic because of the timing of actions. Many water projects would be completed within the first few years, but environmentalists needed assurance that the purveyors would continue to contribute to the mitigation fund beyond that time. The group decided that an environmental impact report (EIR) should be completed and after that stakeholders should sign a Memorandum of Understanding (MOU). They chose this more informal option rather than a contract, which would have taken years to negotiate. They also agreed that environmentalists could sign the MOU, but with the right to withdraw support from any project which did not meet the conditions of the EIR. The Forum also created a complex web of agreements, and in some cases contracts, among individual stakeholders about actions to be taken in dry years. This set of interrelated agreements highlighted the reciprocal relations among players and clarified how each depended on the actions of others.

System adaptations

The Water Forum set up the Successor Effort as they anticipated that implementation would be neither simple nor straightforward. Representatives of all categories of stakeholders were members of this group, which was smaller than the original working group. The Forum recognized the complexity of the situation, the unpredictability of the natural and political environment and the need for adaptability. The group decided that they would rather entrust the spirit of the agreement to a diverse group of stakeholders, who could take each issue on its own terms as it arose. This was a new form of governance and water management, coexisting with the old forms of city and county and special district governments.

The Successor Effort, which was also facilitated by the Center for Collaborative Policy (CCP), developed or assisted longer term activities and institutional arrangements set in motion by the Water Forum. Their five year report[11] shows many actions had been started and moderate progress made on most elements. The Successor Effort engaged with new processes that were outgrowths of the Water Forum. These included the Lower American River Task Force, which works on corridor management planning, water quality issues, and updating the water flow standard, among other things. The Central Sacramento Groundwater Management Plan was critical to establishing a framework for maintaining a sustainable groundwater basin. The Sacramento Groundwater Authority was inspired by the Water Forum and established on the basis of a Joint Powers Agreement among major cities and the county. The coalition has extended its reach to the Consumnes River and negotiated an agreement among the County, The

Nature Conservancy, and the U.S. Bureau of Reclamation to help assure that the river can support the salmon's trek upstream. These spinoff collaborations have produced results, and they seem to represent a transformation in the governance culture for water in the region.

The Water Forum had other spinoff effects that began to pervade the governance culture in other policy arenas. For example, the region had severe problems with traffic and air quality. It was classified by the federal government as the sixth worst place for ozone pollution in the country. Its roads were clogged, interfering with commutes and commercial activity, while an increase of one million in population was anticipated in the following 20 years. A coalition of Sacramento leaders, inspired by the success of the Water Forum, proposed a similar Transportation and Air Quality Collaborative. This initial group of city and county agencies, environmentalists, residents and businesses chipped in to fund a $150,000 feasibility study. Local agencies then funded the process and hired CCP to organize and facilitate a regional effort to move forward on these problems. The initial group drew in other key stakeholders, like the Building Industry Association, the Metropolitan Chamber of Commerce, the American Lung Association, and the Sacramento County Alliance of Neighborhoods. They also drew in representatives from interests typically not included though they are profoundly affected by transportation policy decisions – the disabled, low income neighborhoods and pertinent ethnic groups. This forum involved 100 participants over a period of three years.

Once the Water Forum agreement was near and it was clear how the water would be managed and how much there would be, EBMUD was able to negotiate for its water entitlement by taking it from the Sacramento River after its confluence with the American River, rather than before. While this was a compromise, as the water was somewhat less pure than it would be if it came from further upstream, it was a mutual gain solution as EBMUD had been unable to get the entitlement at all in the past due to unresolved legal challenges. This solution meant both EBMUD and the Water Forum got what they needed. In a further second order effect, EBMUD then decided to hire CCP to help them use collaborative methods in other arenas.

Other system adaptations from the Water Forum's work included working relationships among previously warring players, who began to communicate routinely with one another to anticipate conflicts and to gather information. One lead player from the business community said this process had changed his whole way of working. He began to use the "Water Forum Way" in everything he did – working collaboratively with his employees and customers as well as with his competitors (Connick and Innes 2003). The Water Forum Way became a powerful image for the participants, most of whom told us they were changed by their experience. It established new norms and practices in the water arena, as it did in others where the stakeholders also operated. The experts too were affected by their participation. Normally their model of practice would be that they were hired to do a study and explain it to the client when finished. In this case, they worked with the stakeholders to identify what information was needed. They did data gathering and analysis, but when they reported on their findings they got many questions about the design and data and sometimes went back again to adapt their efforts to better respond to the needs of the group. It was a much more iterative and interactive model of expertise than the traditional one.

The whole effort contrasted significantly with how legislation or policies are normally made. The group collectively spent far more time imagining possible scenarios, developing and detailing solutions and adapting them than elected officials could do. The effort included both scientific experts and people who knew the task and possibilities because of their own praxis. They built a community of inquiry. They had the people at the table that represented those who would win or lose and those who could make or break the deal. They could make a finely honed agreement that would be largely self-enforcing and that contained within it the action-forcing power.

Correspondence with DIAD theory

We believe that much of the success of the Water Forum was due to its coherence with the DIAD conditions. Care was taken in the selection of stakeholders to make sure they mirrored the full diversity of interests in Lower American River water. Their interests were interdependent because they all needed a good supply of clean water and because each had some capacity to affect that supply. They came to understand that, for the most part, they would be more likely to meet their interests if they cooperated because they could produce a package of actions that would be more beneficial to each than if individuals tried to go it alone. They were able to find mutual gain solutions because of their reciprocal interests and the fact that each valued water in different places at different times. Their dialogue very much matched the conditions of authentic dialogue, as we saw firsthand. Everyone had equal access to shared information; the facilitator made sure everyone was listened to and taken seriously; and the free flow of ideas uncovered information errors and generated creative problem solving ideas. The dialogue helped assure that participants understood and were invested in the outcomes and largely played their parts in the implementation. Moreover, this process resulted not only in specific actions, but also in adaptations to the larger system, including new norms of interaction and inclusion and changes in practices.

Reducing racial tensions: the Cincinnati Police Community Relations Collaborative[12]

The context

In a poor, largely African American section of Cincinnati, Ohio, known as Over-the-Rhine, a bitter conflict simmered between residents and police. In March 2001 community leaders in the Black United Front, along with the American Civil Liberties Union, filed a federal class action lawsuit against the city and the Fraternal Order of Police over what they claimed was racial profiling. Racial profiling refers to police practices of using racial or ethnic characteristics to decide if someone is a suspect. In the Cincinnati case it was the practice of pulling drivers over and searching their cars or the drivers themselves that was most at issue. Many in the black community felt this was done to them when they were not doing anything wrong, contending that their only offense was DWB (Driving While Black). To stop people because of their skin color is racial discrimination, and unconstitutional in the U.S. The Cincinnati Police Department denied that they did racial profiling, and the Department had a formal policy against it. The claim of racial profiling is almost impossible to prove, but the perception of its existence was causing public anger and contributing to poor police community relations in Over-the-Rhine.

Getting started

Presiding judge, Susan Dlott, who was familiar with mediation from her previous work in family court, did not think the adversarial court process would serve the community, much less resolve racial tensions. Someone would win and someone would lose, but the dispute would not be over and anger would remain. She asked the opposing counsels to work out an alternative way to resolve this. The lawyers were able to obtain funding of $100,000 from the Andrus Foundation to get started on settlement mediation. The Foundation recommended international peace negotiator Jay Rothman to be the court's special master[13] and to guide a collaborative process leading to a settlement. This situation changed everyone's BATNA because the judge had the power to direct the outcome if the parties could not reach agreement.

Rothman's experience in the Middle East, Northern Ireland, and Cyprus with mediating major conflicts had led him to frame the issues in terms of identities (Rothman 1997). He used the strategy he had developed for identity based conflict, which entails hearing groups' concerns through stakeholders' narratives about their past and hopes for their future. Just as Rothman was beginning his work in April 2001, the simmering anger in the community broke out into riots, triggered by a police shooting of an unarmed black teenager during a pursuit. This young man's death was the last straw in a neighborhood where there had been 15 police killings during the previous 8 years, all involving black males. The riot lasted 3 days and was the worst in the U.S. since the devastating Los Angeles riots of 1992. The conditions and BATNA were suddenly further changed for everyone, and the collaborative process became even more urgent. Business was affected; residents were afraid; and the police were having difficulty doing their job. During May and June a large scale collaborative was established with additional funding from many sources, along with in-kind support from businesses and others in the community. The U.S. Department of Justice initiated its own investigation of Cincinnati Police practices as part of a study of several cities where discrimination complaints had been raised.

Structure and process

Rothman was determined to make this a broad based effort, engaging citizens with many different perspectives and concerns. The first stage of the project in May and June began with a broad public awareness campaign and an emphasis on outreach and relationship building with the media. The purpose was to explain the planned process of gathering visions from all sections of Cincinnati for future race relations in the city. Between June and September Rothman, his staff and many volunteers gathered information about people's goals. They used interviews and both web-based and paper and pencil questionnaires. Ultimately they got 3,500 responses across the range of major identity groups. This was a simple survey with only three questions:

1   What are your goals for future police–community relations in Cincinnati?
2   Why are these goals important to you? (What experiences, values, beliefs, feelings, influence your goals?)
3   How do you think your goals could be best achieved? (The more specific your suggestions the better.)

These questions, which reflect best practices in the mediation field, call attention away from the past, with all its bitterness, and toward the future. They encourage constructiveness, though they do not eliminate anger and blame. They seek to reframe thinking so it is more possible to move forward. The why question elicits stories of pain and loss as well as hope and aspirations. It gets at the all-important task of surfacing needs and values. Citizens do not typically think in terms of interests, as do professional stakeholder representatives like those in the Water Forum. Asking them the why question and focusing on their own experiences and beliefs helps the mediator articulate the underlying interests that are motivating them. The mediator can then help them to move from positional bargaining to interest-based negotiation. The request for specificity in suggestions forces a practical perspective and helps to create a pool of ideas to work with as they move toward settlement.

The ARIA group[14] analyzed and organized these responses so they could serve as the basis for discussion in a series of planned 4-hour feedback sessions. They organized eight groups in terms of affinity, including religious and social service professionals, African Americans, white citizens, city employees, city police and their families, business leaders and foundation professionals, youth, city leadership and other minorities. These groups represented people with differing interests and positions in the system, and they included many of the people who could actually bring about change. As in the Water Forum, both deal makers (the city, the police) and the deal breakers (those who might bring lawsuits or sponsor boycotts) were involved.

The first pilot feedback group was held in June 2001 with 120 religious and social service professionals. ARIA staff, with the help of volunteers, facilitated small groups for a morning, sharing stories, frustrations and hopes. The group came up with seven proposed goals. These included strengthening community-based policing, improving recruitment, training and accountability procedures for the Police Division, building relationships of respect, cooperation, and trust between police and the various communities, and educating the public on appropriate law enforcement. These became the basis for a single text negotiating document that was to evolve as it passed through each of the groups.

In the meantime ARIA staff and volunteers continued outreach efforts. The next meeting was with youth. From the 750 people aged 14–25 who responded to the survey, about 125 signed up to participate in a feedback session (though fewer showed up in the end). This group developed additional goals emphasizing responsibility and respect. Holding the group sessions in serial fashion allowed the staff to learn from each experience and to transmit the earlier group's agreements to the next affinity group. These group sessions continued through November, each with 75 to 100 or more people. In the process goals evolved. Remarkably in October when the police officer was acquitted in the earlier shooting, the city stayed calm. As the process moved along, the group also did research on best police practices across the country to use in the settlement.

First order results

At the end of the feedback sessions staff took the materials from the surveys and the sessions and produced a set of five shared goals:

1   Get police officers and community members to become proactive partners in community problem-solving.
2   Build relationships of respect, cooperation and trust within and between police and communities.
3   Improve education, oversight, monitoring, and hiring practices of the Cincinnati Police Department
4   Ensure fair, equitable, and courteous treatment for all.
5   Create methods to establish the public's understanding of police policies and procedures and recognition of exceptional service in an effort to foster support for the police.

Staff also developed a set of value statements and motivations for each of the groups. They invited the 60 representatives who had been selected by the identity groups to be part of the Integration group, which was charged with reviewing the goals and reaching agreement on them. ARIA then linked these goals with information about best police practices and presented them in January to the parties to the dispute, who then took on the task of negotiating a settlement agreement by March.

The parties reached a complex and detailed agreement, building on the goals. The settlement negotiations were difficult right to the end. There was no admission by the police of profiling or bias and no provision for stopping the boycott. Nor were the 19 related complaints of specific racial profiling incidents resolved. But there were several specific agreements that the Mayor characterized as steps toward basic change. The police agreed to use Community Problem-Oriented Policing as their principal crime fighting approach. Bias in the police would be addressed through training and data collection. Evaluation would be done to determine if these measures resulted in improvement in outcomes. Finally an independent citizen review board would be established to deal with complaints.

All parties signed this collaborative agreement (CA), including the Fraternal Order of Police, the city, and the Black United Front. Judge Dlott ratified the agreement on April 5, 2002, almost a year after the riots. Friends of the Collaborative, a community advisory committee, was established to advise and support the parties in the implementation process. At the same time the U.S. Department of Justice and the city and police department signed a Memorandum of Agreement (MOA) that would require new policies on the use of force, reporting and investigating citizen complaints, new training requirements, early intervention, and risk management. An independent monitor was hired to oversee implementation of both agreements.[15] The agreement did not state everything that would be done in detail, but it provided direction and established new relationships, institutions, and processes to see that the spirit of the agreement was carried out.

This intensive collaborative process had several immediate impacts. First, it cooled tensions in the city and offered hope for a way out of an impasse that affected everyone. The protest leaders became engaged in building solutions. Second, the process helped the identity groups to think through and articulate their interests, getting past the inchoate anger that had gripped many of them. It began to separate the facts (whether racial profiling was actually happening) from the feelings and helped identify that a key issue for both blacks and police was being treated with respect. This was useful information as it is at least potentially possible to change the situation with training and consciousness raising. The information got the community talking and thinking in new ways. It got people from different backgrounds to begin to put themselves in each other's place. For example, white and black city staff shared their experiences, and a white staffer realized that, although the police treated him well, they did not seem to treat his black colleagues the same way. The dialogue helped to create shared meaning around racial profiling. Whether profiling existed or not, it became clear there were good reasons for the perception of profiling and empathy emerged for those who may have been unjustly stopped.

Implementation

These two agreements (the MOA and the CA) were complementary and, in combination, offered a unique model for police community relations issues. Most such MOAs involve only the federal Justice Department, the city, and the police department and focus on police accountability only on specific issues under dispute, such as the use of force (Green and Jerome 2008). They provide the parties, the public, and the court with the ability to gauge whether the police department has complied with the terms of the consent decree. They do not, however, attempt to fundamentally change how policing is done, nor try to evaluate the extent of change. With the combination of agreements in Cincinnati there were more parties participating than normal, and the larger community was included in designing the solutions and participating in their implementation. There were interlocking provisions between the agreements, requiring them to be interpreted and implemented together. The CA adds to the MOA by focusing not just on the procedures, but also on the whole style of policing. It holds all parties accountable for improvements and sets up monitoring and evaluation activities on both the community and the police. This makes monitoring more challenging as parties with previously rancorous relationships now have to confront each other face to face on a regular basis. It also opens up lines of communication.

In 2004 the parties contracted with the RAND Corporation to conduct the evaluation. The first annual assessment was a complex study involving both qualitative and quantitative methods. The researchers conducted a survey of citizen satisfaction with the Police Department; a survey of citizens who had interacted with the police through arrest, reporting a crime, or being stopped for traffic violations; a survey of CPD officers about perceptions of support from the community, working conditions and other factors related to job satisfaction and performance; a survey of officers and citizens involved in a sample of citizen complaints, an analysis of motor vehicle stops for patterns of racial disparity, observation of meetings between citizens and officers during motor vehicle stops, and analysis of Police Department staffing, recruitment, retention, and promotion patterns. They also examined video tapes of traffic stops. RAND completed annual evaluations and prepared a final report in 2009 (Ridgeway, et al. 2006; Ridgeway, et al. 2009; Riley, et al. 2005; Schell, et al. 2007). In addition the Independent Monitor published interim reports and a final report in 2008 (Green and Jerome 2008) building on the RAND work and on the author's direct observation and interviews. These evaluative and oversight activities played a part in the longer term outcomes and system adaptations.

System adaptations

The linked agreements established new publically transparent procedures and ongoing dialogues among the parties. New expectations were established of the police and there was new awareness among them of how they were seen. Annual evaluation reports created a new, albeit temporary, institution and the norm that there should be facts before accusations. The evaluations did not find evidence of racial profiling and after two or three years citizens' perception of profiling declined. The police department adopted policy changes and equipped officers with TASER devices that have changed practices on the use of force. They monitor officer performance and installed video recorders in police cars. The most important system adaptation may be the introduction of Community

Oriented Policing and the establishment of the Community Police Partnering Center. The latter was born of the frustrations of the police because they were being held accountable for change under the agreements, but the community was not and because many community leaders wanted to participate in change. The Center has sponsored high visibility training in problem-oriented policing and the role of the community, and it has become a place where citizens and police sit together on a regular basis to discuss issues with civility and respect (Green and Jerome 2008; Rothman 2006). The Independent Monitor report says the Cincinnati Police Department is a different organization today, using better targeted strategies of crime prevention. Crime has declined. There is greater awareness that citizens and property owners have to be part of the solution. There is a new reward and accountability system for police and more police participation in community forums. This unique set of agreements, along with the process that led up to them, and the monitoring have resulted in one of the most successful police reform efforts in the country and has likely changed policing in Cincinnati for the long run.

An assessment by the Andrus Foundation[16] concluded that, although the immediate crisis was addressed and there have been no further police killings that the community felt were unjustified, the deeper problems were not resolved. This was, in the Foundation's view, because of the focus in the mediation on the future, when there remained significant past grievances around police killings and suspected racial profiling incidents. The levels of trust and respect between the police and the black community have not improved in the Foundation's view, and the police seem not to understand why. The Foundation's hypothesis is that the lack of accountability for the past deaths and earlier interactions was what was standing in the way. This surfaces a common dilemma in collaborative problem solving, where an emphasis on the future may neglect all that led up to the problem and interfere with building a sound foundation for a way forward. On the other hand emphasis on past grievances can interfere with moving forward at all.

Correspondence with DIAD theory

In terms of our DIAD model, the important stakeholders were gathered together. They were interdependent, as their welfare depended on one another. The ARIA group made sure that there was authentic dialogue throughout the year. There was substantial learning in the dialogue about the issues, about individuals' own concerns, and the concerns of others. The project did discover reciprocity, for example, between the interests of youth and of police. Both wanted respect and each could give it to the other. New relationships were built in these discussions. The business community began working with other leaders to restore the economy. The system adaptations have already had effects on the way problems are addressed and have built new heuristics. There remains more to accomplish but the direction has changed and the momentum may continue.

Cross acceptance: the New Jersey state planning process[17]

Context

The state of New Jersey implemented one of the earliest and most ambitious collaborative consensus building processes that we know of. Indeed it was research on this process that set author Innes on the track of trying to understand consensus building. It began with a landmark state Supreme Court decision in 1983.[18] This decision, known as Mt. Laurel II, followed an earlier decision that concluded it was a regional responsibility to provide affordable housing.[19] That decision had national ramifications, as many other states reached similar conclusions. Mt. Laurel II said that the state should develop a statewide plan as a tool to allocate affordable housing, based on a calculation of regional fair share. The court did not believe that disjointed decision making of 567 municipalities was leading to regional fair share decisions; rather it continued to result in exclusionary zoning and racial polarization. Low density suburban development was leaving behind the aging urban core and amounted to exclusionary zoning from the court's perspective.

In response to Mt. Laurel II, the legislature enacted the New Jersey State Planning Act[20] in 1985. This set up a 17-member State Planning Commission as a semi-autonomous body, including Cabinet members, county and municipal representatives from both parties and six public members, including one professionally licensed planner. This act was supported by a remarkably broad coalition, including local government officials, professional planners, affordable housing advocates, environmentalists and developers. They were all looking for a planning process to inform local decision making and improve coordination across state agencies. The act mandated that the plan be developed with active engagement by jurisdictions across the state in a process it called "cross acceptance," which would begin with localities comparing the state plan to their own plans.

Getting started

The process of state planning began collaboratively with the writing of the legislation itself. The governor agreed to support legislation that was produced by consensus, and a self-selected group of influential stakeholders representing business, environmental concerns, developers, and the League of Municipalities, after months of discussion, prepared the basic legislation that became the state plan law. The act garnered support from a broad coalition including local government officials, professional planners, affordable housing advocates, environmentalists, and developers, who all saw it as in their interest to have a state planning process that would coordinate across state agencies and inform local decision making.

The law established a stakeholder-based State Planning Commission (SPC) with members drawn from the state cabinet, municipal and county governments, and the public, including environmentalists, business interests, affordable housing advocates, Republicans, and Democrats. The Office of State Planning (OSP), which staffed the SPC, was placed in the Department of Treasury. Cross acceptance meant that jurisdictions would compare and contrast their own plans with the state plan prior to its approval. County planners would be the brokers between the state and municipalities. The legislation mandated eight goals: revitalize the state's urban centers; conserve the state's natural resources; provide for beneficial economic growth; protect the environment; provide adequate public services at reasonable cost; provide adequate housing at reasonable cost; preserve and enhance historic and cultural values, open space and recreational lands; and ensure sound and integrated planning statewide.

Though many New Jersey municipalities had master plans and land use regulations prior to the law, they were not required to alter these. Cross-acceptance stressed a kind of tiered collaboration, bringing localities together at the county level to prepare a report on the plan and their concerns, rather than requiring separate local responses. Despite the fact that this was a voluntary process, most participated, as one staffer told us, out of fear of what might happen if they did not. Localities depended heavily on state decisions on infrastructure and environmental regulation. Local property taxes were already high; localities were often too small to deal with major facilities needs; and few regional bodies existed to facilitate communication or cost sharing among the communities. Though local leaders were skeptical about the ultimate influence of the state plan on state investment decisions, they concluded it was better to be at the negotiating table than not. Moreover, if the state made a decision on whether to invest in infrastructure in a particular area, it would be in the locality's interest to adapt its own plans to reflect that reality.

The first step was to create the state plan, which was done in a process of trial and error. External consultants produced a first draft. Staff developed a second version based on conversations with state agencies and counties. This was sent out for peer review by experts around the state and nation. It was a third iteration that became the basis for cross-acceptance. This preliminary plan – a three-volume document of policies, criteria, and standards (New Jersey State Planning Commission 1988) – included a tier map, which divided the state into seven categories of land use, including "redeveloping cities and suburbs," "suburbanizing areas," "exurban reserves," and "agricultural areas." The plan included statewide and tier-specific policies on such topics as population densities, housing, and capital facilities.

Structure and process

The SPC set up a three-phase cross-acceptance process. In phase one municipalities compared the preliminary plan to their own plans, conditions, and projections, and counties prepared reports incorporating the municipalities' findings, identifying points of agreement and disagreement with the state plan. OSP summarized and organized these into carefully framed issues for discussion. Phase two involved negotiations between a subcommittee of the SPC and representatives of the municipalities in each county. These negotiations transformed the vast majority of differences into agreements through the reframing of issues, clarification or modification of the plan, and even major changes that later became part of the interim plan (New Jersey State Planning Commission 1991). The third phase – issue resolution – addressed the remaining disagreements before the preparation of the final plan.

The philosophy of consensual groups permeated the New Jersey planning process. The SPC, having decided that its 17-member commission was unwieldy, divided into smaller working subcommittees to handle policy development. These subcommittees worked through issues, sometimes in day-long retreats. They operated in an open way, usually including members of the public in their discussions. Typically their recommendations became SPC policy. Throughout the cross-acceptance process a parallel set of processes also operated. SPC set up advisory committees, each to review the plan from one perspective such as urban, suburban, or rural policy; agriculture; regional design; housing; or infrastructure. Members included knowledgeable and interested parties in state and federal agencies, environmental groups, academics, urban issues, business, and farming. The reports of these stakeholder/experts played key roles in the revision of the plan.

SPC staff gave careful attention to the design and management of groups. The state provided modest training in group process to state and county staff and to citizen participants, though facilitation practices were as yet undeveloped. Staff selected members of advisory committees, they said, to represent a "microcosm of the larger public debate" in the hope of "building creatively on tensions" among the various interests. In the groups, staff worked to create communication among all parties. They listened, learned, responded to participants, and built trust. They facilitated meetings, provided information, clarified communication, reframed issues, recorded discussions and agreements, and prepared position papers on request. In one meeting attended by author Innes, for example, the director frequently articulated and reframed his interpretation of the meaning of group members' statements until all parties were satisfied that they understood one another.

The plan involved both policies and – because the court decision seemed to demand it – a map, though staff knew that would be controversial. There were eventually, as a result of the dialogue, 300 policies in categories ranging from equity, urban revitalization, housing, public investment, air and water resources to open lands and energy. The plan envisioned five planning areas and a hierarchy of centers. The map, however, crowded out much of the public discussion on policies (Bierbaum 2007). It relegated some communities to little or no development. Some interest groups and communities challenged the plan's density standards. Some business interests contended the plan would destroy the economy and demanded an economic impact statement. Business leaders and developers feared having to channel their activities into troubled older cities instead of affluent suburbs. Farming interests said it would unfairly take away property rights. The municipalities and counties were concerned about criteria for land allocation to agriculture or exurban reserves. How would the criteria actually apply in various contexts? Should they depend on the type and viability of the agriculture? What if an island of office development already existed in the center of an agricultural area? As is often said in collaborative processes "the devil is in the details."

Groups discussed standards, both to understand the theory behind such ideas as "carrying capacity" and to explore the implications of applying standards in different contexts. For example, which is more appropriate in reserve areas: three- to five-acre lots or cluster zoning? Groups questioned the meaning of concepts and challenged the language in the plan. When is a suburb really "built out?" Were the tiers tantamount to zoning? If so, were they intrusions on home rule? City representatives objected that the proposed "municipal distress index" would harm their image. Many discussions entailed efforts to give meaning to such elusive ideas as "rural character." Counties and municipalities were concerned that the plan did not spell out implementation procedures and hesitated to agree to the plan without knowing the specific costs and effects. They had contradictory fears about both rigidity and ambiguity. The cross-acceptance process allowed them to address these questions by talking them through, developing trust, and compromising.

Simultaneously, the advisory committees engaged players new to planning in learning about the issues and each other's concerns and, in the process, developing new ideas. City representatives learned that the state plan was not simply concerned with growth at the fringe. The rural policy committee outlined criteria for determining densities in rural areas. The regional design committee proposed making "communities of place" focal points for settlement, rather than the tiers, and outlined a hierarchy of such communities, including urban centers, corridor centers, towns, villages, and hamlets, each with its characteristic size, density, jobs, and other activities.

In the negotiation phase, SPC staff, in consultation with county officials, identified not only the issues of disagreement, but the interests of the participants. The focus on interests rather than positions permitted the "getting to yes" model of negotiation (Fisher, et al. 1991). The discussion forced the SPC to clarify its policies and develop more specific implementation strategies. Sometimes talking through the problem revealed that there was less disagreement than participants originally thought and that a minor change would resolve the issue. Sometimes reframing the problem eliminated the conflict.

First order results

Cross-acceptance resulted in significant changes in the plan. SPC eliminated the term "tiers" and changed the plan to emphasize communities of place as the focus for development. Group discussions had revealed that labeling cities as "distressed" was undesirable as was distinguishing between exurban reserve and agricultural areas. The final plan resolved these issues by outlining a smaller number of planning areas and dropping the distress index. This plan added statewide policies for agriculture, redevelopment, and overall growth patterns. Standards and guidelines were removed and put into an advisory manual.

The SPC unanimously adopted the state plan on June 12, 1992 five years after it began. This action was eloquent testimony to the success of their collaborative model of planning. Even the secretary of agriculture supported the plan on behalf of his constituency, which was the last major holdout. All municipalities and counties had participated in cross-acceptance. In further testimony to the success of the process, supporters of the state plan prevented passage of a bill to require legislative approval before the plan could take effect. The executive director of the New Jersey State League of Municipalities testified against this bill, saying the plan was a "remarkable achievement," and, as put together through cross-acceptance, more representative of the will of the people than it would be if adopted by the legislature. By 1992 only some builders and realtors remained vocal opponents, with virtually all other interests backing the plan.

Cross-acceptance engaged tens of thousands of New Jerseyans who learned about each other's interests and perceptions, as well as about the problems of growth and tools of planning. The participants included citizens and professionals in public and private sectors, leaders of the business and environmental communities, and elected officials. These people were directly and intensively involved at various levels of government, through formal and informal committees and task forces. The process created an alliance of key players and leaders who spoke for the plan.

The philosophy of SPC is summed up in a report of one of the advisory committees:

> Wise decision makers know that consensus fares better than edict where there is limited or no authority to enforce. In New Jersey jurisdictional arrangements there is . . . minimal authority for regional growth management . . . Thus is born the imperative for collaboration . . . Collaboration involves equality, mutual respect, and full representation to be effective. All levels of government the private and nonprofit sectors, and citizens and interest groups ought to deal as equal partners. Full representation also includes a wide array of professional assistance, beyond planners, landscape architects, engineers, and lawyers.
>
> (New Jersey State Planning Commission 1990)

Len Leiberman, member of New Jersey's Chamber of Commerce, in his farewell speech on leaving the SPC in May 1990, said:

> I think the plan will come to be understood as revolutionary in the creative sense. We are moving to a new way of defining the boundary line at the core of representative government, the line between freedom for every individual and the needs of society and between the public and the private interest . . . I originally came loaded with prejudices. Government was bad and we should beat up on them so they can let brilliant people in the private sector do what they do. For me learning how good public servants can be was the most transforming experience.

Implementation

The plan making process was successful in that it garnered widespread support across sectors and scales of jurisdiction. Some agencies had already begun cooperating on key issues. But this process, unlike the Water Forum, had done little to consider implementation or establish a process for it. Republican Governor Kean, who instigated the process, was no longer in office when the plan was approved, and shortly after that Democratic Governor Florio cut the budget for OSP and the director left. No new director was appointed for another year, and the plan was left on the shelf. With little provision for implementation contained in the plan and a lack of interest and funding from state leadership, little action was taken. The next governor, Republican Christine Todd Whitman, took little interest in the plan at first, and her Treasury Department threatened more cuts in OSP, which were only averted by heavy lobbying. OSP began to encourage municipalities to designate "centers" to which they would direct growth and many did so, motivated by the thought that if the state certified their centers, they might be eligible for some kind of funding in the future. Staff convinced the SPC to begin a second round of cross-acceptance, as required by the legislation, in 1995. This process then gained Whitman's attention, and she began campaigning for open space bonds and making speeches about the value of the plan and its smart growth agenda. Though the plan had been dormant, it had not died. Whitman made it into a major rallying cry of her administration. She was to receive an American Planning Association Award and then go on to be the federal Environmental Protection Agency (EPA) administrator, in part on the strength of the environmental credentials she developed in New Jersey.

Under the Whitman administration planning and redevelopment agencies were consolidated under the Department of Community Affairs, a dynamic environmental attorney was appointed head of SPC, regulatory changes were made to the Coastal Area Facilities Review Act tying real estate development to the state plan, and regulations were changed to slow growth in areas not served by sewers. Three million dollars was appropriated for Smart Growth Planning grants for cities. These grants were reviewed by OSP for consistency with the plan. An Urban Coordinating Council was established and brownfields were placed under the aegis of SPC to emphasize redevelopment rather than simply cleanup. In the meantime consultants and municipality staff began to learn more about the plan. It became an education in smart growth planning. Finally the Governor reversed a decision to move a state revenue facility outside of Trenton, in the spirit of the plan objectives to encourage growth in the cities, rather than spreading it to the suburbs. This was a symbolically important move for many bureaucrats and the private sector (Bierbaum 2007).

The state agencies however remained at odds over some issues, and it became clear that there would have to be a shift in thinking by key state departments to see how their missions could be consistent with the state plan and each other. Focus groups with participants selected from departments by Commissioners started what amounted to a state agency cross-acceptance process. These groups raised issues such as the lack of availability of resources to support this activity, limits on department authority to address issues with such scope, limits in departmental knowledge bases, need to improve communication within and across departments, and uneasiness with political conflicts, among other things. As a result of this, Implementation Action Teams were formed for each agency as was an expert advisory group, which offered insights and recommendations. The Action Teams, which varied in effectiveness, did such things as designing marketing and training programs on the State Plan, developing new tools, publicizing showcase projects, creating forums for interdepartmental problem-solving and establishing baselines and target indicators to measure success. Then ad hoc interdepartmental teams formed around specific projects to overcome bureaucratic fragmentation and assist localities with implementation. The plan was being implemented collaboratively in a way parallel to the Water Forum.

The second state plan was approved in 2001. In the nine years between the first and the second plan, priorities and issues had changed so that environment had begun to be seen as more urgent and salient than housing issues; unanticipated urban redevelopment had begun; and new technologies like Geographic Information Systems and computer modeling had changed the possibilities for planning. It was testimony to the importance of flexibility and adaptiveness of the plan making and implementing process that these changes could be accommodated.

System adaptations

At the present writing a new cross-acceptance process is underway on a third plan under Democratic Governor Corzine. While OSP has been much weakened and pared down by antagonistic or indifferent leadership, the law requiring cross-acceptance remains. Some of the ideas of the second state plan have found their way into other plans put forward by the Governor. What is clear is that somehow the idea of the plan and cross-acceptance survived. The whole process, starting in 1988, has been a learning process, as not only staff, but other players learned about each other, about what was possible, about what it takes to collaborate, and about what each other's concerns and interests were. They have adapted their practices over the 20 years since the process began. Each time there was a challenge to the plan, the coalition that had backed the plan originally fought off the attacks, though in some periods the process stalled. The repeated resurgence of the process is a reflection on the robustness of the original agreement and the political and social capital that key players shared.

Martin Bierbaum, deputy director of OSP in its early stages and later consultant to the state, identified a number of lessons from this story of state planning in New Jersey.[21] First, leadership was critical. The plan moved forward with it, but it did not when high level leadership was not there. The attention to local jurisdictions through cross-acceptance was important, but public education and outreach was crucial, "taking the plan retail" as the Director called it. Certification of consistency with the plan and celebrating this as a municipal achievement rewarded desirable behaviors. The provision of technical assistance tied to this certification allowed for face to face interactions between state and local people and helped to build local capacity, especially in counties which had taken little initiative before. The State planning grants helped to get munici-palities on board, and Bierbaum believed that if they had been established earlier, much of the original resistance would have been eliminated. He faults the plan for lacking performance targets, which, he argues, would have helped address the disruptions in the process as administrations changed and new players entered the fray.

Two reflective sessions engaging state staff members in 2000 and 2003 identified other lessons and changes that had occurred. For example, while staff felt the first cross-acceptance process was driven by fear, the second one was not, as it reflected new relationships that had been built. Moreover, by that time it was evident that players had come to understand the planning concepts better and moved to focus more on urban redevelopment and on a reflective understanding of the regional perspective, rather than solely a parochial municipal one. In addition, the second process was less contentious than the first, as more was understood and agreed. The quality of the dialogue however was not what had been hoped for. The staff concluded that cross-acceptance required building partnerships from the beginning and that additional resources needed to be allocated to this type of collaborative process.

A more recent assessment (Harrison 2007) contends that since the Department of Community Affairs[22] issued the state map and required municipalities to update their master plans every 6 years, regional planning is more of a reality as local plans that do not conform are subject to review. Sticks include proliferating regulations and carrots for conformance include grants and technical assistance and the fact that state agencies will all sign off on conforming plans. The Executive Director of OSP is also the Director of the new Office of Smart Growth. The process has survived several governors, evolving and becoming more sophisticated. It remains precarious however, despite its court and legislative backing. Its implementation has been subject to the personalities, ambitions, and ideologies of elected and appointed officials with varying attitudes toward planning, environmental protection and affordable housing.

Correspondence with DIAD theory

This process was a fairly good fit to the DIAD model. It was based to a considerable extent on authentic dialogue among diverse stakeholders engaged in face to face discussions. Without much professional facilitation, however, it appears dialogues did not necessarily meet the basic conditions we have laid out for collaborative rationality. These stakeholders were interdependent because the localities would have to depend on what the state would do and the state could only implement its policies with agreement from the localities. Many issues required, for example, the joint participation of infrastructure agencies and environmental regulatory ones. On the other hand it appears that private sector stakeholders did not have much role in the deliberation, and some later came out objecting to aspects of the plan. In these collaborative dialogues, nonetheless, players developed social and political capital and shared understanding of

New Jersey's challenges and opportunities. Moreover, the planning process over time changed practices of players in the growth arena, ultimately leading to changes in institutions and norms. The state planning process is a work in progress still, as befits a complex adaptive system.

Interagency collaboration in CALFED: informality as a planning strategy[23]

Context

In the 1990s CALFED[24] was perhaps the largest and most comprehensive water and ecosystem management program in the nation. While it was not fully collaboratively rational, it was a self-organizing and adaptive system as it coped with dozens of stakeholders and interests, changing conditions, and evolving science. The program was complex with many moving parts and shifting task forces. It addressed extraordinary challenges, beginning with the reality that vast portions of California are without rain for six months of the year. Challenges were compounded by the way water resources are distributed. Much of the water comes from gradually melting snowpack in the northern Sierra, funneling through the California Delta before it heads to the San Francisco Bay Area, the Central Valley or the huge urban regions of southern California via a massive infrastructure of pumping facilities, dams, and conveyance systems. This situation, combined with periodic droughts, has set up bitter competition among water users, particularly among water utilities that serve urbanized and agricultural areas. Environmentalists have entered the mix because the Delta provides crucial habitat for endangered species, including salmon and water birds, and its wetlands nurture the food web that supports many more species. The environmentalist cause has advanced through lawsuits and court decisions which, in effect, require that additional water be made available for the needs of key species. In addition the state has a complex, overlapping, and often contradictory system of water rights and contracts from federal and state governments, not all of which can be exercised at once in drought years. The situation has pitted farmers, who represent the state's largest industry, against developers and real estate interests. The problem is further complicated by rivalry between northern and southern California.

Policy paralysis had set in by the 1980s, with the interests at an impasse, but increasingly recognizing that the state had to get onto a path to sustainable water resources. Lawsuits and competing legislation had stymied action while failing to address the core problem. Politics as usual had manifested itself in project-by-project decision making, rather than in considering the whole water system. Top-down decision making meant that each regulatory and water-providing agency created and administered regulations, designed projects, and allocated resources according to its mandate. Often these were conflicting mandates, however, with one agency representing, for example, hunting and fishing interests and another urban water demands. None of the existing governance approaches offered the opportunity for discovering interdependence among interests or for doing joint problem solving.

Getting started

In the early 1990s leaders of the primary stakeholder interest groups, agriculture, urban, and environment, began to meet informally in what was known as the "Three Way Process" to look for reciprocity among their interests and agree on a general approach instead of continuously undermining one another's initiatives. They did not have much luck. Agency and court decisions under the Clean Water and Endangered Species Acts were beginning to curtail exports of Delta water to agriculture and urban districts. At the same time the federal agencies involved in regulating or supplying water began to meet in a group known as Club Fed, and the governor called together state agencies in a Water Policy Council. When the bond rating agency, Standard and Poors, threatened to downgrade the state's bond rating if it did not address this impasse, the urgency of the problem became starkly clear and the threat brought the business community on board. The state could set up its own regulatory program if it met federal requirements, but in 1993 the Governor refused to do this because applying federal standards would mean reducing water flows to his agricultural constituencies. The federal government was then going to have to step in with its own plan. At this point it became clear that the agencies and interests were interdependent and could not solve their own problems alone.

The stage was set to create a single, inclusive forum. In December 1994 the Governor and Cabinet level federal officials announced an end to the California water wars with the signing of the State/Federal Agreement on Bay-Delta Environmental Protection. This was a set of principles to guide the effort to find long term resolution of Bay-Delta issues. It provided for stringent protections for the Delta and Estuary and called for both flexibility to reduce impacts of water supply problems and a consensus-building approach to the issues. One of the architects of this extraordinary accord offered four reasons why this agreement was possible at the time: a favorable interest group configuration of players looking for solutions; a substantial incentive for all to support the water quality standards; the federal leverage over state policy; and a "far-sighted decision by the environmental community to negotiate a compromise" (Reike 1996). In addition, committed leadership at the cabinet level by both state and federal resource agencies played a significant role. The leading agencies set up CALFED by a Memorandum of Understanding among themselves. No legislation was involved. CALFED was a voluntary activity.

Structure and process

CALFED was headed by a Policy Group of high level state and federal officials who, as a group, were answerable to the federal Secretary of the Interior and the Governor. They were directors who could speak for their agencies and make decisions. The Management Group of deputy directors attended these meetings and met later to work out the operational details of the policies agreed on. The leadership also set up the Bay Delta Advisory Committee (BDAC) of stakeholders to be a sounding board for the emerging ideas. Stakeholders could not attend Policy Group meetings due to the lawyers' interpretation at that time of the Federal Advisory Committee Act, though eventually these were opened to the public.

Perhaps the most important aspect of CALFED was the many task groups set up to work on issues like ecosystem restoration and water operations. Groups were inclusionary, involving a range of stakeholders and agency members, and they relied on staff borrowed from the agencies. In many cases they produced the ideas and approaches the Policy Group adopted. In particular the water operations groups developed several important innovations, including a flexible, just-in-time adaptive system for water management and a system of water banking for the environment called the Environmental Water Account (EWA). Expert consultants were recruited as needed, but members also had specialized expertise among themselves.

These dialogues were not professionally facilitated, and they varied in the degree to which they met the conditions for authentic dialogue. In the Policy Group, at least until it was opened to the public, the dialogue was free ranging, frank, and participatory. Participants laughed and joked and developed social capital, even among leaders of agencies with conflicting missions. The first CALFED Executive Director played a role a cross between facilitator and a conventional meeting chair. He made sure participants were heard and that they had the opportunity to get clarification from one another. They were not shy about speaking up or asking for clarifications among themselves. Each meeting began with presentations and explanations of the many technical issues that faced their effort so all would be operating with the same information. But the meetings were far more controlled by the Executive Director than they would be by a facilitator. The whole process lacked many of the steps that would be needed to achieve collaborative rationality, such as opportunities to brainstorm, discover reciprocity and work through differences.

In many of the small working groups, however, the dialogue met most conditions of authentic dialogue to a considerable degree, unless there was a controlling chairperson. Sometimes the chair would push things forward without checking for real assent or allowing for open-ended discussion. Some groups were highly creative, informed, and effective while others were not. BDAC was run very much in a controlling style, with stakeholders each making statements or asking questions, but without interactive discussion, much less discovery of reciprocity of interests or building of shared meaning. BDAC was a place for rhetoric and exchange of information, with most statements addressed to the chair and audience. In the one case where a committee had been assigned a facilitator, the group did not use her services. It is not unusual for collaborative efforts involving knowledgeable stakeholders or agency staff not to use facilitators, as they often believe they know how to facilitate themselves.

First order results

As a whole, CALFED during the period of our study can be credited with a series of immediate results as well as long term changes in water policy making and management. It broke the stalemate that had existed for so long and got warring players to talk and discover reciprocal interests. It created learning about the issues and social and political capital among participants. Indeed many of these previously antagonistic players joined to support a series of state bond measures worth three billion dollars to support ecosystem restoration and other CALFED activities. These bonds gave CALFED some independence from its component agencies for a time and reflected the joint learning that ecosystem restoration was necessary if anyone's interest was to be met. The agencies pooled some of their grant funds to distribute under the CALFED aegis according to collaboratively developed guidelines. CALFED began a decentralization effort, designed to empower and educate players in regional watersheds to develop their own tailor-made programs meeting CALFED criteria. CALFED developed a more transparent and participatory decision making system than had existed in the past and created new heuristics for operating in the water arena. Working collaboratively with other players and coordinating actions became more of the normal practice.

The adaptive real time water management system was perhaps the most important innovation. This effort, which emerged from four linked work groups, relied on stakeholders and agency staff in conferences calls who had done local observations of water conditions around the state. One of the remarkable aspects of this was that environmentalists trusted farmers and others to provide accurate information they could collectively put together to get an overall statewide picture. They could develop consensus on adaptive actions in the face of new data and implement the actions without fear of lawsuits and without the lengthy rule making procedures that had made water management chronically months behind the events that triggered the need for changes. The EWA offered a way of shifting water supply in time and space to better assure it would be provided where and when it was needed. It made water borrowing and lending possible, reducing some of the conflict and allowing better compliance with federal and state mandates for fish protection.

In 2000 CALFED adopted a sort of plan, which they called a Record of Decision (ROD). This was not a blueprint, and it did not require specific actions by particular agencies. Rather it was a record of what had been agreed so far, and it provided principles for the players to use in working together to address key issues like water quality, water supply, levee improvement, and habitat restoration. Though CALFED was far from finished with its tasks, the group prepared the ROD as a message to the incoming federal and state administrations, hoping they would not undo the work and agreements they had achieved. Because CALFED had been established informally with only an MOU and was not established by or with any authority other than what the agencies had individually, there was no one to officially adopt the plan. To give the plan some sort of official standing, the group decided to link it to a programmatic environmental impact assessment required by state and federal law. The last step in such an assessment is a review and decision by the responsible agency called the Record of Decision. What CALFED did was to adapt this concept and produce the assessment along with the ROD. It was not, strictly speaking, what the ROD was supposed to be but no one minded and the ROD became the guideline for action in the following years. This is but one example of how CALFED coped with the contradictions of being an informal system while also intended to instigate action by formal agencies.

Implementation

By 2002 CALFED began to have problems. Adopting the ROD had been much easier than the implementation phase, just as adopting the first plan in New Jersey was easier than the next phase, because power and resources were really on the line. Like New Jersey, CALFED faced changes in administration, which meant it did not have the high level champions or the funding it had in the first stage. When it went to the state legislature for funding, legislators were puzzled, even indignant, because they could not figure out who was in charge in this complex, self-organizing system. They established an oversight body, the California Bay Delta Authority (CBDA), with the encouragement of staff who also wanted a clear sense of to whom they were accountable. The Policy and Management groups disbanded, though some working groups remained. The focus changed from searching for reciprocal and joint opportunities for action and joint problem solving among agencies, to agencies making formal presentations to CBDA, some of whose members knew little about the water system. Agencies began to drift away from joint grant making and, in the most egregious case, the U.S. Bureau of Reclamation (BOR) decided to send more water to southern California without consulting CBDA. This proposal caused a furor among stakeholders and highlighted that BOR was a powerful agency used to operating autonomously. Problems with the declining food supply for the fish ended up providing legal justification to stop the action, but voluntary cooperation was breaking down.

System adaptations

Despite these breakdowns in collaboration, the concept, relationships, learning, and heuristics established in CALFED and its predecessor projects continue to influence practice. Its Science Program continues, but now with supporting collaborative expert groups. A number of the task groups continue work, including the EWA and the Operations Groups. Though CALFED itself was stripped of some functions and moved to the state Department of Resources, collaborative dialogues continue involving many of the same players, while also bringing in other commissions and committees and engaging issues like land use and historic preservation. The current focus is around the California Delta at the heart of the water system. The collapse of levees in New Orleans created a new sense of urgency and directed the attention of the governor and legislature to the Delta. In 2008 a series of collaborative groups were at work developing strategies to deal with the interrelated complexity of the Delta, its ecosystem, its role in farming, recreation, historic preservation, flood control, fisheries and water provision for urban use.[25] A major concern moreover is how to establish a governance system that is adaptive and flexible enough to deal with the uncertainty, complexity, and constant change, not only in the natural and human systems, but also in the understanding of them.

Correspondence with DIAD theory

CALFED is a rich example in many respects. Though it was only partially collaboratively rational, it accomplished a good deal. The informality of its arrangements reflects the difficulty of collaboration among bureaucratic agencies, much less collaboration with stakeholders. It operated in its most effective period as a kind of shadow system where things were done unofficially or with some modification of formal procedures. This strategy worked as long as the players felt their interests were interdependent and as long as CALFED had financial backing and support from the highest levels for its work. Without the collaborative Policy Group however, CBDA could not get joint action as the agencies reverted to past practices. Agencies and stakeholders could put pressure independently on the legislature and CBDA. The time came when there was little price to pay for noncooperation.

The process fit our DIAD model to some extent as it engaged diverse and interdependent agencies and stakeholders with reciprocal interests. Its outcomes included new social, political and intellectual capital and new heuristics among the agencies and players, all of whom are continuing to play a role in the cascade of new groups since formed to deal with the Delta. Many of the same players are participating, but new ones have been recruited along the way. CALFED had much of the success it did because of the years of prior dialogues and education in the skills of communication, listening, and presenting their interests. As time passed these skills and knowledge have persisted and spread. CALFED was a complex adaptive system itself, well matched to the complex system of California water and politics. There is continuous pressure, however, to move back to the usual bureaucratic style with legislative oversight. It seems likely nonetheless that many of the cooperative arrangements will continue (like operations management) because of the learning of the players. Traditional and collaborative governance in California water seem likely to coexist uneasily in the coming years.

A coalition approach: the Bay Area Alliance for Sustainable Communities (BAASC)[26]

Context

The BAASC was a regional collaborative of civic leaders and nonprofit organizations in the San Francisco Bay region, whose official mission was to make the Bay Area more sustainable. In practice it has been a hybrid between a collaborative effort and political coalition. The region was afflicted with transportation congestion and sprawling patterns of land use that aggravated the congestion. Environmental leaders wanted to control, if not stop, further development, with its impacts on air quality and the consumption of open space. The business community, especially builders and developers, was concerned about environmental regulation that could stop development. At the same time a nonprofit organization, Urban Habitat, was leading a Bay Area effort for environmental and social justice. In 1997 the idea of sustainability was increasingly seen as a goal for regions, and funding was available through foundations.

Getting started

BAASC started in 1997 when a small group of civic leaders representing the three E's – environment, economy, and equity – inspired by the President's Council for Sustainable Development – decided to provide leadership for regional sustainability. Members of the President's Council from the Sierra Club and Pacific Gas and Electric enlisted the Bay Area Council, representing business, and Urban Habitat, representing environmental justice and equity, along with the Association of Bay Area Governments (ABAG), representing the five regional agencies, to be the Steering Committee. This was the inner circle for collaboration and decision making. They also established an outer circle of 45 members representing nonprofit organizations, which promoted one or more of the three E's, as well as a number of public agencies. These members attended bimonthly meetings, heard presentations and offered comments. The overall concept was an idealistic one of creating a sustainable region by working together. Steering Committee members raised funding from foundations to support the effort through their own organizations, which did most of the work for BAASC. The Alliance itself was a skeleton operation with only one quarter-time staff member.

Structure and process

The Steering Committee (SC) engaged in intensive dialogue during the first five years, reporting to its membership periodically. The founders, according to a long time close observer,

> Did not have a road map for the Alliance; only a good idea and good intentions. They were/are concerned individuals who hoped to move the Bay Area to a more sustainable future. They volunteered countless hours to lead and participate in countless discussions. They did not have the answers; they did not even know the questions.

The group did not have professional help in designing or managing the process or in gathering information. Members relied on the skills and knowledge they had as advocates and political activists. The goal they quickly adopted was to change the patterns and practices of land use in the region to achieve a more compact, transit-friendly form of growth. In one of their first steps they decided on five tasks: develop a vision; create a regional footprint for growth; produce a set of sustainability indicators; and do an action project. They did all this with little preliminary dialogue or brainstorming and no open-ended discussion of the problems or how these tasks would help.

The SC structured the membership into four caucuses representing each of the three E's and government, and SC members became caucus chairs. Much of the discussion took place within caucuses, which took positions about issues and sent them to the SC, usually without much idea about the interests of the other groups. They did not use interest-based bargaining in the style of *Getting to Yes* (Fisher, et al. 1991). The committee kept to a standard of getting agreement among all three E's for whatever it did, though doing so was often contentious. While the members of the SC were all high level regional leaders and they were ostensibly co-equal, the representative for business was a powerful personality who worked hard to get her way. Indeed the whole program had her stamp on it, in its focus on reducing infrastructure costs and on allowing responsible development.

After a year of mutual education, the SC set up diverse working groups of members and others to work out how to go about the tasks. Again these were chaired, but not facilitated. By 1999 the SC was also beginning work on the action project, the Community Capital Investment Initiative (CCII), designed to bring investment into disadvantaged neighborhoods. Quarterly membership meetings were held, mainly for information and feedback to the SC which made the decisions. All staffing and funding came through the SC member organizations, which raised money and implemented projects. Task groups and caucuses were run in different ways depending on the chair's style, though seldom according to the principles of authentic dialogue. BAASC did not hire experts or commission studies to assist in their work, though occasionally experts volunteered their own efforts. There was a sense that the participants knew what they needed to and that the task was more political than analytical. Of all our cases, this one involved the least expertise and spent the least amount of time sorting through information.

The procedure to produce *The Compact for a Sustainable Bay Area*[27] was to make lists of goals and practices, pass them around among members, pare them down, modify them, and eventually get agreement. Developing the *Compact* took about three years, as stakeholders argued over how much growth could and should be accommodated and where, and over whether infill housing would be sufficient. The *Compact* was not the result of an inquiry into the meaning of sustainability, nor was it a vision as it would be in a collaborative process, but a list of do's and don'ts and goals. This list was honed in the caucuses and not by negotiation among the larger group or in small diverse workgroups like those in the Water Forum. The SC eliminated or watered down proposed actions in response to any stakeholder's objections, and they never discussed how the options were or should be interrelated. It was as if each action would take place in a vacuum. There was little chance for making tradeoffs or discovering reciprocity, nor even for the caucuses to understand the reasons for other caucuses' positions. Indeed the focus in the caucuses was on developing positions and even vilifying some of the other players.

The task of producing a footprint for development was transformed when two regional agencies received a large grant to develop smart growth scenarios for the Bay Area. BAASC joined forces with these agencies on this project, which was to involve dozens of workshops engaging hundreds of people around the Bay Area in choosing their preferred land use patterns. Invitations were sent to civic leaders in each county to spend several hours working together in small groups to identify where they thought growth should and should not occur and how dense it should be. These groups ended up being largely self-selected and not necessarily balanced with regard to the relevant interests. Consultants and staff took the patterns identified table by table and county by county and condensed them into three – a sprawling, a clustering, and a high density version. In later workshops participants chose a preferred scenario – not surprisingly the intermediate, clustering one.

A special task group selected regional indicators, caucuses reviewed and argued over the proposed measures, and the SC made the decision about which to use. This was as a citizen-based effort, and did not use experts to assist in selecting data sources or designing the indicators.

CCII was an ambitious and innovative effort, which began with one of the partners, the Bay Area Council, raising millions from investors. The idea was that disadvantaged neighborhoods offered an untapped business opportunity if investors and developers could be assisted by knowledgeable community players in finding these opportunities. Their investments could meet a "double bottom line," with both market rate returns for investors and benefits for the community. If CCII could achieve this, there would be a sustainable flow of community investment. The effort soon spun off with some involvement of BAASC members. It involved a Community Council (CC), a Business Council, and three investment funds, each with different purposes and rules. The process was difficult as assumptions and ways of working of the councils differed substantially, and there was no multiway, face to face discussion among all parties. The CC developed the first draft of criteria for community benefit. The fund managers selected projects and made decisions about investments, but they were not accustomed to checking with anyone, and they argued they had to operate more quickly than the CC, which needed a lot of time for dialogue.

First order results

The original tasks have had limited direct consequences for the region and certainly fell far short of expectations. BAASC adopted the *Compact*, but it was vague and hortatory rather than an agreement that would move stakeholders. It had little if any results in terms of changes in land use or growth patterns. It did more or less work from a political perspective. All stakeholders were able to get something into the *Compact* they liked and eliminate things they did not, so most were able to support it. Some, including those on the Steering Committee, were unable to bring their constituencies on board with it, including the Sierra Club and, to some degree, the Equity Caucus. Among the membership too, support was unenthusiastic.

ABAG used the preferred footprint selected by the workshops as a basis for a new type of population projection based on desired growth patterns, rather than, as before, on a combination of trends and what local plans would allow. In a break with tradition, the Metropolitan Transportation Commission (MTC),[28] agreed to use these policy-based projections in their allocation of transportation funding. This would to some degree limit the transportation projects that encourage sprawling growth, but only after some time, as the pipeline was long. There were no enforcement mechanisms nor any self-implementing provisions, as the people who would have to do this were not at the table.

BAASC eventually published an indicator report and posted it on the web.[29] It did not have the funding to use indicators for the educational efforts it had planned, and skeptics wondered whether the BAASC, in any case, had a viable strategy to assure the indicators had practical value.

Ultimately six projects were built under CCII using the investment funds. The first however was one that the CC objected to, and only one project met all their criteria. The CCII produced some developments in poor neighborhoods that might not have happened otherwise, but critics were unsatisfied with the benefits to neighborhoods. Once the funds were expended, CCII came to an end. It had not satisfied either the investors or the community. Transaction costs were significant and benefits not clear.

One of the most important short term results, however, was the Social Equity Caucus. BAASC raised funding for Urban Habitat to organize a caucus to develop positions on issues. This caucus is a group of small organizations which were not previously linked together but whose shared goal was promoting equity and environmental justice. This organization has a vision for a socially just region as well as a collective voice to promote it. One result was that members of the Environment and Economy caucuses learned about some of the needs and concerns in disadvantaged communities. Once the Environment caucus learned that a top priority of the Equity caucus was housing in neighborhoods, they realized, for example, that they could make an alliance around encouraging infill housing rather than greenfields development.

Implementation

An organization needs a theory of change to help them to turn their visions into reality, but BAASC had at best a sketchy theory, at worst an ineffective one. Their idea was to create a political coalition and influence local governments and the legislature, but their efforts in this regard had little effect. The theory of change seemed to be "think of the idea then use political skills to get it passed legislatively."

The *Compact* did not include an implementation plan or anything like the Water Forum's assurances or the Cincinnati Collaborative's MOA, and it did not have the backing of a state mandate, as in New Jersey. There was little discussion about how the players were to be motivated to act on the *Compact*'s wish list. The players who would have to implement the *Compact* were primarily local governments, which were not part of the BAASC. The *Compact* contained no information about what it would take to get new ordinances passed or changes made to general plans. This exercise had not been joint problem solving, but an effort to get a document that could be used for lobbying. The problem was that with compromise among three divergent interests, the document was not a rallying cry for any one of them. After the *Compact* was in draft, BAASC hired lobbyists with local government connections to go to the cities and counties and try to persuade them to endorse it. This was not very successful as some localities were already working on sustainability or related policies and they were not interested in even hearing a presentation. After months 67 of the 101 cities endorsed the draft version, but their expressions of support were fraught with caveats and did not represent commitments to action. The final *Compact* never went back for final approval.

BAASC also instituted a series of meetings among political and nonprofit leaders in the region designed to promote the *Compact* and the idea of compact growth. These were mostly formal presentations by politicians, with little dialogue among the civic leaders in attendance. Our conversations with the participants suggested they learned little they did not know and even felt their time was wasted. They were disappointed not to be able to engage more directly.

When BAASC got to the point where the indicator data would have to be collected and organized, they hired a consultant. The first consultant they enlisted said he could not work with the indicators they proposed. A second agreed to do the job, but had to make changes, as he said some indicators were inappropriate or impractical. The purpose and use of these indicators was not discussed, and it is difficult to know what part participants thought these would play as a practical matter. They were seen to be part of the *Compact* and to measure progress toward sustainability, but without a definition of sustainability it was problematic to make sense of them. There had only been one indicators report as of 2008, and that was not much recognized or used. The funders were, however, supportive of indicator reports, and their support may have been a reason for this seemingly futile effort.

While BAASC spent time on developing a media and outreach strategy over the years, it appears that their forums and meetings have been preaching to the converted, rather than having a wide impact on public opinion. The few bills the group wrote and advocated for did not get any traction in the legislature.

The CCII soon became a spinoff that involved some of the BAASC members. Working through the process of building this institution was difficult due in part to culture gaps between the community and business which could not be worked out without face to face dialogue, if at all.

While the process has continued for more than a decade, the SC and members did not have compelling reasons to act or reach tough agreements because the region could go on being unsustainable and there would be little direct impact on them. There was no sense of crisis. For many members BAASC was about networking. For SC members BAASC provided the umbrella to get funding and projects. There was little or no focused thinking about the long term viability of the BAASC during the time of our research and no strategy to assure it had useful functions and funding after the projects were completed.

System adaptations

Nonetheless BAASC did contribute to longer term adaptations in the region, albeit unforeseen ones. Despite the fact that it did not involve a collaboratively rational process, it did produce some significant outcomes. The case demonstrates that even flawed collaborative efforts can have some value (though some would question if the results were worth the millions spent on them and the thousands of hours of time of civic leaders). It did build new relationships among players which sometimes became working relationships for other tasks. It did result in learning by the participants about the issues and about each others' activities. It did contribute to a discourse about sustainability in the region. It did educate political leaders about issues. It produced several innovations, all of which, it should be noted, emerged from a few multiway dialogues among players with differing interests. The innovations included the Social Equity Caucus, the idea of using preferred land use scenarios to create policy-based population projections, and the CCII. It brought together hundreds of leaders with differing interests and helped them learn about each other's concerns and develop respect for each others' views. It built social networks and relationships among competing stakeholders who work together today on projects at the intersections of their shared interests.

BAASC helped to develop a discourse among many regional leaders. Over years of discussion its members became what one policy expert has called a "discourse coalition"[30] focused on smart growth and the policies and practices that could lead to it. This sort of coalition is held together by its concepts, arguments and language. Once the discourse is established, its power does not depend on participants' meeting, strategizing, or acting jointly. Its influence comes as the discourse spreads and as it reframes public debate. BAASC's unique contribution in this regard (because others were also talking about smart growth during this time) was to integrate equity into the thinking about sustainability. It helped participants understand that meeting the needs of the disadvantaged was not only a moral issue. All those we interviewed seemed to have become committed to action that served all three E's jointly. This understanding went beyond the members of the BAASC, as each represented an organization with many constituents. A number indicated they had altered their organization's activities based on what they learned working with members of other caucuses.

BAASC helped spread a view of a sustainable region as one with more compact, transit-friendly growth and infill housing. It helped link the five regional agencies in dialogue after their first ever meeting under its auspices in 1997. This meeting opened more lines of communication among representatives of agencies, and the linkage enabled the smart growth/footprint project to go forward. For ABAG, which, as a Council of

Government (COG), had communicated primarily with its constituent local governments, the project opened communication with stakeholders. Evidence of the spread of these sustainability ideas was that Bay Area Rapid Transit (BART) later adopted a policy only to provide new transit stops if substantial development was planned around them.

Broader outcomes include not only the development of new networks, social capital, and partnerships that continue today, but also influence on the trajectory of land use policy in the state. While the Footprint/Smart Growth project did not at the time appear to have immediate impact other than changing population projections, this model was adapted to become a basis for state legislation enabling and funding regional "Blueprint planning." One of the BAASC leaders had moved on to become Secretary of Business, Transportation and Housing, where she led this effort. The Sacramento COG conducted its own Blueprint Planning effort engaging the regional and local leadership in a process that impressed a leading state legislator from that area. He, in turn, negotiated a major piece of state legislation[31] designed to implement smart growth, building on the Sacramento experience. At the present writing, it seems likely that the law will result in new norms and practices in California land use planning. Our research has found that there can be a cascade of changes resulting in part from a collaborative process, as its effects ripple out through the complex system (Connick and Innes 2003). Ironically these and other unplanned outcomes turned out to be more significant than the projects BAASC set out to do.

Correspondence to DIAD theory

This was a process that was more about building a coalition for political influence in Sacramento than about creating an inclusive collaborative learning group to work toward common goals in a self-organizing way. From the point of view of DIAD theory, BAASC included a diversity of interests on their Steering Committee and all of these understood their interdependence around growth issues. This diversity was not, however, adequate to the projects they sought to do, nor to the broader goal of creating a smart growth strategy. In particular, it lacked representation from local government and from MTC, both of which were necessary to implementation and both of which had crucial knowledge about relevant practices and politics.

Second, although in principle the stakeholders were interdependent, the systematic articulation and discussion of interests that are basic to collaborative rationality did not occur. They took positions and seldom explained them. Assumptions remained unquestioned and not necessarily shared. At a retreat near the end of the process, environmentalists and business folks were shocked and angry when the equity representatives said that smart growth was not their priority. They were more concerned about jobs and transportation. Much of the discussion occurred in caucuses rather than multiway dialogue, which meant it was difficult to discover reciprocity or shared interests. Without systematic identification and discussion of interests among the membership or a search for reciprocity, the *Compact* represented the lowest common denominator.

The process deviated from authentic dialogue in other ways as well. Although the SC may have had a collaboratively rational dialogue to some degree, the evidence indicates that its members had unequal power in the dialogue, despite the fact that they did things consensually. One member was a powerful personality and had the most resources. A couple of members were not particularly forceful. There were angry exchanges, but without a chair or facilitator to make sure everyone was heard and treated respectfully, it is not clear that power imbalances were addressed. Moreover, without staffing and expert assistance there was little testing of the accuracy of assertions and assumptions. The CCII proceeded, with the business people sometimes making the investment decisions over the objections of the community people.

BAASC seemed to have the ingredients for a robust result – stakeholders, a mission, all interested in sustainability and an agreement to get all on board for any action. It ended up with weak and poorly developed strategies, domination by business, little exploration of the big picture, and little mutual exploration of interests. The SC proposed solutions and tasks at the outset, without brainstorming or collaborative dialogue. At no time, judging by the detailed minutes, was there a discussion over the meaning of sustainability or of smart growth, much less on how it could be achieved. The process thus was not self-reflective and offered little opportunity for single or double loop learning.

Politics and parliamentary procedure: the East Bay Conversion and Reinvestment Commission (EBCRC)

Context

In the early 1990s, as part of a federal decision to reduce U.S. military bases, the Defense Department selected nine facilities in the San Francisco Bay area for closure. For some communities the bases were the primary economic engine, employing hundreds of residents. Military personnel patronized local stores and restaurants. The law required that bases be turned over to civilian control with the aid of local reuse authorities. This transfer was never simple, and it could take years because it typically involved massive environmental cleanup, multiple public and private partners with conflicting objectives, and protracted negotiation over sales prices. The community was usually in a hurry, but the military was not. In 1993 President Clinton announced a five point plan that implicitly gave highest priority to community economic development, in contrast to the past emphasis on maximizing property sales revenues for the Treasury. Other laws affecting the bases required the reuse to include affordable housing and places for the homeless. In California Indian tribes claimed some of the land.

Getting started

Congressman Ron Dellums' East Bay district was particularly hard hit by proposed closures. As the powerful head of the Armed Services Committee, he was instrumental in creating a National Pilot project to identify and create innovative approaches to the base conversion process. The congressman's office set up the EBCRC with $5 million in federal money. The Commission was a stakeholder group from the region, including mayors of affected cities, state legislators, and representatives of private industry councils, the national defense laboratories, major private businesses, labor unions, and nonprofits representing equity interests like the homeless, Indian tribes and environmental justice. The participants were high level, capable individuals. In Innes' capacity as Director of the Institute of Urban and Regional Development (IURD) at Berkeley, the Chancellor appointed her to represent the University. She agreed because the process seemed to have the potential to provide value for the region and because she wanted to understand more about stakeholder processes. While the only power the group had was to allocate the money, it could have considerable influence because of this diverse and powerful set of stakeholders. President Clinton came to meet with the EBCRC early on to encourage participants and thus made the project seem more promising. One of the co-chairs was an open-minded consensus builder. The other was a political person whose main job was to assist the congressman. The chairs established diverse working committees to deal with specific issues. Innes became chair of the Technical Advisory Committee (TAC) of academics, experts and leading practitioners. She was anticipating a real opportunity to build consensus and achieve innovative solutions to the thorny problems created by base closures. Unfortunately this was not to be.

Structure and process

The first problem was that the co-chairs felt it would be politically prudent to run Commission meetings formally according to parliamentary procedure (Susskind 1999) and open meetings laws, as they involved public officials. These were not official government meetings so these procedures were not legally required. The meetings began with long announcements. The agenda that had been announced publically some days before, in accord with open meetings laws, noted what items were for information and what for action. There was time at some point in the meeting for public comment – three minutes per person. During the meeting, for any of the Commission members to say anything other than to react to what we were given, according to parliamentary procedure they would have to make a motion and get it seconded. Only then could members speak, but only for or against the motion. They could offer amendments to the motion, but these ideas would not be discussed without a second. All of this is standard practice in government bodies in the U.S. and in many board meetings.

The result of applying this procedure was that members quickly divided into camps over each motion. There was no opportunity to find common ground and no opportunity to bring up issues unless they were on the agenda. Innes found herself, like a number of others, irritated at having her motion criticized, sometimes by someone who really did not know what he was talking about. But she would not have a chance to make a correction till her turn to speak came around, perhaps half an hour later. The one time she disagreed with a motion, Commission staff called her at home and told her to work out an agreement before the next meeting with the person who made the motion. They wanted "consensus" but not to air differences publicly. They did not want to have dialogue or open up larger discussions. Innes reluctantly worked out something with the other stakeholder, though neither was happy with the solution. After that she simply kept her disagreements to herself.

The required public comment periods were neither valuable nor productive. Because so many of the stakeholders were represented around the table and in constant communication with their constituencies, the few members of the public who showed up to speak were the usual gadflies who come to meetings and repeat themselves, sometimes unintelligibly. Not surprisingly Commissioners either left early or used the occasion to go in the hallways for private conversations and networking (Innes and Booher 2005).

At one point, in deference to the idea of collaboration, a facilitator was hired to help the group prioritize possible projects. His methods were anything but collaborative, however, and did not involve authentic dialogue, or even dialogue. In a workshop with the thirty stakeholders and two dozen members of the public who happened to show up, the facilitator gave everyone self-stick dots which they were to put on their favorite options listed on butcher paper on the wall. He did this without prior discussion. More dots meant an item would be discussed and fewer that it would not. This procedure fell short of collaborative rationality in several ways. First, it permitted self-selected and not necessarily representative members of the public to "vote." Stakeholders were at least a representative group of interests. The public who attended were heavily weighted toward would-be contractors and people with agendas and readymade positions. These players could and did weight the results heavily by putting all their dots on one item. Second, it moved to this "voting" procedure on the basis of only a sentence or two about each option, so many people did not know what they were voting for. It appeared that this workshop was more about making people think they were participating than really seeking input, much less using it.

The Commission increasingly focused on how to spend the money, and after the first few conversations some preferred projects emerged in a way that was mysterious to Innes. There was little or no discussion of many issues central to reuse planning, like what was the most cost effective way to address displacement. There had been proposals from stakeholders and outsiders, but in the group there was never the collective brainstorming on the issues that is so important to developing creative ideas. Nor did the group assess the ideas and proposed projects in terms of collectively developed criteria, as good practices of consensus building would require. Rather the ideas were selected behind the scenes. Questioning these would be unwelcome, especially since each of the projects had champions on the commission, some of whom stood to gain funding for the project. The process was somewhat parallel to the BAASC, which started out with projects without a freewheeling conversation first about what tasks would best address their interests and objectives. Unlike BAASC, EBCRC did make use of research. IURD, under Innes' direction, provided modest technical assistance, looking at job losses and moves by former base employees. Ultimately the projects were selected not on the basis of analysis, but in the pork barrel mode with each project chosen to benefit a constituency, such as labor unions or business. Each served a constituency including labor, business or social equity.

In the meantime the TAC was engaging in creative dialogue, trying to work through issues like what were the best cleanup and environmental restoration strategies. In the process, however, the committee began to lose key practitioners, the very people who could explain from their experience what would and would not work. They left because they feared that their participation would prevent them from later bidding on the lucrative contracts their organizations hoped for. The remaining academics and experts did not have the necessary praxis for the group to continue the discussion. The TAC enlisted legal experts and developed a proposal for a code of ethics that would serve this type of process and allow dialogue with these stakeholders, whose knowledge would be essential to the development of workable proposals. The Commission would not provide funding for modest legal fees so the TAC disbanded with little left to do.

First order results

The chosen projects were set in motion but as most involved partnerships with other agencies, the time line was long and the projects involved both technical delays and political controversy over the ensuing years. Few of the projects would have happened without EBCRC, however, as no other entity was available to take responsibility. During the course of the meetings stakeholders built new professional and personal networks and learned a good deal about the issues surrounding defense conversion. The process helped to call public attention to defense conversion and EBCRC got localities moving forward on reuse plans.

System adaptations

As of the late 1990s, when Innes lost touch with the organization, there had been some limited evidence of system adaptation. Local governments and the military had developed some new ways of working together and some mutual learning had taken place. Partnerships emerged like that between IURD and the Bay Area Council (BAC), an organization representing big business in the region on the EBCRC, with IURD providing research to assist BAC in refocusing the regional economy. Other working relationships developed among stakeholders who also discovered common causes and interests. Moreover, some relatively powerless stakeholders, like homeless advocates had gained visibility and credibility. Over the years it helped, working with the local reuse authorities, to bring in $50 million in federal funding to close and develop the military facilities. Some of the things it has helped to bring about over the years include making sure local reuse authorities had regional representation to help them avoid interjurisdictional conflicts. They worked on providing worker dislocation assistance, helped with assuring facilities to homeless providers, and offered technical assistance to reuse authorities to manage research contracts. Today the Commission no longer functions.

Correspondence with DIAD theory

The overall process was not collaboratively rational and did not fit our DIAD theory, despite the fact that it was inclusive of stakeholders with potentially reciprocal and shared interests in the region. The Commission discussion was around position-taking rather than meeting one another's interests. Actual face to face, free-ranging authentic dialogue was not possible. Ticklish issues between two stakeholders had to be settled off stage without the participation of others who might themselves have had a stake in the argument. As a result proposals and projects were not necessarily those best suited to the mission, and some important issues fell through the cracks. The process was designed to give the appearance of consensus without the reality. For Innes it became too much trouble to speak out, and the group increasingly proceeded without much dissent. EBCRC zeroed in on projects before exploring the issues or agreeing on goals because of limited time and the desire for visible, short term results to satisfy its political backers.

The group never had a discussion about what desirable defense conversion would mean. Each brought his own individual perspective, but the group never developed shared meaning, much less a shared mission. If no one objected to an idea it became de facto agreed-on. No one wanted to use social and political capital to challenge anything that was not crucial to their organization. The chairs, staff, and powerful players got their way with little challenge. They could say there was consensus, and claim the projects were supported by the impressive list of stakeholders. Stakeholder principals began to send staff to the meetings after a while instead of attending themselves. Meetings became largely pro forma.

Other collaborative efforts

Collaboration in public decision making takes place in many settings and forms (Margerum 2008). Collaboration ranges from partnerships between organizations, like those between a public agency and a private organization for service delivery, in networks linking Silicon Valley companies which allow timely response to emerging technology (Saxenian 1994), in large scale facilitated citizen dialogues like Blueprint Planning community workshops (Barbour and Teitz 2006), or in small informal groups working to protect their neighborhoods. Some collaborative processes involve formally selected stakeholders, whereas others involve individuals representing themselves. Some have broad long term missions, like the Chesapeake Bay Program, and some have short term, limited tasks like developing goals for a city's disused waterfront. Some are ad hoc and temporary like the Cincinnati process, and others may be formally institutionalized like the New Jersey process. Some are sponsored by government and some operate outside to influence public policy or to supplement government with their own civic leadership, as do California's Collaborative Regional Initiatives[32] (Innes and Rongerude 2005). Some are designed to be purely advisory, whereas others are de facto decision making groups, like the BDAC task subcommittees in CALFED. Many of them focus on a shared resource, as did the Water Forum. Many involve place making activities such as urban design, economic development, land use, transportation, or infrastructure planning (Healey, et al. 2003). The range of applications of collaboration is broad, but the percentage that is well managed and meets the DIAD theory conditions of diversity, interdependence, and authentic dialogue is still small. The rest of this book attempts to help increase that proportion.

Conclusion

In this chapter we offered six stories of processes, ranging from highly collaboratively rational in the spirit of DIAD theory, to business-as-usual formal meetings. Our purpose has been to provide an inside look at the dynamics of a variety of processes to help the reader understand why they do or do not work. We have illustrated how to link choices made in process design to the outcomes that result. We have chosen the cases to represent a range of scales and topics, as well as a variety of methods of creating dialogues and reaching agreements. The cases are also designed to show first, second and third order effects, including unanticipated effects and system changes that can occur in well run processes.

Looking across these stories we suggest the following propositions about the relationship between process and outcome. Our overarching observation is that the more collaboratively rational a process, the more extensive and long term are the outcomes. In particular:

- Face to face dialogue among stakeholders is essential to the discovery of mutual gain opportunities and to agreements that are robust rather than superficial or weak.
- Missing stakeholders, deal makers or deal breakers can mean a process is unable to deliver what other stakeholders want.
- Small group, diverse task teams can accomplish things that will be accepted by a wider group.
- The ability to challenge assumptions and conduct freewheeling dialogue is essential to developing effective actions.
- Power differentials around the table can interfere with wise decisions, if not managed within the dialogue.

- The development of shared, explicit knowledge and shared meaning is central in effective processes and in single and double loop learning.
- Staffing is essential for complex tasks and authentic, informed dialogue.
- The longest lasting outcomes and system adaptations build on the relationships and learning that can emerge with a genuinely collaborative dialogue.

Armed with the theory and concepts in Chapter 2 and with these case studies, we can now move on to explore and analyze in more depth the dynamics implicit in these and other collaborative efforts. In the next chapter we look in depth at the challenges of creating collaboratively rational processes in practice. We will explore the nature of collaborative dialogue, and then look at how knowledge can be integrated into collaborative decision making, including how to deal with conflicting science, and finally we will make a case for the importance of local knowledge to robust conclusions and resilience in policy.

Notes

1   A case in point is an example from Australia where community engagement processes around the development of wind turbines were more about placating communities than consensus building Hindmarsh, R. and C. Matthews (2008), "Deliberative speak at the turbine face: community engagement, wind farms, and renewable energy transitions, in Australia." *Journal of Environmental Policy & Planning* 10(3): 217–232.
2   This case is adapted from a dissertation Connick, S. (2003). Innes conducted some of the research on the early part of the case. Additional materials have been used to bring it up to date.
3   We have used this case in many of our writings but one in particular unpacks the dynamics of the interactions Innes, J. and Booher, D. E. (1999b) "Consensus building as role playing and bricolage: toward a theory of collaborative planning." *Journal of the American Planning Association* 65(1): 9–26.
4   Since it began it greatly expanded its scope and it is called the Center for Collaborative Policy. Its mission is to build the capacity of public agencies, stakeholders, and citizens to use collaborative methods to improve public policy outcomes. The experience with the Water Forum was important to helping the Center recognize that they were doing much more than dispute resolution and needed to rethink their mission. This Water Forum case was not about resolving a particular dispute. Rather it was, in a context of many different disputes, designed to anticipate and preempt these long term conflicts by creating policies and practices that could address them and offer a way to move forward without litigation, constant conflict and distrust.
5   For example, she had facilitated several statewide growth management collaborative dialogues which we have documented (Innes et al. 1994).
6   Staff included some who worked directly for the city or county, along with staff provided by the Center. Expert consultants were also hired.
7   A Joint Powers Agreement permits existing agencies to jointly exercise their existing independent powers.
8   The Water Forum Agreement can be found at www.waterforum.org/agreement.cfm (accessed February 15, 2009).
9   The Hodge flow decision, named after the presiding judge, established the principle that environmental protection and in stream flows were significant interests to be protected

under the law. It set minimum flow requirements that would limit EBMUD's diversions from the river. A panel of legal experts convinced Forum participants that this established a legal precedent that would affect all purveyors. This became a major incentive for the stakeholders to work together (www.waterforum.org/DEIR/APPNC.pdf).

10 It got this name because the Water Forum group was adamant that they would not set up a bureaucracy or another layer of government to implement their agreement. Moreover they realized that implementation would be complex and involve many unforeseen circumstances that a bureaucracy could not handle. They wanted a representative stakeholder group to continue to consider issues as they came up, in an adaptive way. See for more details www.csus.edu/ccp/projects/recent.stm#waterforum (accessed February 15, 2009).

11 www.waterforum.org/wfse5yrRvwEvalCover.htm

12 This story is based on a combination of films: including Cincinnati Project, Common Ground Productions, Catalog no. 1628, Voices of Hope Research Findings; *Driving While Black*, Diverse Productions for Open University, TV-4 NTSC; a segment on Public Broadcasting's Newshour with Jim Lehrer April 12, 2002; official documents; many newspaper articles; and conversations with mediator Jay Rothman, whom we thank for his help and comments on the draft story. We are also grateful to Jill Williams of the Andrus Foundation for her suggestions on the final draft.

13 U.S. courts, like those in some other countries, can ask parties to work with a professional master to help sort through the issues. Sometimes the master is a mediator and sometimes an expert. But the court will rely on his or her advice in making its judgment.

14 www.ariagroup.com/jay.html

15 This was attorney Saul Green.

16 Jill Williams, personal communication.

17 This story is drawn from Innes' research in New Jersey in 1989, some of which was published in two articles about state growth management programs (Innes 1992b), and a retrospective article by a deputy planning director for the original state plan, who has continued to follow the implementation of the plan (Bierbaum 2007). A book by Enrico Gualini documents the later evolution of the planning process, (2001).

We are particularly grateful to Martin Bierbaum, who has been professionally involved in later iterations of the State Plan, for reviewing and correcting this account and providing us with more recent information and reports. This has allowed us to offer more on results and develop lessons to be learned from this 20 year evolving experiment.

18 Southern Burlington County NAACP *v.* Township of Mt. Laurel, 67 N.J. 151 (1975) and 92 N.J. 158 (1983).

19 See Kirp, et al. (1995).

20 NJSA 52:18A-196 et seq.

21 Personal communication.

22 www.state.nj.us/dca/osg/commissions/spc/index.shtml

23 This story is told in more detail in several articles, working papers and a dissertation (Connick 2003; Connick and Innes 2003; Innes et al. 2006; Innes et al. 2007). Each of these contains references to other writings that have informed this case. Two other important articles also reflect on CALFED: Freeman, J. (1997), "Collaborative governance in the administrative state," *UCLA Law Review* 45: 1–98.

Heikkila, T. and A. Gerlak (2005), "The formation of large-scale collaborative resource management institutions: clarifying the roles of stakeholders, science, and institutions," *Policy Studies Journal* 33(4): 583–612.

24 It should be noted that at this writing CALFED is in a state of transition and is now located within the State Department of Resources. We will focus here on its period as a largely freestanding collaborative effort.

25 www.deltavision.ca.gov

26 This is adapted from a longer version of the case: Innes, J. (2004). Taking the three E's seriously: the Bay Area Alliance for Sustainable Communities, Berkeley CA, Institute of Urban and Regional Development, University of California.

27   This is posted on the BAASC web site at www.bayareaalliance.org/compact.pdf and published as *Draft Compact for a Sustainable Bay Area* BAASC, Oakland CA 94604, July 2002. A final version was printed in 2004.

28   The region's official Metropolitan Planning Organization, responsible for allocating transportation funds.

29   Bay Area Alliance for Sustainable Communities (2004). State of The Bay Area: A Regional Report. Pathways to Results, Measuring Progress toward Sustainability. San Francisco, Bay Area Alliance for Sustainable Communities. www.bayareaalliance.org/indicators.pdf (accessed February 18, 2009).

30   This is a term used by Maarten Hajer in discussing conflicts over acid rain in the UK and northern Europe: Hajer, M. A. (1995), *The Politics of Environmental Discourse: Ecological Modernization and the Policy Process*, Oxford: Clarendon Press.

31   This was known as SB 375 and it established new incentives for regional land use and transportation planning. http://leginfo.ca.gov/pub/07-08/bill/sen/sb_0351-0400/sb_375_bill_20080930_chaptered.pdf

32   See California Center for Regional Leadership (www.calregions.org) for an explanation.

4 The praxis of collaboration

Effective collaboration depends on praxis. That is, it depends on extended practical experience deeply informed by theorizing and reflection. Those who engage in collaboration build their capacity and intuition about how to proceed, while at the same time building theory about when and how collaboration can work. Praxis is practice interwoven with theory and theory informed by experience in the spirit of pragmatism. Our purpose in this chapter is to build an in-depth understanding of the praxis of collaboration, drawing on the theories we have outlined in Chapter 2, the stories of practice we have told in Chapter 3 and on our own and others' research and practice. We will go beyond the cross cutting lessons in the previous chapter to look in a nuanced way at key elements in any collaboration, including understanding the conditions necessary to initiate a process and move forward, the ways of creating authentic dialogue, and considerations in the design of a process.[1] The chapter can be regarded as a supplement to the valuable handbooks already available.[2] In addition we explore the elusive concept of power and how it does and does not play a role in collaborative dialogues. Finally, we look at the contradictions and paradoxes within and around the praxis of collaboration and make the case that, not only will these never be resolved, they are an essential part of the power of collaboration, and we must find ways to embrace them.

Necessary conditions for successful policy dialogues

From our perspective a successful policy dialogue is one where deep and durable agreement was reached, actions were taken with strong support; outcomes included addressing the original problematic situation; and system adaptations ultimately resulted. Successful cases create social and intellectual capital and build institutional capacity. They are adaptive to changing circumstances and evolve along with knowledge and conditions. The most successful produce spinoff and second and third order consequences such as institutional change.

Our findings on the three most successful cases outlined in Chapter 3 – the Water Forum, the Cincinnati dialogues, and the New Jersey State Plan – are consistent with other case studies we have done (Innes, et al. 1994) and with Booher's practice experience. The first three cases share critical features like inclusion and authentic dialogue. The limitations in the latter three cases can largely be explained by a lack of some of these features, such as a strong incentive structure bringing people to the table, sponsors and effective initial leadership, inclusion of diverse stakeholders, sufficient infrastructure to support the process, the use of a negotiating document to focus the dialogue, and a self-organizing adaptive process that evolved with new information. These conditions take many forms, which we elaborate here. Meeting these conditions, however, is not sufficient for a successful dialogue. Its contents and management are also crucial. We discuss this aspect later in the chapter.

Incentive structure

Each of the comparatively successful collaborative dialogues had a compelling incentive structure that encouraged the necessary players not only to participate, but to stay at the table and work toward agreement. In the language of negotiation theory, the stakeholders' BATNA was not as good as the opportunities presented by multiway dialogue. In the Water Forum not all stakeholders felt their BATNAs were poor, as some thought they might get what they wanted through litigation or legislation. Such options are uncertain and would be fought by other stakeholders. An agreement in the Water Forum would hold more certainty, though it might not provide everything a stakeholder wanted. It was an example of Axelrod's rational cooperators (Axelrod 1984) whose experience was that they could get more of what they wanted by working together than by going it alone.

Stakeholders in the Water Forum were well aware that they had to share a limited supply of water. The fact that two of the major water users and suppliers, the City and County of Sacramento, were the sponsors who would set their policies for water management on the basis of this dialogue was even more compelling. The stakes were raised further when a court decision reduced the supply by requiring release of more water for the fish. Stakeholders came to the table to protect their interests but also kept their options open, constantly scanning the political and judicial environment to see if they could do better going it alone. Some even brought lawsuits against others during the process or pursued their own legislation. While such actions caused consternation in the group, the facilitator reminded them that they lived in two worlds. She insisted on complete disclosure and continued with the dialogue. These outside activities intensified the incentives for participants to reach their own internal agreement accommodating all the stakeholders.

In New Jersey state law required the state plan, though participation by the localities in cross-acceptance was voluntary. However, once local jurisdictions saw the preliminary plan, they realized their interests were at stake. While they did not know whether the plan would be implemented or if the state would make investment decisions based on it, just the chance it could happen was motivation enough to participate.

Moreover, court decisions were behind the plan and the courts might get involved again, with unpredictable consequences. Uncertainty is often seen as the worst option. In Cincinnati, the riots and potential for more, as well as the economic boycott and the lawsuit against the police, gave most of the players reason to work out an agreement. The police were the most resistant because they could continue as always without an agreement. Their BATNA was status quo. It is difficult to prove racial profiling so they were unlikely to be penalized for it. But the Mayor's support, a federal inquiry, and the fear of many police as they patrolled Over-the-Rhine was enough to get them to participate, albeit without enthusiasm.

In CALFED the external incentive structure was the political paralysis that was preventing any stakeholders from getting what they cared about, while court decisions protecting endangered species were ratcheting up the stakes. State and federal money and substantial bond funding guaranteed in the early years that CALFED would be where the action was – where projects would be designed and decided upon. Once the funding began to dry up and some of the early objectives were met, the incentive structure deteriorated, and agencies and stakeholders began to drift away. It is not unusual that as a process begins to have results, the reasons for staying in it become less compelling. On the other hand, early successes can have the opposite effect, keeping people at the table as they see progress.

EBCRC brought people to the table because defense conversion was a major regional economic and social crisis as well as an opportunity for new industries and development. Most stakeholders were not directly affected by the crisis, so their incentives were weak. Moreover, the potential reciprocity among the players was not discussed so the advantages of staying were unclear, as was the potential benefit of reaching agreement. EBCRC kept some people at the table because there was funding to be given out, but those who were not getting funding had little incentive to stay when the activities boiled down to a distributional issue. Finally, our earlier study (Innes, et al. 1994) of California cases of consensus building found that a major motivation for staying at the table over time was that players were building relationships and learning. They enjoyed the interchange in ways that EBCRC stakeholders did not.

The BAASC also had little incentive structure. While its key stakeholders agreed that existing land use patterns were not sustainable, nothing had changed in the environment or laws to compel them to work for a solution, much less to do things differently. This was not an urgent problem, but one that everyone had lived with for a long time. There was no sponsor to act on what they did and no clear benefits to individual stakeholders associated with reducing sprawl. There was minimal exploration of reciprocity or the potential for mutual gain solutions and, in any case, no opportunity to adapt the original tasks.

In another example, civic leaders in San Diego California instigated a collaborative dialogue to develop a growth management strategy when the state threatened to impose its own legislation (Gruber and Neuman 1994). Instigating a successful collaborative process normally requires a change in the status quo that is threatening to the players – something that would make matters worse or raise new risks. People adjust to an unsatisfactory status quo and know what its costs are. Change brings uncertainty and perhaps worse outcomes.

In many cases the existing incentive structure is not sufficient to bring together the necessary players. One or more stakeholders may lack the incentive to join or conditions may not seem pressing enough to demand that stakeholders take the time and energy. It is often possible, however, to change the incentive structure through legislation, lawsuits, protests, or boycotts. These strategies brought many people to the table in Cincinnati and created the New Jersey process. High level, visible government sponsorship can also be significant, as it was in CALFED and the Water Forum.

Leaders and sponsors

External incentive structures are not enough. A collaborative process needs leadership to get started. Someone has to have the idea and the ability to engage other leaders in designing and setting up the process. Someone has to line up project sponsors and find the resources to fund the effort. In the Water Forum it was the City and County staff; in New Jersey it was the team of leaders who prepared the legislation and the state planning director; in Cincinnati it was the presiding judge, who ordered mediation and located a major funder; in the BAASC it was two San Francisco members of the President's Council on Sustainable Development; an Assistant Secretary of the U.S. Department of the Interior and a Director of the State Resources Department got things moving in CALFED; and in EBCRC it was the Congressman's co-chief of staff and the Director of a regional social equity advocacy group. In most cases other leaders emerged along the way and played pivotal roles.

The leadership that we find in successful collaborative processes is generative-training and encouraging other leaders and getting others to take initiative (Bryson and Crosby 1992; Chrislip and Larson 1994; Chrislip 2002; Roberts 1997). It is not about having a vision and implementing it, or being the "czar" or decider. On the contrary, collaborative leadership involves getting something started and then encouraging, rather than controlling, building capacity among others, and initiating networks. Most of the leaders in the successful processes we are aware of were instigators and inspirers, rather than people looking for followers. As the process moved forward they stepped back, allowing other leaders to emerge and the process to take its own course. One exception was in BAASC, where one of the Steering Committee members emerged as a major leader, pushing hard on her agenda and interfering with the development of other leaders and with the potential for an adaptive process.

Inclusionary decision making

The most successful cases we are aware of included most or all relevant stakeholders. They typically started with a core group and, as they found other players with a stake, they invited them in. A collaboratively rational process has to engage all those who have pertinent knowledge and a stake in the issue. Feasibility and legitimacy of collaboratively produced plans require this engagement. Identifying and drawing in the stakeholders can require substantial effort. The deal makers and the deal breakers are obvious choices, but the stakeholder group also should include those who could benefit and those who could be harmed by any agreement. It needs to include the strong and the weak, as well as all the major perspectives. It is no mean feat to identify all these interests, find people and organizations to represent them, and then to get them to come to the table. If key stakeholders cannot be persuaded to join, then it is unethical to proceed, in our view and in the view of the facilitation profession. It is also a waste of time as an agreement is unlikely to hold if key stakeholders did not buy in.

The Water Forum staff used a technique that all professional facilitators use: conflict assessment.[3] They interviewed possible participants to find out their perceptions of the issues and what their options or BATNAs were. They found the players who had a stake and invited them in. The facilitator in Cincinnati did something similar, spending the first two months identifying stakeholders, finding out about the issues and widely seeking advice on who should participate. In New Jersey, not only did OSP include all jurisdictions, it engaged private stakeholders such as business and environmental representatives in a variety of ways. CALFED began with a small group of the most powerful agencies representing urban, environmental, and agricultural interests, and it continued to incorporate agencies and private stakeholders as it went along. The BAASC, however, decided from the outset that the negotiators were to be five individuals from specific organizations and that there would be a second tier membership of nonprofit groups representing business, social equity, and environment, who would provide input, but not engage in dialogue. They left out local government.

An inclusionary strategy is important to developing a policy or plan that will work. A case in point was an effort to develop a health impact assessment of development plans and proposals in San Francisco so that it could be part of the city's decision making process.[4] Health department organizers resisted advice to include developers because the small nonprofit providers and advocacy groups and the health department staff regarded them as the problem. They suspected no agreement could be reached with the business community. Moreover, these NGOs wanted the chance to network among themselves and build their own capacity and learning in a safe setting. In this case lack of inclusion of developers stymied the original purpose of the assessment to integrate health impact assessment with planning and development decisions.

Theoretical considerations play out in practice to help assure feasible and innovative results. Theory tells us that challenging given knowledge and the status quo is critical to achieving collaborative rationality. Only by uncovering what is hidden under socially constructed understandings can there be any hope of seeing past the disempowering language and expectations of society and getting out of impasses. Diverse stakeholders assure that the difficult questions get addressed. In many cases entirely new approaches and ways of thinking may be needed. A diverse and conflictual group trying to reach agreement often comes up with ideas that are not merely marginal adjustments but creative solutions to problems (Hong and Page 2001). Internal tensions, agonism, and a dialectical process not only help participants to move out of self-fulfilling, self-referential discussion, they reveal the many sidedness of a problem.

Diversity works to produce collaboratively rational results because collaboration uses a different logic from representative government, where a quorum is enough for a decision and where a majority rules. Agreement has to be broader and deeper to approximate the conditions of Habermas' communicative rationality. In practice, stakeholders themselves determine what will count as agreement, based on the principle that it has to involve a supermajority that is inclusive of interests. For example, a typical approach is to require between 80 percent and 90 percent agreement so long as all major stakeholder categories are included. An agreement might require acceptance by a majority or 75 percent of each different caucus or interest cluster. The idea is to make sure no interest is left out and that no agreement is reached until every effort is made to bring all stakeholders on board. Opposition can often be reduced to a small percentage, and sometimes the effort to accommodate these stakeholders can mean that they will not too actively oppose the result because their concerns were acknowledged.

While this decision model acknowledges the importance of preventing a small minority from holding the group hostage, minority opinions must be listened to and taken seriously, especially if they are strongly held. In such opinions are knowledge, insights, and values that a group ignores at its peril. For example Innes was involved in a group that did collaborative dialogue around an assessment of academic departments. Normally decisions were taken consensually after lengthy dialogue, but in one controversial case, after many hours there remained one last holdout. This person was not the most forceful or knowledgeable in the group, and eventually the group overrode her objection. Not many months later the group was threatened with lawsuits because of the decision. Her objection, members realized in retrospect, had been valid, and not heeding it meant they spent months undoing the damage of their decision. The model of decision-making by majority rule not only may not take into account key perspectives, it results in winners and losers, often creating enemies, as Innes found in the EBCRC (Fisher, et al. 1991). Decisions can be unstable, not only because 51 percent can easily be shifted to 49 percent, but also because players are not bound together through reciprocity.

Dedicated staffing

There is much to be done behind the scenes as well as in meetings to make a process successful. All of our most successful cases had significant, trusted staff support, in contrast with the less successful ones. Robust agreements and collaboratively rational decisions and capacity building do not solely occur around a table. There are agendas to be written, meeting summaries to prepare and distribute, experts to invite, information to gather, phone calls to be made to participants to ensure their needs are being met, and meetings to attend or facilitate, as well as data to gather and analyze. A major staff job is to keep participants informed, make sure they feel heard, and help them work through concerns that they may not feel comfortable discussing in the meetings. Staff meet with key stakeholders, group leaders, and among themselves to track the process and consider alternative ways to design the meetings and tasks, or to discuss the best way to deal with a difficult player. Staff provide crucial support to conveners. The Water Forum, the New Jersey process, Cincinnati, and CALFED had ample staff to do these things. It is the ideal for collaborative processes to have dedicated staff if they are to build trust. Though CALFED's staff were technically employed by one or another of the agencies, they were mostly trusted by all the stakeholders, as CALFED was their main job. BAASC and EBCRC had minimal dedicated staff and accordingly were handicapped. Staff can make agreements happen by providing support, encouragement, information, and by putting out fires when there are the inevitable blow ups. Their creative ideas and shuttle diplomacy may well be what gets a process back on track when it goes off the rails. They do not impose solutions, but they can assist stakeholders to discover what will work for them collectively.

A negotiating text and evolving agreement

Collaborative decision making is best understood as a path rather than a destination. A single text negotiating document is an effective way to deal with this, as our three most successful cases demonstrate. In New Jersey it was the preliminary state plan; in Cincinnati it was the goals statement; and in the Water Forum such a document evolved out of a "trial balloon" floated by staff after a couple of years. A negotiating text provides confidence to participants that their ideas are being incorporated and clears away confusion about what has been decided. It is not a draft, nor anyone's proposal, but a tool to focus the issues under discussion. It is a running record of what has been agreed and remains tentative till the final round. It reduces complexity and makes the arguments more tangible and easier to play around with. It leaves open the potential of changing things as negotiations evolve. As a new issue or problem is uncovered, it may shift perceptions and suggest a new configuration for the emerging agreement.

The negotiating text is also a vehicle by which dialogue can continue outside the face to face discussion. Stakeholders can take it to their organizations and constituents, bringing others indirectly into the deliberations. In the course of such discussions stakeholders' own ideas evolve and they reflect in new ways on their work to that point. The document allows wider distribution of emerging ideas, commentary on those ideas, and reshaping of the stakeholders' thinking. The next time the document goes out, someone will discover that a new detail requires other changes. When it comes back again, others will see it differently as well and want other changes. These complex, evolving agreements reflect the reality of interconnections among the issues – that one choice affects others, as, for example, a proposal to encourage multifamily housing needs to link to transportation options. As one of our interviewees said, "consensus building is forever."

All this suggests that we need to regard an "agreement" emerging from a collaborative process as more like a punctuation mark than an end point. This was the

case with the ROD in CALFED, or the goals agreement in Cincinnati. New Jersey anticipated going through a new planning process every three years. The Water Forum reached
an agreement that participants knew would have to evolve so they set up a successor
effort to collaboratively address unanticipated future issues. Each of these examples
reflects the recognition that conditions will change and that implementing an agreement
will require learning how to do it, revisiting what should be done, and coping with
unforeseen challenges.

Adaptiveness

A complex adaptive system is one that involves diverse agents, interaction among them,
seeking of information from the environment, and agents enabled to alter their behavior
as they get feedback from the environment and each other. As discussed in Chapter 2
this kind of system can be productive and innovative (Axelrod and Cohen 2000). New
Jersey, the Water Forum, Cincinnati, and CALFED cases were all highly adaptive, altering
the tasks and designing their process as they went along. No outside player or agency
told them what their product had to look like, how they should go about producing it, nor
who should be involved. This freedom allowed them to add stakeholders along the way,
to take on unanticipated issues, and to rethink their product. Much other experience
indicates that this ability to self-organize is a feature of successful collaborations (Innes,
et al. 1994). The collaboration itself reveals much that was unanticipated about issues,
stakeholders, and opportunities. The great strength of a collaborative process is its ability
to mirror and adjust to the constant change of contemporary conditions.

We can see the importance of the capacity to adapt by looking at BAASC,
which was rigid in its approach, changing few goals or tasks over 6 years, even when
its strategies were not working. It started with a 5-person Steering Committee from
predefined organizations, never reconsidering its membership even when the founding
individuals left and were replaced by others who were less powerful or less committed.
It identified its products at the outset and decided its strategy was to create a coalition
to go to the legislature to lobby for these. When lobbying failed to produce results, it did
not rethink its theory of change. The SC did not gather information that could have shown
it was following an unproductive path. When the *Compact* became a proposal with little
substance, the SC still pushed it forward, even in the face of doubts. BAASC did adapt
the Footprint concept to work with the regional agencies, but they did not adapt the
regional indicators project, and it had little impact. The CCII had a sharp separation of the
community and investment decision makers, and it never adapted this design, though
there was poor communication and little mutual understanding. BAASC was not adaptive
without the full diversity of relevant players; with inadequate interaction among them;
and little flow of information from outside the system. They did not learn how to do things
better as they went along, and they did not consider changes in their purposes that might
have made their project more likely to engage support.

Authentic dialogue: the praxis of process

These conditions are not sufficient for effective collaboration. What is needed in addition is authentic dialogue. Creating such dialogue is an art form, however, which typically requires training for both process managers and participants. There are principles and practices that can guide this effort, but ultimately the dialogue must be created anew in each new situation. It is more than following a handbook. It involves praxis of process managers, facilitators, and participants. That is, an effective dialogue depends on participants learning how to communicate productively in a way that becomes second nature. Such dialogue can occur without special training in small groups of people who know each other well and feel comfortable together, or in groups where members have learned how to do this in other settings. For example though CALFED offered little training or facilitation, many of the players had been talking in group settings for several years on other water projects and had learned skills of productive dialogue. Nonetheless the authenticity of the dialogue and accordingly the value of the outcomes depended on whether the chair was controlling or genuinely facilitative.

Authentic dialogue is not just talk, and it does not emerge naturally in large groups, at least in industrialized countries. The norm is a formalized, almost ritual, "debate" like that in the EBCRC, where interests are concealed rather than shared and where compromise, logrolling, and tradeoffs behind the scenes are the modes of reaching agreement. These methods prevent the discovery of reciprocity and mutual gain opportunities. Dialogue is such a powerful and little understood component of collaboration that we will devote a full chapter to exploring how it works to create new ideas, change participants, and transform world views. In this chapter we will look at the strategies for creating authentic dialogue.

Many of the techniques for achieving authentic dialogue do not come naturally to many of us. Indeed some group leaders may not actually want authentic dialogue, preferring to dominate the discussion rather than allow it to take its course. They want to keep certain voices silent, or at least not offer them legitimacy. Authentic dialogue can be unpredictable, and it requires a chair or facilitator who can both "go with the flow" and keep things focused and moving toward agreements. Needless to say this is tricky, but training and experience improve these skills. Authentic dialogue is always a work in progress. Every project is different, and every day is different. The process manager has to be constantly alert, scanning the group, paying attention to external events and internal dynamics and reassessing how things are going to see whether the tasks need revision or the group needs to reframe its approach. In large, diverse and conflictual groups this may require the use of formal techniques and professional facilitation assistance.

Speech conditions

Authentic dialogue requires that Habermas' ideal speech conditions are met to a substantial degree – that is, that all claims are accurate in a scientific sense, comprehensible, sincere, and legitimate. He is drawing on positivist epistemology for the first concept, interpretive thought for the second, sociological and political theory for the third and fourth. Many commentators have expressed doubt that meeting these conditions is possible, but we can say, based on our research, experience, and observation, that well run processes like the Water Forum come very close to achieving these conditions. Indeed the best practices (Society of Professionals in Dispute Resolution 1997; Center for Collaborative Policy) of professional facilitators in the policy field are a mirror of these conditions.

The claim of accuracy is one that can be tested by expert knowledge, if necessary triangulating among experts or finding trusted science and not allowing the claims of any one stakeholder to prevail without it. With inaccurate, biased, self-serving or inappropriate information, the entire dialogue can be a waste of everyone's time and it will not lead to successful adaptation and problem solving. This question of knowledge is so critical that we devote Chapters 6 and 7 to exploring how it can be a constructive part of the discussions and how to address differences.

The claim of comprehensibility is somewhat easier. The facilitator or chair must try to assure that everyone understands each other's statements. Often this means repeating an unclear point in slightly different words and checking with the speaker if this is correct. Or it may mean querying the speaker until his meaning becomes clear, asking perhaps for examples. It can mean encouraging others to ask such questions. Often people speak without being certain themselves about what they mean, and this sort of interchange can be part of a learning process for them and the group. It is part of a social construction of the many facets of the complex problems they may face as a group. Comprehensibility is often a moving target as ideas and understandings change, and it has to be constantly checked within the group.

Sincerity in many ways takes care of itself over time. It is hard to lie repeatedly to a group of people who are sitting around a table face to face. The face to face aspect of collaborative dialogue is critical, not just so everyone can hear and question each other's statements, but also so everyone has the opportunity to judge each other's sincerity. The ability to judge sincerity in collaborative processes is greatly improved by informal opportunities for participants to chat between formal dialogue sessions, in meal breaks, retreats or field trips. In these periods stakeholders learn something about each other as people, and they learn what they share on a social level, like issues with school or children, favorite activities and so on. This informal interaction builds social capital and makes it more difficult for stakeholders to behave insincerely. This interaction never happened in EBCRC because this organization, like many supported by federal funds, was not permitted to provide food. This lack of food was an additional problem as meetings were held at dinner time and people became cranky and impatient to leave. Small group working meetings, however, tend to produce social capital as these tend to be informal and people get to know each other, as they did on the EBCRC Technical Advisory Committee. When social capital exists, people are more likely to acknowledge their real concerns. Often stakeholders who are opponents on the policy issue speak up for each other in meetings to make sure each other's perspectives are taken into account. People on opposing sides have been known to become fast friends, without changing their minds about the issues. While such social capital can be a key to transparent, interest-based negotiations, the pitfall is that these relationships may interfere with the willingness of players to challenge each other's assumptions.

Legitimacy for a speaker takes a number of forms. One is that a participant speaks for a constituency, as evidenced by being chosen by that constituency. It is strengthened by evidence that he or she has communicated with the organization members and received guidance. This allows the stakeholders to truly engage with one another, discover reciprocal interests and offer a credible promise that agreements can not only be reached, but implemented. These criteria only apply in situations where there are organized constituencies or where interest groups can be organized or public agencies identified with missions of relevant interests. The Water Forum had agency participants, representatives of water utilities and advocacy or lobbying groups so most at the table were skilled at representing an interest. The Forum was particularly assiduous about this, creating many requirements for the stakeholder representatives to report to their organizations and even requiring principals (directors of the organizations) to attend special meetings.

Lobbyists can be excellent stakeholders as they are skilled in representing their interest, they know the constituency, and they know how much leeway they have. They can separate their personal views from their professional responsibilities; they are not reluctant to speak up when it might create discomfort and tension; and they routinely report back to their constituencies. Upper level bureaucrats have similar capacities and some are accustomed to working with others outside the agency. But the requirement that participants represent interests is frequently not met in ostensibly collaborative processes. EBCRC, for example, had no explicit expectation of representation, though people around the table purportedly were there to speak for Native Americans, economic development, environment and so on. What they said could be purely idiosyncratic and individual. Innes, for example, had no idea what the university's interest, if any, was in defense conversion and accordingly offered her own views of what would be good for the region.

Legitimate speech claims also can be made by stakeholders who are giving voice to an interest rather than taking direction from a constituency. Stakeholders can be individuals who can speak for the knowledge, concerns, and interests of a category of people who are not or could not be organized. For example, a respected nonprofit with the mission of promoting environmental justice could represent that interest, even if it does not have an organized membership group, as Urban Habitat did in BAASC. Environmental justice is a broad societal issue and those with direct interest in this are diffuse and do not necessarily share enough to be organized.[5] Alternatively, a legal advocacy organization that defends Mexican-American interests was enlisted in the California Statewide Growth Management Consensus Project to speak for these interests. This sort of representation does not commit anyone to any specific action, but it does inform a larger collaborative dialogue and it can be sufficient for a group whose function is primarily advisory.

Finally, a participant may have legitimacy to provide input grounded in his own praxis. For example, a stakeholder representing agricultural interests might actually be a farmer and thus able to speak legitimately about the particulars of irrigation methods or drought experiences. A realtor might represent real estate interests with firsthand knowledge of the housing market. The personal role of the stakeholder as an individual living, working and moving around in a region may come into play.

Learning new ways to think and talk together

Authentic dialogue requires collaboratively adopted ground rules that will enable a productive dialogue. The rules typically include an injunction against criticism of others; acceptable ways to deal with the press; avoiding repetition; and not dominating the conversation. Dialogue is apt also to require admonitions about listening respectfully. Many people come in with their own ideas and spend meeting time rehearsing to themselves what they want to say, rather than listening, much less keeping an open mind. Changing these habits may require training exercises. It definitely requires keeping a record of what has been said that all can see.

People around the table often censor themselves, not saying what they are thinking because they fear it would offend somebody or they think it is too radical or peculiar. Long years of conflict avoidance and going along with peer pressure make this kind of behavior difficult for individuals to change and difficult for them to recognize. Moreover, some participants assume that since collaboration is about finding common ground, they should not bring up anything controversial. But without sincerity and without the questioning of given knowledge and assumptions, a dialogue cannot be collaboratively rational. It will not break through the socially constructed and often disempowering assumptions that may be the cause of a problem's intractability. Dealing with this reluctance to speak out can be one of the most difficult issues for a process manager. Encouraging brainstorming and publicly recognizing creative ideas can help, along with making sure that the conversation is safe for all participants.

There are nonetheless stakeholders who are confrontive and fight for positions rather than listen. Some are highly emotional and angry. While process managers need to try to get these individuals to speak in terms of interests rather than positions and avoid attacking others, it is equally important that they not gloss over the conflict. Sometimes managers may even have to surface and address hidden conflicts to assure the dialogue does not result in what many critics are concerned about – a lowest common denominator agreement, with peer pressure stifling unpopular voices – like BAASC's *Compact*. Hidden differences can lead to an agreement that is thin and fragile, rather than one that has engaged the deep issues and bound the stakeholders together in reciprocal arrangements.

The goal of a collaboratively rational dialogue is not to choose who or what is right, nor even what is true or best, but to find actions that all or most can support and that are workable, so creativity is often necessary. This requires setting up a special dynamic that typically does not emerge in ordinary conversation (Mutz 2006). Participants do not have to agree on reasons, goals or values. They do need a shared understanding of the issues and interests; they need to have high quality information; and they need to work hard to meet the needs of each interest. If they do so, it can make the results rational. If a problem has been tackled from so many perspectives, with so much information and so many challenges to assumptions and different viewpoints and all in the end agree on something, the result is likely to be robust and feasible.

Achieving diversity

Initiators of a collaborative process are often resistant to the idea of inclusion. It is easier to make a decision if one does not include a difficult stakeholder or an interest that seems antithetical to the goals the organizers have. It may seem unnecessary, moreover, to include disadvantaged interests, as they probably will not be able to stop any agreement from going ahead, particularly if those interests are neither organized nor placing any pressure on the process. Why go out looking for new stakeholders when the problem is already complicated enough?

Contrarian and disadvantaged stakeholders are necessary to help achieve robust agreements that break open the unacceptable status quo that brought people to the table in the first place. These individuals and interests see the world from a different perspective than others and ask the questions or make the challenges more mainstream stakeholders do not. In the BAASC the Social Equity caucus, after internal dialogue, concluded that the smart growth objectives of the other two groups were not significant to their welfare. When they announced this, others responded with indignation. Smart growth had been an unquestioned value for them, and BAASC was built on promoting this idea. BAASC searched for a growth strategy that would benefit the social equity participants, which became the CCII. They developed this innovative way of acting on smart growth ideas as it became clear that promoting infill was not enough. The goal was inner city development that did not gentrify and push the poor out, but development that benefited all three interests, channeling development away from greenfields, helping to revitalize poor neighborhoods and creating new business opportunities.

Legitimacy and feasibility of proposals are also at stake. If a disadvantaged interest is not at the table for a decision it can undermine the potential to get legislative or other support for a proposal. A collaborative policy dialogue, the Growth Management Consensus Project (GMCP) starting in 1990, designed to produce state growth management legislation in California, made extensive efforts to incorporate social equity stakeholders (Innes 1994a). Booher participated in this group of statewide interests in growth, environmental protection and development. The original reasons for seeking out equity stakeholders were strategic. First, some of the group believed that whatever they came up with would be more legitimate in the eyes of the Democratic legislative leaders if it was supported by the disadvantaged groups that they viewed as their constituency. Organizers also had the idea that they could get around some of the environmentalists by playing off their issues against the equity interests. It turned out, however, that the group members learned a good deal from one another and evolved in their thinking. The equity stakeholders, along with the others, learned that they had a stake in growth management, and some went on to be leaders in their regions on this and related issues. Other stakeholders came to see equity issues as central to growth management.

Diversity and inclusion create the potential for reciprocity and the discovery of mutually beneficial activities, as the BAASC case demonstrates. The leadership required the inclusion of a social equity voice originally because the project was built on the notion that sustainability required accommodating environment, equity and economy. Moreover the BAASC theory of change was that if they could produce a political coalition among all three, they could get smart growth legislation passed. Though they did not succeed in that regard, it turned out that all the caucuses benefited from the inclusionary policy. Although the social equity representative could not force environmental or economic stakeholders to act against their interests, and in some ways the equity group was the least empowered of the groups, the requirement for consensus among the interests meant they were listened to and at least some of their interests were attended to. The head of Urban Habitat, an African American leader whose primary interest was environmental justice, said it was empowering to him and the equity caucus simply to be able to sit at the table and be heard by leaders in the business world, environmental world and government. They in turn learned about his perspective for the first time and discovered reciprocity among their interests. The business community got assistance in finding investment opportunities in poor neighborhoods in return for providing some community benefit. Environmentalists realized that they had common cause with the equity stakeholders around the strategy of building infill housing rather than housing in rural greenfields.

As a practical matter it is difficult to recruit or retain disadvantaged and minority stakeholders. They are often not organized into interest groups and even if a nonprofit or advocacy group can be identified, it typically will not have the resources to send people to meetings, much less provide them with the professional assistance and research they may need to hold their own with better funded and more sophisticated interests. They may be unaccustomed to representing their interests in such forums, which can be intimidating for anyone. Volunteer representation from disadvantaged interests is hard to assure as the poor may be working multiple jobs or not have resources for babysitting and transportation. One part of the solution is to raise funds so these people can get to meetings, especially in statewide or regional processes, and to help them with the data and analysis they may need to participate on an equal basis with others. In the U.S. foundations have supported some processes. In processes where some of the players are financially capable, that money can be put into a central pot for supporting facilitation and participation of disadvantaged stakeholders. In CALFED special effort was made to enlist stakeholders in the environmental justice issue. It is also appropriate for sponsoring government agencies to assist these stakeholders.

Choosing and keeping stakeholders

Critics of stakeholder-based collaborative dialogues often assume that initiators or professional staff choose the stakeholders and therefore have power that undermines the legitimacy of the results. However the instigators can in practice only begin with what seem to be obvious leaders and stakeholders. Additional stakeholders may be identified by a conflict assessment that reaches widely into the community or by working with the core group to identify others with interests and the ability to influence. Moreover as a process proceeds and learning takes place, it is common for a group to identify other stakeholders who offer missing perspectives or knowledge. Outsiders may observe the process and seek to join later when they decide their interests are at stake, as did Sierra Foothills interests in the Water Forum. They may see a decision emerging and want to avoid being left out. Typically a group will honor requests because, if such players are kept outside, they might harm the credibility of the process. Stakeholders may be refused inclusion if their basic interest is already met by someone already at the table or if the group is already large. Finally, an emerging solution may create new stakeholders. In short, membership in a collaborative process should not be regarded as fixed from the outset, but should respond to learning and the evolution of tasks and perceptions.

Stakeholders may be reluctant to join, even when a negotiated agreement could be in their interest, and they often operate with one foot out the door, constantly threatening to leave. There can be many reasons for this, including a fear of not being able to hold their own in the discussion, being "rolled" by the opposition because of their inexperience, or being co-opted or peer pressured into an agreement that will not be good for their constituency. They may have a well grounded fear that they will be viewed as collaborating with the enemy just by showing up. This fear has been especially common among environmental groups whose leaders may contend that in collaboration the environment always loses.

Stakeholders come to the table for many reasons. They do not come out of altruism, solidarity, or community values, as some commentators assume. Critics right- fully point out that such motives cannot be the basis for a robust agreement. Stakeholders come because there is potential benefit for their constituency, though this is not enough to keep them there. Stakeholders are people with personal and professional lives. They may not show up for dull meetings where little gets accomplished. While most originally come for instrumental reasons related to achieving interests, according to our research, they often stay at the table through long and difficult meetings, for personal reasons. The meetings help them learn about the problems and issues and build their professional capacity. They build relationships with others around the table that also help them professionally (Innes, et al. 1994). For example in the collaborative San Francisco Estuary Project, a Corps of Engineers stakeholder told us he routinely began calling the Sierra Club representative when the Corps was proposing a dredging project to find out the environmentalists' perspective on it and modify it if necessary (Innes and Connick 1999). Sometimes these professional relationships also become personal ones, with stake- holders going to each other's weddings, christenings, and birthday parties though they continue to push for their interests around the table. As stakeholders move forward they may develop a sense of solidarity, a joint commitment to collective action, loyalty to fellow participants, or a belief in some shared values. They may come to develop a sense that they are doing something worthwhile. Much depends on how the process is managed.

Stakeholders can lose their original commitment if the incentive structure changes. For example, in CALFED, as the state and federal administrations changed and as the high level encouragement and commitment largely disappeared, it began to appear to some participants that there was less advantage to participating and little sanction against going it alone. After the first six years the money started to run out, so the advantages of participating grew even fewer. The drought had ended, and programs like the EWA had lessened the crisis and conflict. Once the Policy Group ceased to meet, much of the solidarity of participants melted away.

Agonism

The importance of agonism (Hillier 2003), the continuing tension among points of view in a collaborative process, can hardly be emphasized enough. Such tension can make a process challenging to manage, but it is an essential source of the creativity that allows forward movement in the face of stalemate (Forester 2006). Conflict and tension among participants is essential to the practice of collaborative dialogue and at the core of collaborative rationality. Agonism enables the dialectical process, which in turn allows us to get past the taken for granted understandings that conceal power relations and support the status quo. It is a way of getting at the "many sidedness" of the world, of uncovering its contradictions and working through how to move forward. The contradictions and differences are a permanent component of our complex, constantly changing world, and they need to be surfaced if a group is to come up with feasible strategies.

The most creative moments typically emerge in a dialogue after an impasse is reached. It is as if the participants, in their frustration, reach deep into themselves and get past norms, platitudes, and unexamined assumptions to find an idea they did not know was there or never considered before. The group then builds on it to construct a new approach. We have seen this happen often. In all the successful cases conflict erupted at times. The underlying tensions were such that the Water Forum facilitator used to tell stakeholders to leave their guns at the door. They carried on their conflicts in a more civil setting, but without letting go of their interests. Participants felt passionately about their issues. Success did not require eliminating conflict, but channeling it into constructive conversation. While it is tempting to pressure those who disagree to back off, to do so would be self-defeating. Instead there needs to be creative generation and exploration of ideas that could make a package not only more palatable to dissidents, but also more feasible and robust for the longer run.

When participants recognize a stalemate has been reached, this can be the moment when a change of direction becomes possible. Susskind, for example, tells of a collaborative process designed to resolve a dispute over the location of a transit station in a wetland area near Boston. Environmental advocates were at loggerheads with the transportation agency and both were in disagreement with neighborhood groups. It seemed as if there was no solution. The transportation agency had the power to do what it wanted, though transportation planners had hoped for a consensus. An environmental leader in the group went off with some colleagues for their own discussion, out of which emerged a proposal that had not been on the table – a proposal that the transit agency would restore and improve the wetlands while building its station (Susskind 1981). While this type of mitigation approach is common today, it was innovative at the time and it allowed all the interests to get much of what they wanted. They created a new component in the mix so it was no longer simply a zero sum game with winners and losers. That station has been built and the wetland restoration completed.

We have seen many other examples of this dynamic where an impasse opens a new way of seeing. For example, the Water Forum was stalemated around the problem of funding habitat restoration, with some stakeholders insisting they were already paying for this via the federal water supply system, which charged them fees, and others saying the Forum needed the funds to implement its proposals. This frustration stymied the process for a while. Finally at one meeting a stakeholder announced that they should not pay this federal fee at all – that they could be like the Boston Tea Party and refuse taxation without representation. While this idea of civil disobedience was not followed up in the end, it broke open people's assumptions and challenged the status quo. This challenge in turn led to an outpouring of creative ideas in the meeting as the facilitator wrote across the board "BREAKTHROUGH."

Similarly in CALFED at the end of the Clinton Administration, the Secretary of the Interior came from Washington to help facilitate an agreement before an entirely new set of administrators was appointed who might dismiss emerging agreements. At the eleventh hour when stalemate continued on key issues, Secretary Babbit suddenly designated two of the most vocal antagonists, an environmental leader and a director of a major water agency, and told them they had an hour to sort out their differences. They came back with an agreement that the rest of the group ratified. This became the basis for the ROD, CALFED's plan.

Agonism and its frequent companion, stalemate, can be, if processes are well managed and there is social capital and a shared interest in reaching a conclusion, the stimulus that changes the dynamic. Being stuck is not only frustrating, it may give stakeholders permission to let go of assumptions, revisit their own attitudes and objectives, and search for new strategies. It provides the opportunity for double loop learning, where the group members reexamine, not just the particular solution ideas, but also their values and goals. They may reframe the task, redefine the goals, and be able to move forward in a productive way.

Process design

To achieve collaborative rationality, face to face dialogue is essential. Serial dialogue or shuttle diplomacy may be better than no multiway dialogue for achieving acceptable agreement, but collaborative rationality requires that all participants must hear all other major points of view. If not, agreement will be flawed and certainly not well informed. This dialogue allows the discovery of reciprocity and multiway agreements that can serve all or most participants and potentially provide broad community benefits. It is necessary particularly to achieve the speech condition of sincerity. The challenge is that there may be many more stakeholders or participants than could possibly be included in a single dialogue. In this kind of situation an approximation to fully face to face dialogue can be achieved with different forms of smaller, but also diverse, groups linked together in various ways and reporting to one another or to a central collaborative committee. We saw this in all our cases.

Collaborative dialogues can be structured in a variety of ways (Straus 2002). In the spirit of self-organization their forms need to develop out of the specifics of the issue and context. They need to evolve like a complex adaptive system, as conditions and knowledge change and as partial agreements are reached or new tasks and information needs emerge. There is no one-size-fits-all approach. Process design is an art form that has to be undertaken continuously. There is seldom an obvious boundary around a planning or policy problem, nor around the appropriate participants. Process design may involve a series of experiments. Professionals may propose the design, but it has to be developed and revised with group members. Stakeholders tend to be impatient with process discussion, however. Typically they want to get on with the substance rather than discuss ground rules, organizational design or procedures. They groan and complain. But this is not a reason to skip these important steps. If the process is later perceived to be flawed or illegitimate, it can undermine both the feasibility and legitimacy of the outcomes.

For most stakeholder-based dialogues a diverse central committee is needed to agree on and legitimize a proposal. This committee, often made up of leaders in their fields, usually is too large and busy to work through complex or technical issues in detail. They set direction and make difficult decisions. Task forces and working groups in the Water Forum and CALFED were delegated to work on tasks like managing water operations or designing a set of conservation best practices, and to report back to the oversight group with their proposals. To maintain authentic dialogue and be credible with the central group, these small groups had to be diverse in their interests and knowledge. Indeed CALFED required that they be certified as meeting the standards of the Federal Advisory Committee Act (FACA), which, among other things, requires such diversity of representation. In the Water Forum participants met both in interest-based caucus groups to decide on what positions they would take in upcoming dialogue, and in diverse task groups including members from all the caucuses to work out a consensus based strategy.

Small groups provide an opportunity to reach further out into the community to include more stakeholders and people with other forms of knowledge, as they did in

CALFED. The members may serve simultaneously on other groups as well, building networks among themselves and developing shared heuristics. The Technical Advisory Committee in EBCRC became such a group, including people not in the main stakeholder group, who were valuable to developing a knowledge base. These included developers and brownfield experts, for example, and engineers who could talk about the practical and technical problems and opportunities in base cleanup.

In New Jersey, commissioners, rather than delegating to caucuses or working groups, used a radiating circles design, spreading across the state from the County down to the municipal scale, with staff and representatives of the state agencies participating. They also used working groups to bring in people with special knowledge. In this way they achieved widespread participation that was of a higher quality, better informed and had more give and take than traditional methods like public hearings.

BAASC had working groups in the early years, but the SC worked through the major issues by themselves, bringing them to the members only for feedback in formal bimonthly membership meetings. BAASC used a caucus model as the main way dialogue took place among the members. The idea was that each caucus would develop a position on the issues which the head of the caucus would take to the SC. There were several downsides to this strategy. First, it encouraged position taking, which then could not be negotiated in terms of interests. It contributed to the lowest common denominator results and made it unlikely that anything innovative or risky would be proposed. It made taking advantage of reciprocal interests difficult because the caucus members mainly talked among themselves about the issues they valued, not about the issues that others valued. These downsides became clear when, after five years of discussion, environment and economy caucus members discovered in a retreat that equity members put a low priority on smart growth and preferred to address issues of jobs and affordable housing. The Water Forum also used a caucus model, but paralleled this with diverse task groups. This approach allowed caucus members to develop their shared interests and to discuss emerging proposals among themselves, while they were also in regular dialogue on tasks with members of other caucuses. This method allowed for the development of shared understanding and avoided the polarization in BAASC.

Small groups are where the most productive dialogue can take place, particularly in the absence of professional facilitation. Caucuses have a role, but used alone can interfere with achieving constructive, mutually beneficial outcomes and contribute to stereotyping among stakeholders. Task groups can be the most effective venue for working through the technical and detailed aspects of issues, but they need to be diverse and credible from the view of the governing committee and other observers because these may be the venues where, de facto, many decisions are made, as were the task forces on water operations and the EWA in CALFED.

Beyond the structure of interlinked or overlapping dialogue groups a second crucial element of process design is the partitioning of a large objective, such as devising a state plan, or developing a strategy to protect a river, into smaller do-able tasks. Stakeholders need a concrete sense of making progress if they are to stay at the table. This task partitioning is often where experienced facilitators and staff can make their most valuable contribution. Process managers need to send people home from meetings with evidence of specific movement toward an objective that can be named and recorded. This can include conflicts reduced or options created, consolidated or prioritized as well as agreements reached.

While participants need to have goals and visions to inspire them and make them feel that their participation is worthwhile, they still need to work through incremental steps. In New Jersey the first task was to compare the state plan to the local ones. In the Water Forum the first task was to come up with a shared mission. Later tasks were more specific, like "propose a set of best practices for water conservation." As the processes proceeded someone had to devise more tasks as issues emerged and progress was made. A facilitator or process manager often has to be a bit of a cheerleader, reminding participants of what they have accomplished and, at the end of each meeting, agreeing on the next task and objectives for the next meeting. This is one of the ways that a successful collaborative process evolves and remains dynamic.

Collaborative dialogues and power

The question of power is a leitmotif throughout both the practice of collaboration and the literature, particularly in critiques.[6] Do collaborative dialogues have too much power, given that participants are not democratically elected? Or are they pretty much a waste of time because they have so little power? They typically have no authority to make or implement decisions, but have to turn to public agencies or other formal authorities, which may or may not support their recommendations. Do the organizers have undue power because their choice of topics and of participants can shape the outcomes? How can dialogue of any kind make a difference in the face of raw interests? Those with power will do as they wish regardless of the dialogue. How can Habermas' idea of equalizing power in a discussion make any sense in a world where power differentials among players are patently significant? The power of economic structure is so fundamental, according to some neo-Marxist critics, that it is naive for theorists to contend that collaboration can produce any real change.

In practice, stakeholders worry that if they participate they will have to give up power to the group and succumb to peer pressure. They worry that participation will reduce the options available to them. Elected officials and professional staff worry that their own power will be undermined if a diverse group agrees on something. Such tacit concerns about turf and authority interfere with productive action. In one case that Booher was involved with, for example, an entire plan was created for a collaborative dialogue around a major state issue and agreed on by key participants, but legislative staff killed the proposal because they felt it was their prerogative to prepare legislation. In another case, where he facilitated a dialogue in Davis, California, the opposing stakeholders agreed on policy addressing controversies around growth and the city budget. The city council, which had commissioned the group, at first dismissed the result until Booher included them in the dialogue. Sometimes in our experience, professionals set up purportedly collaborative processes but maintain control of the agenda, information, options and decisions. This tends to backfire as publics see through it.

One problem is the elusiveness of the concept of power and the fact that it holds different meanings for different people in different contexts. The simple view is that power is a force or leverage that one player holds over another. Power is better understood, however, as a relationship which can shift with the context as well as with the participants. It is inter-subjective and socially constructed. The idea of power exists because people are part of a community where they interact and interpret what is going on. Power is a social construction, not a brute fact. It is not something anyone possesses autonomously or something that can be transferred intact to any other context or relationship. It is contingent. Power is not a zero sum game in which the more power one player has, the less others have. On the contrary, a collaborative dialogue can generate what we have called network power (Booher and Innes 2002). As the participants get to know and understand other stakeholders and issues, they become more powerful themselves. As they develop common heuristics and shared purposes, each is empowered by the others. Power flows through the network, and each participant's gain in power is not necessarily a loss to others, but also a gain.

Bryson and Crosby (1993) offer a helpful perspective on power, arguing it has multiple dimensions. On one axis is the power of deep structure – the power of the economic and political dimensions of society, such as capitalism and market structure or perhaps a religious institutional structure. This tacit power exists in the background. No one holds it, and it does not take human form, though it constrains what actions can be taken in practice. This structure comes with norms that can be in themselves powerful, if not sacred. If one pushes too far, as for example in trying to promote government funded health care in the U.S., one comes up against deep seated norms that contend government is inefficient and the private sector can do it better. Or when the Bush Administration sought an economic stimulus package, as it did in early 2008, the assumption was it had to work through the market, so tax rebates should be given to everyone to encourage them to shop and prop up the retail sector. It took a disastrous economic collapse for the deep structure conditions to change enough for a government investment program like that during the Great Depression to be on the table in 2009.

A second sort of power is that of individuals to make decisions at the margin, the kind of power that legislators, public officials, and corporate leaders hold. It also includes the decisions of members of the public to vote one or another way, to purchase something, buy a house, take a trip, or sign an agreement. These choices are framed within the limits of deep structure so many options never make it to these individuals.

Mediating between these two sorts of power, one tacit and in the background and the other explicit and in the foreground, is the power to produce ideas, rules, modes of doing things, methods of inquiry and discussion. This is the sort of power that professionals, bureaucrats, and scholars hold. It is not the power to make a particular thing happen, but the power to direct attention and even action in one way versus another (Forester 1989) or the power to determine who participates, according to what agendas, and under what rules. This sort of power comes into play in collaborative processes, but it is shared among the participants. A collaborative process operates primarily in the intermediating role, though sometimes it can be a decision making process.

Bryson and Crosby argue that there are three types of venues where power comes into play. First, there are forums where meanings of events, problems, and potential actions can be developed. Collaborative dialogues are perhaps best adapted to the forum role. These meanings then have their own power in the next phase, which is the confrontation of various players in an arena where negotiations take place and decisions get made. A collaborative process can also be an arena, where issues get fought out and allocations of resources and attention are decided, as they were in the Water Forum. The third venue is a court, where the legitimacy of a decision is determined or where residual issues are decided. These are functions needed in formal government as well as collaboration. In local planning in the U.S. a planning commission might act as a forum to deliberate goals for the plan; the city council might act as an arena, deciding whether a plan proposed by the commission should be passed. Sometimes the decisions are challenged in court, or assessed in the court of public opinion or even come before the city council or an administrative hearing board. In the case of the Water Forum, leaders brought the emerging agreement to the larger community for legitimation before it was implemented. In New Jersey the process itself offered all three venues, with the court that set it up looming behind the process.

Collaborative dialogues, while not being deterministic or authoritative, do have the capacity to establish agendas for decision makers, norms, priorities and new shared meanings and even language for discussion of issues (Kingdon 2003). They can only do this within certain parameters however, as only some ideas can be heard at a point in time. Dialogues put ideas forward that decision makers may respond to and they influence the powerful participants who may see and act on issues differently. Business and environmental leaders in BAASC, for example, came to understand more about the needs of the equity interests and discovered reciprocal interests on which they could work together. In the Water Forum, group solidarity forced the most powerful federal agency, the U.S. Bureau of Reclamation, to change its flawed forecast. In Cincinnati, networks were created linking the police and local business and community leaders. New shared objectives altered the perspectives and options of all.

A critique of collaborative dialogue from neo-Marxists is that it is naive because the structural reality of society is such that it cannot make much difference (Fainstein 2000). They are quite right that the immediate power of collaborative dialogue is at the margin. Dialogues cannot directly change the deep structure of power. They cannot directly change the power of key stakeholders, nor get them to do things against what they perceive as their interest. They cannot come up with too radical a proposal if it is to be taken seriously.

However we contend that the changes that emerge from collaborative processes in the agents and in the actions can have second and third order effects which do affect structure. While the structure of a society constrains agents, what agents say and do alters structure (Giddens 1984). It changes norms and practices as well as organizations and expectations. Admittedly structure changes slowly, but effective collaborative dialogues tend to speed the process. The Water Forum, CALFED, and other collaborative dialogues have slowly but surely altered the way that decisions are made in California water management. In 2009, when the Delta's future is under discussion, there is no longer any question that it needs to be governed in an adaptive, inclusionary way and that it cannot be managed by a top down bureaucracy. The powerful interests – most notably agriculture and urban water – no longer control the water scene, as environmental groups and local communities are also players. The court decisions about water flows have been important, but they were the triggers for change and do not account for the ways that new players and new values have influence today. The legitimation of collaborative decision making in this arena has opened up "power" to many other interests as other research vividly demonstrates (Healey 2006).

Collaborative rationality requires an equalization of power inter-subjectively created around the table. Skilled facilitators make sure that everyone is heard respectfully, that all have the same information, and that all have the capacity and the support to speak freely. Process managers have to address external power differentials to keep the power around the table as equal as possible. For instance threat making is not normally permitted, and a skilled facilitator will call this to the attention of the group if it happens. If someone tries to assert facts that are questionable or to which others are not privy, the facilitator may ask the group if it wants to inquire into the data. If the facilitator or group leader notes that a particular stakeholder is not communicating effectively in the group, either being extremely difficult or very quiet, she might speak to his principals, so they can make a change if they wish. Facilitation is about managing interactions so that all the interests and knowledge are given adequate recognition, and free inquiry is not stifled. The equalization of power means everyone has the right to a point of view, no one is to dominate and all are engaged and interacting. In this situation understandings and even values can be changed through a joint learning process, as they were to some degree in all our successful examples.

Participants are well aware of stakeholders' potential power, but this power is not exerted within a collaborative dialogue. Habermas contends that in such a situation the power of the better argument wins (Habermas 1981), but in our observation the sort of debate that he envisioned is not what happens. Collaborative dialogue is a much more freewheeling, storytelling process, as participants speak of their views and experience, and the group tries to find a common story line that builds on these. The power in the dialogue is that of the silver tongued or those with the most powerful stories, rather than the most logical master of debate or the most economically powerful. Sometimes the most effective person in the dialogue can be one representing the most disadvantaged group. On the other hand, many of the more powerful stakeholders have highly skilled professional representatives who can be eloquent spokespersons.

The reader may object however that, even if one can equalize power in this limited way around a table, one cannot equalize it outside. This is of course true but beside the point. Powerful stakeholders come to the table because there is something they want from the other players. For stakeholders to recognize power outside the table is critical to realistic agreements at the table, and this reality of context must figure in the discussions. Disparities in resources, authority, or power outside the process may actually be central to the dialogue. For example, in one collaborative process that Booher co-chaired, it was common to hear people comment that the California Teachers Association (CTA) "will never go along" with one or another idea. Everyone knew that without this politically powerful statewide player their project could not go forward, so the group made a particular effort to craft a proposal the CTA could accept without compromising others' interests. The CTA, however, could not dictate the solution.

Seemingly powerful stakeholders join such efforts because their BATNAs do not allow them to get what they want without participating. This situation gives other participants a kind of balancing power in the reciprocity they may be able to offer. The powerful may be persuaded to make some changes in their positions or actions if at the table they can discover it would be in their interest. They may, working with others, discover options that are only open if they can create an interlocking package of proposals, in accord with the theory of interest based bargaining.

As for whether the policy/planning professionals who are involved in these processes lose or gain power, the answer is both yes and no. They may lose the power (such as it is) to advise decision makers quietly or to design plans or policies with minimal public input. Some leaders of advocacy groups may lose the power to protest if they join a collaborative group as a stakeholder. But both of these forms of power are unreliable. There is no guarantee advice will be taken, plans will be implemented, or protests will change the decision dynamic. Professionals have different sorts of power when they are involved in collaborative processes. It is shared power, but it may well have more impact. If they play a part in setting up a process, choosing core stakeholders, and designing tasks, they can be influential. It is harder for them to bias a process with their personal views, but they can use their professional knowledge to help shape the collective views. Such a shared view can potentially create a more robust result than one produced by an individual. Professionals also can represent particular interests that they may believe in and because of their professional skills, assure that those interests are more powerfully represented than otherwise.

Professionals have many roles to play in collaborative processes – as insti-gators and process managers, staff, expert consultants, facilitators, and stakeholder representatives. Collaborative processes enlarge the scope of what professionals can do and allow them to be more creative and engage in new ways with issues, interests, and communities. There is no simple answer to whether they have more or less power in these roles than in the more conventional ones.

Contradictions and paradoxes

Along with the Frankfurt School theorists, we believe that contradictions are the norm in the social and political world. This world is in constant motion, and everything we admire has a dark side, which may emerge at any time. The yin and yang of collaboration cannot be avoided so it must be embraced. Agonism can be creative, spurring us to address dilemmas and problems, and keeping us from complacency. Contradictions mirror complex dynamics of the world for which we hope to make policy. There will be no moment when we can rest on our laurels and no definitive answers.

The idea of collaboration itself is a paradox. During World War II collaborators were reviled for working with the enemy, and it is arguable that the Germans could not have occupied most of Europe for as long as they did without them. On the other hand collaborators saved lives and helped maintain the integrity of the occupied nation states. Today this duality continues. Collaboration can create societal value, improve social and political relationships, generate more robust and meaningful knowledge and move communities and leaders to constructive, consensual public action. By the same token it can co-opt players and provide less benefit for some participants than they would have going it alone. Participants can, for a variety of reasons, go along with actions that are not in their own, or even a broader public's interest. The fact that the policies were made through collaboration can make them durable, but it cuts both ways as such policies can be difficult to change. Collaborative rationality, however, does provide some protection against injustices, practical mistakes, and uninformed choices.

Today collaboration is more often viewed as a virtuous activity, helping to make things happen in a diverse and conflictual world. At the time of this writing there are calls for post partisan politics in the U.S. The public is tired of political paralysis, but they can become equally disgusted with leaders they regard as selling out. Environmentalists have been particularly frustrated, as they wend their way between protesting and collaborating. Just as the critical theorists contend, everything implies its opposite. There are always multiple sides and multiple ways of seeing the same thing. It is our view that one cannot and should not try to reduce these perspectives into a single view. We have to find ways to build on the tensions, as it is out of these that constructive approaches to societal problems can be identified and innovations can emerge.

Stakeholders live in two worlds. Participation is voluntary so they constantly scan the environment for better options or even actively develop other options. They may "check their guns at the door" and operate in a civil fashion at the table, even if not always outside it. Environmental groups, for example, bring lawsuits while simultaneously discussing options collaboratively. This "one foot out the door" stance is both disruptive to a collaborative process and a source of creativity. Those who want to keep the stakeholders at the table are forced to find new strategies. The very notion that there are at all times at least two possible arenas where action can be taken, at the table and away from it, lends urgency to the search for a mutual gain approach. This duality helps participants improve and clarify their BATNAs and simultaneously raises the standards for an acceptable solution.

There is a fuzzy line between collaboration and cooptation. Both these concepts are socially constructed among the stakeholders and their constituencies. In fact the line itself may be unstable. In the U.S. the dominant norm is an individualist competitive ethic, which implies that collaboration is unacceptable, but stakeholders learn how to stand up for their own interests without denying others the same opportunity.

Competition and collaboration are closely joined in practice as, for example, California's Silicon Valley demonstrated when competitive firms collaborated with one another to make this area the world's most innovative and healthy high technology region in the 1980s and 1990s (Saxenian 1994).

While many collaborative processes produce agreements, these are not permanent. They may need to evolve if they are to remain agreements when new challenges arise and new information appears. Both the Water Forum and CALFED participants understood this. The Water Forum had a successor effort to assure continuous adaptation of the agreement and the implementation effort. The ROD in CALFED was more a set of arrows pointing in the direction of wished for outcomes and a set of heuristics for getting there, than it was a blueprint or plan in a conventional sense. Planning and policy making is a journey (Thompson 1997) as we keep dealing with what we meet along the way.

Collaboration involves two often contradictory ideas of meeting one's self-interest *and* attaining the common good. It is the ultimate in addressing the contradiction of the Hobbesian every-man-for-himself world (Hobbes 2009) and the communitarian nature of the social world. As Ostrom tells us, self-interest can come to be seen through the lens of collective interest as a group works together to protect a limited common resource (Ostrom 1990). Though she is a believer in individual rational choice based on calculations, her research shows how norms develop that change that calculation. The norms are about the community, but the actors and the structure of management of the resource addresses the self-interest of each of the individuals.

We have indicated that collaborative planning has to proceed independent of trust. To do so an agreement typically has to include assurances. These are reciprocal agreements among different parties that are tied together so that one party has to do something the other wants to be able to get what the first party needs. Proposals come in packages, and groups do not agree to one part by itself but to the combination. So the design of agreements can proceed without personal trust. On the other hand collaboration often ends up building trust nonetheless, though assurances are also necessary. Trust is intersubjectively created, but self-interest is always at play. It is important to recognize collaboration is not about making tradeoffs and logrolling, which do not build trust, though they may depend on it. It is about creating agreements that are self-enforcing and do not require trust. Ironically however trust is typically an outcome.

While collaboration in our view must be about challenging the status quo, commentators often note that collaboration may simultaneously protect and enable the status quo. It can reduce disruptive tensions and find actions that make the status quo more tolerable. It can put a halt to radical social movements by doing part of what they seek and incorporating, or even co-opting their leadership. On the other hand participants may challenge the status quo and accepted norms may be altered through the dialogue. There is no moment when we can hold this dynamic constant and make a judgment about its effect on the status quo. Collaboration is likely to play a part in changing this, but at the same time it creates a new status quo. It forces us into the paradox of a status quo in motion.

This dynamic is nowhere more evident than when a process starts to succeed and achieve some of the goals of its participants. While this success may have been due to the collaborative work of its agencies and stakeholders, it can in turn undermine the continuation of the process, as it did in CALFED when the problems began to be solved and seemed less urgent. At that point key stakeholders began to drift away and operate independently. But on the other hand success can be what keeps people at the table, as it did in the Water Forum. In a parallel way a process can make tremendous efforts to be inclusionary and bring in the powerless. As the process continues and preliminary decisions are made and actions taken, however, it can create new stakeholders who were not originally included. A collaborative process cannot simply stay on a course, but has to be constantly in motion rethinking its tasks, membership and its incentive structure. There is no resting on laurels. There is no resting.

Building consensus is a profound example of the dialectical process. There is always tension between agonism and the desire to all hold hands and get along. There is both internal and external pressure to agree, while there is equally pressure not to give up one's own view. There is typically a shared desire to reach agreement, but at the same time a need to reach out to naysayers. It is about being in a space where all these tensions coexist and maintaining constant awareness of them. It means resisting the impulse to ignore or collapse differences. It means finding ways to learn from them and move to higher levels of performance because of them. It also necessitates a constant search for double loop learning, rethinking and reframing one's understanding rather than simply improving one's strategy at the margin. Complexity theory tells us of the dilemmas of fitness landscapes, using the image of hills and valleys. We have a tendency to get comfortable at the top of a hill, though there may be a higher hill beyond. To get there, however, we have to risk descending into the valley first. The challenge of determining whether to be satisfied and make a decision or to continue the search is one that dogs collaborative processes. Such processes need to be both able to decide and to keep options open.

When collaborative dialogues are appropriate

Our major caveat is that collaborative policy dialogues like those we describe in the previous chapter are not a panacea, nor even appropriate for the vast majority of public decisions. There is no point in attempting something complex and potentially costly if the issues are well understood and there is considerable consensus around the solutions. An ordinary legislative/bureaucratic approach is fine under such conditions. Nor is there much point if the cost of doing the dialogue is more than the cost of making a mistaken decision. For busy stakeholders or citizens to come to the table often over periods of months or years, the issue must be of significant and long term social, economic or political importance. If it is impossible to get all the key stakeholders to the table, then collaborative dialogue is not appropriate. At that point one can either go to more standard decision making procedures or come up with a way to change the stakeholders' incentive structure through new legislation or court decisions. But we note that most of the questions for which planning and policy professionals are called in are wicked problems, where there are no simple solutions, no known answers, and no consensus among leaders or the public (Rittel and Webber 1973).

For collaborative decision making to be worthwhile, given the time and energy it requires, the problem should be a complex one, with multiple elements. If it is merely a question of allocating a fixed amount of a resource or funding, then it involves only distributive rather than integrative bargaining. If it is a zero sum game it requires only negotiation rather than wide ranging, exploratory collaborative dialogue. If there are multiple issues that can be looked at as an interrelated set, however, and multiple stakeholders whose interest in each of these issues differs, there is the potential for the reciprocity that we discuss in our DIAD theory. That is, if it is possible to enlarge the pie by mixing and matching various elements creating a new package, collaboration can give more total benefit to the parties than they would have had without the opportunity for multiway dialogue. This is beneficial to society and is a principal justification for collaborative dialogue. While many decision situations do not offer this opportunity in contemporary public policy and planning, the number of complex, controversial and important issues in which many have a stake is increasing steadily in our globalized and rapidly changing world. We believe that collaborative policy dialogues are both called for and practicable in many situations where they are not now being used and where often self-defeating efforts are underway, relying on decision making as usual.

Conclusion

There is no recipe for successful collaborative planning, but there is ample experience and knowledge on which practitioners can draw, not only in this book, but in many others. Each situation requires a unique and nuanced approach adapted to the context, players, and problem. While one can start from known best practices and follow some broad steps, the particulars of each situation are critical and normally will require deviations from guidelines. Inevitably, engaging in collaboration is, and should be, a "learn by doing" process – a process of experimenting, testing, and adapting. It requires working with power but not being dominated by assumptions about power, which shifts and flows in and around these processes. It requires accepting contradictions rather than glossing over them. It requires praxis to deal with its ambiguities, nuances and unexpected turns. It is unfamiliar to many players and threatening to those in power. Collaborative planning will remain challenging until and unless our norms of decision making evolve further.

Notes

1   Useful books looking in some depth at the praxis of collaboration include: O'Leary and Bingham 2003; Wondolleck and Yaffee 2000.
2   These include *The Consensus Building Handbook* (Susskind, et al. 1999); *Managing*

Public Disputes (Carpenter and Kennedy 1991); Kitchen Table Sustainability (Sarkissian, et al. 2009); The Collaborative Leadership Fieldbook (Chrislip 2002); Creating a Culture of Collaboration (Schuman 2006); The Handbook of Dispute Resolution (Moffitt and Bordone 2005); and The Deliberative Democracy Handbook (Gastil and Levine 2005).

3   For an overview of how to conduct a conflict assessment, see Chapter 2 in the Consensus Building Handbook (Susskind and Thomas-Larmer 1999).

4   Innes and Booher were involved in advising this process and Corburn has addressed it (Corburn 2009).

5   Mancur Olson explains this phenomenon (Olson 1965).

6   A sampling of the literature: Amy 1987; Bryson and Crosby 1992; de Sousa Briggs 1998; Fung and Wright 2001; Hillier 2002; Hoch 1992.

Dialogue as a community of inquiry

5

Communities of inquiry

Solving mysteries

Mystery buffs can understand dialogue as a community of inquiry. Sherlock Holmes has Watson with whom to discuss cases; Hercule Poirot has Hastings; and Nero Wolfe has Archie. Police detectives, in real life as on television, work in pairs talking through their ideas about the significance and implications of the evidence. When they get stuck they talk to their bosses, who push them to get creative and solve the case. When they go into high gear something happens as they are more willing to let their imagination work. The learning and discovery process has false starts and wrong assumptions, but a seeming dead end can lead to a new way of seeing the situation. In one Sherlock Holmes story for example when there seems to be no one who could have been the murderer, suddenly Holmes, using tiny clues that have been around from the beginning, develops a new way of making sense of the evidence which allows him to see how the victim staged her own murder to frame her enemy. He has a sudden aha experience, but only after listening and reacting to the less brilliant theories of Watson and the even less brilliant theories of the local constabulary (Doyle 1922).

Dialogue requires that four functions be fulfilled (Isaacs 1999b). There has first to be a mover – someone who sets direction. In mystery novels that is the brilliant detective. There has also to be a bystander to provide perspective, an opposer to find the flaws and force more rigorous thinking, and a follower to help complete the process – someone to say "yes, that is it." In the mysteries the detective's sidekick may perform all of these functions at different times, as do the local police who ultimately take the culprit off to justice. In a way these stories are like ballets, where all the players work simultaneously together and at odds, but in the context of a large conversation out of which truth eventually emerges. The long term popularity of these classic mysteries in great part reflects their use of this community of inquiry method, which draws readers into the exercise. There is something fundamental about this way of learning and discovering which taps into human experience and which is engaging and enjoyable.

Dialogue as a community of inquiry

The idea of a community of inquiry draws on the work of American pragmatists, Charles Sanders Peirce and John Dewey (discussed in Chapter 2), who explicitly used the concept, as well as on Habermas' notion of communicative rationality. Peirce posed the ideal of a self-critical community of inquirers, and Dewey recognized how this had consequences for education, social reconstruction and a revitalization of democracy (Bernstein 1971). Peirce defined inquiry as a struggle to move from the uneasy and dissatisfied state of doubt to the calm and satisfactory state of belief. This doubt is essential to drive a community of inquiry as well as to provide for openness to other views. Pragmatists argued that inquiry must be based on science and on an empirical and experimenting approach to the world. This is not the same as the test tube model of experiments conducted by the neutral observer that is part of our mythology about how to uncover truth. Instead learning from experience plays a fundamental role in developing knowledge. Unlike the positivists, who depend on abstract analytic categories and logical deductive arguments, in a community of inquiry participants bring their experience, their theories, and their praxis. They seek out facts, place them in context, try out actions, and jointly assess the results. This dialogue is continuous and oriented to solving problems (Shields 2003).

Dialogue is at the core of collaborative rationality. It is within dialogue where ideas and choices emerge and where confusing and conflicting views and knowledge can be transformed into something that is both rational and meaningful. Dialogue is neither debate nor argument. In its simplest definitions it is conversation, an exchange of ideas, or a discussion between representatives of parties to conflict that is aimed at resolution (Merriam Webster 2003)

One scholar says it is the "art of thinking together in a relationship" (Isaacs 1999a). Another (Yankelovich 1999) refers to it as "seeking mutual understanding" and argues it has the power to transform participants. Martin Buber (1958) contends that participants in a genuine dialogue (as opposed to merely a conversation) have a real openness to one another. Rather than tuning out each others' views and marshaling arguments to counteract what each other says, participants internalize the views of others to enhance their mutual understanding. In dialogue, participants penetrate each other's polite superficialities and defenses and, in responding to one another in an authentic and empathic way, forge relationships. They reach beyond themselves in a way that Buber contends reflects deep human needs.

The late physicist David Bohm, who has influenced many scholars and practitioners with his reflections on dialogue, contends it is a

> stream of meaning flowing among and through us and between us . . . out of which may emerge some new understanding. It's something new which may not have been in the starting point at all. It's something creative. And this shared meaning is the "glue" or "cement" that holds people and societies together.
>
> (Bohm 1996: 6)

It is ironic but telling that a great scientist would be a passionate advocate for a mode of inquiry that differs so significantly from the popular image of scientific rationality as involving a linear and often solitary process of conducting experiments, analyzing data, and reaching conclusions about the facts based on logic. Bohm contends, in the spirit of the critical theorists, that dialogue is a way of dealing with contradictions and differences and that the results are more powerful than the working of an individual mind. He says,

> The spirit of dialogue . . . is . . . the ability to hold many points of view in suspension, along with a primary interest in the creation of a common meaning. It is particularly important, however, to explore the possibilities of dialogue in the context of a group that is large enough to have within it a wide range of points of view, and to sustain a strong flow of meaning. This latter can come about because such dialogue is capable of having the powerful nonverbal effect of consensus . . . In true dialogue there is the possibility that a new form of consensual mind . . . may be a more powerful instrument than is the individual mind . . . Fixed and rigid frames dissolve in the creative free flow of dialogue as a new kind of microculture emerges.
>
> (Bohm 1996: 246–47)

Thus dialogue can lead to what Schon and Rein (1994) call "frame reflection," or the ability to act from one perspective, while in the back of our minds we hold onto an awareness of other possible perspectives, in a sort of double vision. Crucial to the usefulness of such double vision and, more generally to reflective policy inquiry in Schon and Rein's pragmatist view, is the link to actual practice. Dialogue that is grounded in practice helps participants avoid being trapped in their own thought and failing to see possibilities.

William Isaacs differentiates dialogue from negotiation designed to reach agreement among parties who differ. He contends,

> The intention of dialogue is to reach new understanding and, in doing so, to form a totally new basis from which to think and act. In dialogue, one not only solves problems, one *dis*solves them. We do not merely try to reach agreement, we try to create a context from which many new agreements might come. And we seek to uncover a base of shared meaning that can greatly help coordinate and align our actions with our values.
>
> (Isaacs 1999a: 19)

He argues, like Bohm, that dialogue is a flow of meaning. It is

> a conversation in which people think together in a relationship. Thinking together implies that you no longer take your own position as final. You relax your grip on certainty and listen to the possibilities that result simply from being in a relationship with others.

In ordinary conversation the word dialogue tends to be used interchangeably with debate (a contention by formal argument), discussion (consideration by a group of persons of the reasons for and against a measure), and deliberation (discussion that is careful and deliberate) (Merriam Webster 2003).

But these are different from genuine dialogue, which is by nature more spontaneous and creative, less focused on an a priori question and more broadly aimed at learning, evolution, and action. In Bohm's view discussion is more like a ping pong game where people are batting the ideas back and forth and the idea is to win points (Bohm 1996: 7). Dialogue on the other hand is not about winning or making your own view prevail. When someone's mistake is uncovered in a dialogue, everyone gains, as in a mutual gain negotiation.

From opinion to judgment

In policy dialogue participants come to develop more reflective and informed judgments and make more sense of public affairs in the course of developing shared meaning. (Shared meaning does not necessarily mean agreement.) Public opinion expert Daniel Yankelovich in his classic book *Coming to Public Judgment* (Yankelovich 1991) makes an important distinction between mass opinion and public judgment. During the 2000 U.S. presidential election campaign, polls suggested there were rapid pendulum swings in public opinion on a weekly, if not daily, basis. Public opinion on many issues is not grounded in a genuine understanding of the issues so it can fluctuate almost at random or in response to minor news events. Yankelovich poses the hypothesis that this unstable state of public opinion can be changed through dialogue, which can help people to develop grounded understandings and link them to their own values.

He and associates have explored this idea through structured, daylong dialogues where participants move from initial raw opinion to considered judgment about a complex issue. We observed these dialogues as implemented in San Diego around the contentious topic of growth management. Many sets of 10 randomly selected local residents talked among themselves for a full day, starting with simple data and information about the arguments for and against various solutions, from stopping growth, to improving transit, to having a regional coordination system. To assure that the arguments and data offered were fair representations, people on various sides of the issues had reviewed them. Most participants moved during dialogue from preferring a no-growth policy to preferring a regional management one, though most had opposed the latter at the outset. We watched as the groups worked through issues, building on their collective personal knowledge and experience and began to realize they could not stop growth and began to think through what managing growth would be like. Each group became a community of inquiry, with members sharing a goal to work out what would be the best policy for the city. With only a few guidelines about how to talk to one another (no criticizing, for example) their conversations evolved into authentic dialogues. They got past the assumptions that had dominated their thinking, not unlike the detectives, as they challenged each other and drew on what they each knew. They developed camaraderie which made it easier to converse. In the assessment phase at the end of the day participants gave moving testimony as to what the dialogue experience meant to them. Some learned that they could actually understand public issues and policies; some decided to vote for the first time; others saw they could make a difference by becoming more politically active. The researchers found, among other things, that even those who entered with a strong political ideology were "far more interested in finding workable solutions than adhering to a particular ideology" (Rosell, et al. 2005).

Dialogue is transformative

Genuine dialogue can transform beliefs and values. In the San Diego dialogues people learned that their assumptions about how the city worked were not accurate. They went through a single loop learning process (Argyris and Schon 1996). They discovered that the growth process did not work as they assumed, and they adjusted their opinions about what to do as a result. A few went through a double loop learning process. Instead of just changing their opinions about the best way to manage San Diego's growth, they rethought their whole approach to public issues and decided they wanted to play an active rather than passive role in public decision making. In double loop learning players do not just adjust their actions to adapt to new information, they change their goals and reframe how they look at the problem.

Both single and double loop learning occurred in the San Francisco Estuary Project (SFEP), a regional collaborative process set up by U.S. EPA to develop a comprehensive management plan for this extensive waterway. This complex task involved stakeholders from the fishing, agricultural, and development industries, as well as environmental groups, local government and state and federal agencies. After two years of dialogue and data gathering and analysis (Innes and Connick 1999), players learned that, contrary to many of their assumptions, fisheries in the estuary were declining and there was a significant water quality problem. They realized there *was* a problem they needed to tackle. The trouble was that standard solutions like controlling end-of-the-pipe emissions would not solve the problem, as there were many other unknown pollution sources and a complex pattern of tides and currents.

Moving on from this recognition, stakeholders came to understand that the estuary was a complex, dynamic system, where the outcomes of introducing specific pollutants or other actions could not easily be predicted. As they could not identify fixes for the problem, they focused on developing a way to monitor the health of the estuary. Choosing a measure was contentious, however, as much was at stake. Accordingly SFEP assembled a group of scientists representing all the key stakeholders and sent them to a facilitated 3-day retreat telling them to come up with an agreed upon measure. Instead of producing an index of pollutants: the scientists created a salinity index and identified a location within the estuary where the index should meet a certain standard of fresh and saltwater mixing for the optimal conditions for maintaining biodiversity. Thus in a process of double loop learning they moved away from conventional measures to thinking about the task in terms of outcomes instead of inputs.

Collaboration in high performance groups

An extensive literature in social and educational psychology focusing on group dynamics helps to understand how and why dialogues can produce such results. A commonly used text reviewing this literature (Johnson and Johnson 1997) lays out the theory based on empirical evidence. First, the authors argue that man is fundamentally a group being and that cooperative efforts over the millennia have contributed to human progress. High performance groups – that is groups that are effective and achieve remarkable things – are made up of members who commit themselves to the common purpose of maximizing their own and others' success. Members of such groups hold themselves and each other accountable for achieving goals. They do real work together, share information and perspectives, and give each other assistance and encouragement. They reflect on what they are doing and seek to continuously improve (Johnson and Johnson 1997: 17–18). The authors identify five elements of group effectiveness, which resonate with collaborative rationality and our DIAD theory. These include: positive interdependence among participants; individual accountability; face to face interaction; social and interpersonal skills, many of which can be taught; group processing of goals, events, and their group dynamics (Johnson and Johnson 1997: 24–31). In effective groups there is active participation by all members; clear communication of ideas and feelings; influence based on expertise, ability, and access to information, rather than on the basis of authority or power; flexible decision making procedures responsive to the needs of the situation; use of critical analysis of each other's conclusions and reasoning to promote creative decision making; and explicit recognition of conflicts, with efforts to resolve them constructively.

Unpacking collaborative policy dialogues

In our observation dialogues where creativity and transformation occur involve several activities: framing and reframing of the issues; storytelling; role playing; and bricolage (Innes and Booher 1999b). We do not contend that such familiar discussion methods as making tradeoffs, taking moral positions, or using logic and invoking scientific evidence are irrelevant in consensus building – indeed they are all part of the overall process. We do contend, however, that in controversial, complex, and uncertain conditions these familiar approaches are usually not enough to produce agreement. Often they interfere with dialogue. None of them encourages the innovation and collective commitment to a new idea that is necessary to emerge from paralyzing disputes and agree on a constructive solution. None of them provides opportunity to address emotions or to use imagination and speculate on the future. Argumentation in the traditional sense of starting from basic principles, making claims, providing evidence and theories and drawing logical conclusions about what is right is not typically part of collaborative dialogue in our observation.

Framing as a source of conflict

One of most important dynamics of dialogue is that it can address the frames that participants tacitly employ – the frames that interfere with collaboration, learning, and creativity and that are largely invisible in other types of discourse. A frame is the way people see an issue, situation or practice. These frames, because they are usually invisible to people using them and because they are embedded in whole sets of practices and institutional arrangements, are often behind what is referred to as intractable conflict (Lewicki, et al. 2003). With differing frames participants cannot even meet in the same discussion territory, much less work through the pros and cons of a course of action.

For example, 15 years after part of the San Francisco Bay Bridge collapsed in the 1989 Loma Prieta earthquake, no new bridge had been built despite the dangers of the old, flawed bridge. The delay can be largely attributed to differences in framing. The two mayors at either end of the bridge saw it as linked to the economic future of their cities, with Oakland's mayor arguing for a beautiful bridge that would improve the image of his city and San Francisco's mayor demanding that a new bridge should not interfere with his development plans for Treasure Island at mid span. Other players framed the issue as safety or cost effectiveness. Without full dialogue among the stakeholders (including the commuters who risk their lives each day) paralysis, finger pointing, and indecision continued for years.

Once the design decision was made and work began, huge delays and cost overruns became evident, and the bridge building stalled. Again framing interfered with agreement. Some said it was because the chosen design was too expensive and it should be changed. Politicians framed the issue as one of who should pay, the state or the users. Players framed the toll issue in a range of ways, from comparing the existing toll to the much higher ones on New York bridges, to the question of fairness for commuters and the poor. Some blamed the high cost on Bay Area politics, saying that implied that local people should pay for the bridge, while others saw it as a matter of incompetence and deception by the state transportation agency, which concealed cost overruns for months, and therefore should mean that the state should pay more. The governor finally announced, in an effort to break the gridlock that the focus should be on how to pay for the new span and not on conflicts over the design. This effort at reframing was met by his political opponents with relief, as financing provided a more manageable frame for the dispute.

This example suggests how much is implied in a frame, including values, assumptions, causal relationships, and ideal visions for the future. One mayor framed the bridge design as being about aesthetics and a long term legacy. It was about making something for the region to be proud of, so cost was not important. The other mayor framed it as being about his decision making rights as mayor to develop his city and its economy. Neither cost nor design was part of his frame. Engineers too disagreed over the relative importance of safety, cost effectiveness and aesthetics. Some framed the financing question in terms of geographic fairness, others in terms of ability to pay, or who was to blame for the cost. Because of these framing differences, there could be no single goal for the bridge or its financing so neither top down planning nor linear analysis could resolve the issues. There were some limited dialogues along the way among a committee of high level local officials, but these did not include many key stakeholders and did not have officials from outside the area. Once the design was selected, the dialogue stopped, but the bickering continued. It was clear people were not "on the same page" so moving forward was not possible.

According to Gray, framing is a

> process of constructing and representing our interpretations of the world around us. We construct frames by sorting and categorizing our experience – weighing new information against our previous interpretations. Through this process we focus attention to elements within the frame . . . Framing also involves a representational process in which we present or express how we make sense of things. Constructing and representing, however, are not necessarily separate activities. It is often necessary to represent our thoughts in words to know what we really think of a situation.
>
> (Gray 2003: 12).

In productive dialogue much of what goes on is often about exposing frames and reflecting on frames, as Schon and Rein (1994) would have us do. As the people in the dialogue represent their frames, they may collectively construct new ones. The exposure of the frames is in itself valuable as the tacit values and understanding are put on the table for exploration. In one case in the Netherlands stakeholders worked explicitly and symbolically with the idea of a frame to change the public discourse (Hajer 2003a). The future of an agricultural area was up for debate, with conservationists wanting to return it to its "natural," former state of wetland and others wanting to develop it. The farmers erected a huge frame in the fields which, in effect, was a picture of agriculture. This

> caught policy makers by surprise. Up to that moment policy formation had been a smooth process, with experts and policy makers agreeing on the need to move beyond mere nature "conservation." Policy makers had invented the vocabulary of "main ecological structure," "networks of nature," and nature development . . . Moreover the policy was facilitated by the widespread societal support for sustainable development and the need to enhance biodiversity. What could the problem possibly be? Farmers were well aware that their agricultural practices were not economically viable.

The frame in the fields first of all confronted government with the limited effectiveness of its traditional strategies of "conceive–decide–implement" in a network society. Top-down implementation strategies faltered on local protests.

The frame in the fields showed that environmental policy should not be regarded as a fixed programme for ecological improvement that "only" needs to be implemented, that politics was not merely a matter of doing "more" or "less" for the environment (Hajer 2003a: 91).

In short the frame was a graphic way of calling attention to the unexamined frames the government was using and illustrating the frame of the local population. Without dialogue a dramatic gesture was needed which set in motion a process of frame reflection and change.

Frames are important according to Gray (2003: 17) because they define issues and shape action as a result. For example, battles over a scenic waterfront in Albany California have raged for decades with no resolution, as some frame this as about dealing with the city's need for revenues, and others frame it as being about protecting a beautiful regional resource. These framings have polarized debate, though dialogue could reframe these as mutually supportive toward responsible development.

People also use frames to protect themselves, contending an issue is a matter of rights rather than merely interests. Framing was one of the biggest obstacles to reaching the Water Forum agreement because California has a complex (and often contradictory) system of water rights, that had long been a major obstacle to cooperative action to manage water more efficiently. Those with water rights cling to them, despite the reality that under many conditions they may not be able to exercise them. Frames also shape what we believe ought to happen (e.g. if the local officials run up the cost of the bridge, local people should pay) and affect what we think is right and wrong. They provide a socially constructed reality and self-fulfilling prophecy, as we internalize and enact frames. Finally, frames are critical to social movements and mobilization, helping to create a common cause or mission among a group of people. For example, the framing of developers as greedy and indifferent to the environment can mobilize environmentalists to oppose development, just as framing of environmentalists as ideologues can encourage cities and developers to try to limit the forums where they speak and not take their concerns seriously. Frames of this sort involve fixing blame and invoking collective action against the culprit.

There are many types of frames, but Lewicki and colleagues found three to be particularly common in the environmental disputes they studied (Lewicki, et al. 2003: 21–32), as we have in our experience. The first is an identity frame. This can be powerful. "Identity is iterative: shaping and being shaped by the individuals' social and cultural experiences and memberships" (Hoare 1994). We identify ourselves as Bostonian or Californian, professor or practitioner, environmentalist or homeowner, and with this identity go certain expectations that shape our attitudes and views of us by people in other categories. In controversial situations identities may be threatened, and this is likely to make the controversy more intractable. It is difficult for someone who self-identifies as an environmentalist and works with others to fight environmental depredations, to turn around and collaborate with a developer, even if it is to create something more environmentally responsible than the toxic wetland that is in place. In Albany people on both sides of the waterfront issue identify themselves as environmentalists, which means that when someone says their proposal is not environmentally sound it makes them angry. It is not an issue for inquiry.

A second type is a characterization frame, which is particularly problematic when people have strong group identity frames. This kind of frame characterizes and often blames others. The repeated use of characterization frames polarizes already antagonistic relationships. In water disputes agricultural interests are outraged if they are accused of wasting water, as that is not their self-image. Other participants use "pro-development," and "tree hugger," as epithets and stereotypes. In facilitated dialogues this kind of labeling is generally avoidable, but it may be an undercurrent until people begin to relate to each other as individuals. A third type is a conflict management frame, which is about what is the appropriate way to deal with conflict, such as avoidance, joint problem solving, authority, political decision making or adjudication (Gray 2003: 25).

We have found many examples of competing frames in planning and policy processes. At the Bay Area's Metropolitan Transportation Commission (MTC), which prepares the regional transportation plan (RTP) and allocates funding, for example, we found that players disagreed with each other less about desired outcomes and more about how to frame the task of planning (Innes and Gruber 2001; Innes and Gruber 2005).[1] One group saw it as a technical bureaucratic task involving data analysis and matching projects to eligibility criteria; another, the leadership, saw planning as a political divide-the-pie effort; a third group was a social movement which saw the task as visioning and advocacy; and the fourth wanted to plan through collaborative dialogue.

These differing frames led to real clashes. A case in point was when a small working group of Partners[2] sought a better way to prepare the RTP than simply packaging project requests. At first they had a constructive dialogue among themselves and staff, as they brainstormed, speculated, and collectively thought through their concerns with the existing planning process and ideas about how it could be improved. These meetings were cooperative, energetic, and filled with humor. The process reflected the model of dialogue we advocate, as people chimed in with ideas in a rapid fire way and sought ways to accommodate each others' concerns. Partners wanted the plan to be created through dialogue, and they proposed that project sponsors should have to answer a series of open-ended questions about the value of the project to the region and how it would mesh with MTC goals. Partners believed this approach would get away from top down planning and into a dialogue based on values and goals. This group was self-organizing, with the partners preparing agendas and materials rather than, as in other MTC meetings, having everything carefully planned and scripted by staff (Innes and Gruber 2001: 204–40).

Once the group proceeded to the details of the questions and how they would be used, however, they ran up against a conflict in cognitive models between the staff and partners, which, without a facilitator, could not be overcome. Staff were looking for certainty, precise questions and answers, and explicit steps laid out on how to get from an answer to a decision. They wanted narrow questions focused on limited legal man-dates. On the other hand partners accepted the inevitability of uncertainty and ambiguity and the desirability of nuance. They wanted open-ended questions focused on what would be best for the region. Staff complained that the partners wanted a process that involved value judgments and appeared not to understand when partners argued that staff were also using value judgments, albeit cloaked under the guise of objectivity. The dialogue foundered at this stage and became rancorous as staff and partners could not get past this conflict in framings. Staff took over and partners backed off from collaborative dialogue almost entirely. A skilled facilitator might have been able to see this difference in tacit cognitive models of planning and help the group to overcome the impasse, discuss their assumptions, and potentially move forward. Cognitive models can be deeply ingrained and almost invisible to the people who use them. Lewicki and associates recommend dealing with frame conflict through dialogues such as study circles, listening circles, narrative forums and visioning or search processes.

In the planning for the new city of Ciudad Guayana (Peattie 1987) the professional planners framed the task as designing for a future middle class population and developing the "amenities" they would want, like parks and shopping plazas. The local residents were focused, however, on transportation, child care, and social services. Anthropologist Peattie framed her task as planning with the workers and squatters who were already living there, but the professional planners' frame did not include them. Peattie also shows us how different professionals represented the issues – essentially how they framed them. She shows us the bird's eye view of the future city that the architects used, with few perspectives actually at the level of a person living or working in the city and little evidence of actual people in the views. It seems that the architects' frame was to build a place that would be aesthetically satisfying to architects and attractive to show on brochures. The economists prepared massive tables projecting investment, value of output, labor force, power usage and so on. They framed the task as creating an economic engine and getting the right mix of inputs and outputs. Neither design nor people (except as labor force) showed up in their analyses.

Metaphor in dialogue

Frames are often expressed in dialogue or discussion through metaphors, which like frames, can advance or hinder dialogue. Like frames they are typically invisible to participants. We use metaphor all the time when we communicate but, typically, not consciously or deliberately. A metaphor is essentially understanding and experiencing one kind of thing in terms of another, perhaps more familiar, thing. It gives us a way of making sense of experience. It can govern our thought and everyday functioning. For example, we typically see argument as war. We do not call it that, but we use the metaphor to frame our conversation. We say "your claims are indefensible," "his criticisms were right on target," "I have never won an argument with him," or "he shot down my arguments" (Lakoff and Johnson 1980: 4).

Thompson in his observational study of cognitive models in environmental disputes (Thompson 1997) found that newspaper accounts on land use debates in Riverside County California, repeatedly used war metaphors in their reports, e.g.: "The County becomes a battleground of nature and man," "Unless a peace plan can be found soon, Riverside County can look forward to escalating conflicts," or "also on the front lines are developers" (p. 228). This metaphor was so taken for granted (p. 230) that reporters interviewed did not believe its use violated principles of objective reporting. Participants in the disputes also used the language of war. They talked about their "opponents," about "forcing a showdown," "firing off" critical letters, and "waging long and hard political and legal battles" (pp. 230–31). Similarly, in public hearings a "common strategy was to rally the opposition, turn out in force, and defeat the project" (p. 232). These players were not just using words poetically, they were defining the character of the interactions, helping to elicit emotions of antagonism and characterizing people with different views as the enemy. On the other hand, among practitioners the metaphor was often that planning is a journey, a long term, purposeful activity that goes along a path and has stages and destinations (pp. 233–4). In collaborative planning Thompson finds the use of a building metaphor, as participants talk of working together and creating things. The language and metaphor frame the mindset of the players and reinforce practices and attitudes.

Metaphors, and their more explicit version, similes, are also important in dialogue for another reason. Using such comparisons can generate great creativity. Comparing one problem or task to a physical thing or to another task, can open up new ways of seeing. It can get participants in a dialogue unstuck when they reach an impasse or cannot find a way to address a problem. Schon (1979) offers the example of a group of product development researchers trying to improve the performance of a new paintbrush with synthetic bristles that was delivering the paint in a discontinuous "gloppy" way. They tried every technical fix to the bristles they could think of and remained stuck until someone said "you know a paintbrush is a kind of a pump!" This insight led them to look at the problem differently and think of different types of solutions that could improve the brush's performance. Schon's point is that metaphor can be generative of ideas. Without our necessarily fully understanding what the points of comparison are at first, the metaphor can generate a new line of thought. This was the case in the Water Forum when participants were stuck on trying to figure out a way to pay for habitat conservation, given that the utilities were already paying into a required federal conservation fund. When one person proposed they respond in the mode of the Boston Tea Party and refuse to pay into the federal fund the idea shocked participants at first, but quickly they got into imagining what that would be like. While they did not choose civil disobedience, the idea that it was possible pointed to solutions they had not considered. This comparison generated new energy and ultimately an unexpected solution.

Storytelling as argument

The "reasoning" or argument that goes on in dialogue is very unlike the conventional image of stating positions and giving reasons for them, or drawing logical conclusions based on value premises and supporting data. In dialogue much of the reasoning is accomplished through storytelling, People work out what they think through a sort of mutual adjustment of stories that produces a collectively shared sense of events. John Forester has vividly illustrated this process in a story of a planners' dialogue (Forester 1993: 193–4). Half a dozen planning staff are discussing several development projects in the context of recent political attacks on them. The director offers his version of the story.

It is a story of brave and ethical planners having invoked the ire of the public. It never says this in so many words, but the story says it in a way that is richer and more vivid.

> I think the Mayflower project . . . was pivotal. That is the first time we took a very high profile position on a very unpopular issue. We were outvoted on the council seven to three; we were pushed to the center of that controversy. We tried to hold what we thought was the right line, and we really lost a great deal of support in the general public because of our position.

He goes on with the story saying that the second project made things worse because people were really angry though he thinks they "were not taking the heat" for the third one. Others amend his story, saying they think they are taking the heat for it. Another provides more evidence with a counterfactual story "I mean I don't hear anyone saying 'The Board of Public Works really screwed up'." The director says "This is interesting because we did not screw up." But then a staff member notes that the planning department did not point the finger at the screw up, suggesting (politely) that they had not done their politics well. The director continues elaborating his story to account for why planners seem to bear the brunt, even if they are not culpable.

> My perception is that people just think about any kind of change and then they think about planning and then they think about planners.

A staffer builds on that.

> If something goes wrong the planners did it. If something goes right, the City Council members claim credit for it.

The director allows that he has always resisted staff requests that he come out and answer these things. He notes he has always said "you don't want to get into a cursing war with a skunk; you know you just get more heat that way." But after this dialogue he proposes a new scenario.

> I think we have to set out a strategy over the next year or two of how we are going to sell the department and how we are going to position ourselves to get to those people whose minds are not already made up . . . If we could get to them with reason and explain to them what our job is and how we came to the conclusions that we've come to . . .

A staff member builds on this and proposes preparing a position paper on the projects telling the story of each one. Their strategy will undoubtedly continue to build and evolve through this collaborative storytelling and brainstorming process.

> This group was conducting a joint reasoning process that eventually moved into a strategy of action by telling stories about their perceptions of events, trying to develop a common story and then telling stories about possible new ways to deal with their problem. Through the story they have tacitly defined their problem as being blamed for doing their job ethically. They do not do a formal causal analysis, get data, or lay out and compare all the options, which would be time consuming and probably not

worthwhile. They are using a kind of pragmatic community of inquiry as they look at the empirical situation through their experience. They translate this into stories and conclude that the problem is due to being misunderstood and misrepresented. They move into an experimental strategy to try to change this.

Stories and storytelling remain, with some key exceptions, not widely recognized tools or practices in the literature of planning and policy analysis. Forester's later work continues to explore the roles and functions storytelling plays in many planning situations (Forester 1999). Communities tell stories about themselves, their history, the way they have been treated, how they are different from others, as a way of building individual and community identity, particularly where members are outside the mainstream, like the gay community, retirement communities or evangelical communities (Fitzgerald 1986). They tell stories that imagine a better future. These stories organize their lives and give them justifications for what they do. They express the ambivalent emotions in such communities and hold them together. Stories, social learning and other ways of knowing are, according to Sandercock,

> displacing the sole reliance on the powers of positivist social science as a basis for action. Local communities have grounded, experiential, intuitive and contextual knowledges which are more often manifested in stories, songs, visual images and speech than in the typical planning sources.
>
> (Sandercock 1998: 205).

Storytelling is integral to planning and politics as Throgmorton shows in his detailed study of the decision making around Commonwealth Edison's proposals for expansion of its power capacity in Chicago. All the players had their own story lines. In this case it was mostly not a dialogue but a battle of stories conducted in the public arena (Throgmorton 1996). In a historical analysis of U.S. policies promoting homeownership de Neufville and Barton found that the Jeffersonian myth of the independent yeoman farmer as the ideal citizen had captured the imagination of decision makers to such an extent that even in contemporary times justifications for maintaining the home mortgage tax deduction or subsidizing the creation of suburbs made at least oblique reference to this story (de Neufville and Barton 1987). Their analysis showed that the story itself helped to frame the problem definition that policy makers were using and in turn to point the direction to solutions. It also showed that some stories, especially those that invoke the origins of a nation or a community or even of a local issue can take on mythic qualities. These qualities mean that they cannot easily be challenged in ordinary public discourse. A myth has a sacred quality and it does not have to be literally true to have influence. It has the truth of literature rather than the truth of science. Moreover, it touches deep values and emotions. It makes sense of things in a way that provides inspiration to act.

Storytelling is thus central to how dialogue builds meaning and identity, transforms participants and even moves them to action. These stories provide lenses to try out as ways of understanding events or imagining futures. They provide a way to disagree without arguing, to build on and from the perceptions of participants, while bringing in multiple kinds of knowledge. They help to express the storyteller's emotions in a manageable way while also conveying emotions of those in the story. Storytelling does not require turning the analysis into something "objective" and distinct from the lifeworld. It plays a big part in framing what is problematic about a situation and getting agreement on that. It conveys moral messages in a contextual way. Without asserting an action was good or bad, storytelling puts together a way of making a moral case while leaving open the ambiguities and contradictions of a situation.

Storytelling does put a particular frame on things, but it can be challenged by other stories. In a dialogue the effort is to find compatibility among stories – at least enough to move forward into practical action. Storytelling provides a way of talking about possible futures. A story can reframe a situation, predict a result, allow free flow of speculation and exploration of what would happen "if." It can help one to see the missing part of one's logic. The crime scene investigation dramas currently popular on U.S. television illustrate the power of reasoning through storytelling and simulation. Using the physical evidence from a victim's body and the scene, investigators jointly construct a possible scenario, sometimes even enacting it themselves. When they do, they find the flaws in their theories and develop new ones. They look for other evidence and try out new scenarios till the evidence and the scenario match. Storytelling is a way to keep reframing the issues and evidence until a satisfactory conclusion or action plan can be reached.

In collaborative dialogue storytelling is pervasive in all phases of the process. For example, community leaders or project organizers may begin by describing the situation and explaining why they set up the project, telling stories about the situation and the gathering of stakeholders and the scenarios for its dynamics. Then stakeholders talk about their reasons for coming to the table and their interests. Typically they do this by telling stories about their view of what has been happening and about the stakeholder group they represent and their experience with the issues. Even in the education phase, which may involve charts, tables and analytic conclusions, experts have to outline their understandings of the situation and explain the implications of the data. Given the diversity within a stakeholder group, participants typically have to use examples and offer an overall story line to illuminate their argument.

Role playing and drama

> If looks could kill they probably will
> In games without frontiers – war without tears.
> > Peter Gabriel, *Games without Frontiers*

Argument also takes place in dialogue through role playing. Role playing allows participants to reflect on their own frames and imagine others. It is a way of addressing emotionally charged situations in a way that keeps participants one step away from the tensions because it is a sort of game. It helps stakeholders to separate themselves as people sitting at the table from the people or organizations they represent. In the course of engaging in various roles, participants develop identities for themselves and others and become more effective participants, representing their stakeholders' interests more clearly.[3] Role playing allows for collective scenario building, like the crime scene investigators reenacting a possible crime.

We have learned a great deal about role playing and scenario building in recent years from the working of interactive, real time role play games that became popular for a whole generation of young people (Innes and Booher 1999b). The refrain from Peter Gabriel's popular song captures what is so important about the games for how we conduct collaborative policy dialogue. Role playing allows participants to explore their urges and personas, including the dark ones, and to play them out against other personas. They allow them to battle with opponents without actually harming them. They can do so without boundaries or the usual social expectations, and they can do so without attacking the individual but by operating in the world of "what if?" In these games they engage in a heroic quest, as participants in a dialogue do, meeting challenges along the way and building their skills, knowledge, and repertoire of actions. These are cooperative games in the sense that they are not about winning or losing but about learning and developing and making the game interesting for all participants. The juxtaposition of subjunctive and future tense in Gabriel's song reflects the interplay of imagination and reality in these games.

Simulation has long been regarded as a legitimate tool of analysis, even in positivist, instrumental thought, but the role playing advocated here is far more dynamic and less controlled than conventional simulation. Its purpose is not simply to work out what the future might be like, but also to help participants learn to respond to unexpected and complex possibilities, and to produce innovative strategy. Because these simulations include real life actors, the exercises themselves and the learning associated with them are part of the product. Players learn how the dynamics of their own ideas and actions play out in a complex world of interlinked players and unanticipated events. Scenario building can make collective sense of complexity and help to predict possibilities in an uncertain world. It can allow the playful imagination, which people normally suppress, to go to work.

Whatever else collaborative policy dialogue may be, it is definitely role playing. Participants come to the table representing stakeholders with different interests. It is each one's job to play the role of that stakeholder in the discussion, just as in games where one person may play a vampire and another a werewolf. In these roles they speak in the voices of their respective groups – as they believe their members would if they were to hear the discussion or proposal. Participants also shift into other roles during the discussions – roles that reflect themselves as individuals. One may have a role as lobbyist or agency staff member. In that role the person may tell the other participants about the difficulties she will have selling a particular idea to her constituency, though the person may simultaneously contend the idea is excellent and support it in her role as a professional and member of the group. These professional and collegial roles are crucial because they build and maintain trust even when the group cannot agree on what seems reasonable. Players also may take different roles as participants in the dialogue, choosing to be for example, the naysayer, the skeptic, or the enthusiast. Some try to generate new alternatives, and still others see their roles as clarifying emerging arguments or noting the connections among the players' views. All of these roles can be helpful to moving a process along.

Finally, participants also bring to the table personal roles as parents, commuters, suburbanites, bicyclists, or people who care about the environment. They often contribute valuable knowledge and opinions from these roles. Sometimes they even advocate steps that the stakeholders they represent would oppose, like the urban transit manager who opposed efforts to expand transit funding because, as a suburban dweller, he sympathized more with the need to improve highways, or the suburban transit manager who pushed for bikeway funding because he was an avid cyclist. In a dramatic moment in the Water Forum, a frustrated water provider representative switched into his personal role as environmentalist and citizen, and challenged the other providers who were saying their boards would not agree to install water meters.

> We sound like a goddamn school board talking about the algebra schedule. It seems we have a consensus here that we need to put meters on everyone's home here. I am serious (passionately) . . . We need to have the gumption to say to our boards "we need to do this."

Another player replied in a distressed tone, "But we have to feed our families!" He retorted, "But are *we* here to protect ourselves?"

Proposals for action can stimulate one or another player to weave a scenario of what would happen in his or her community if a particular idea were implemented. One Water Forum utility manager, for example, drew a vivid picture of the irate citizens of Sacramento marching on the water district office if meters were installed suddenly without public education about the need to control water use. Environmentalists told parallel tales of what would happen if meters were *not* installed, noting which well-financed environmental organizations would file lawsuits or get legislation passed, bringing all water projects to a halt. As players offered their own images an outsider would have had a hard time following the conversation, which was in no way linear or close to an argument based on principles and logic. Players did not disagree directly nor make universal claims that proposals were good or bad. Instead, they usually claimed that someone's proposal would, for themselves, be a disaster or a waste of time and money, and did so by telling a story, not by just making an assertion. For example, some water districts contained mostly commercial property, which is easy to meter, while in other more residential districts both the technology and the politics would make metering far more difficult. Districts that could install meters for major water users could make more rapid progress in conservation than could those with small users. The stories of each of these districts showed how complex the overall situation was and how one-size-fits-all solutions would not work.

Drama and engagement are important in dialogue to move and change the players. Emotions run high in creative dialogue on contentious issues, not necessarily through confrontation, but through participants' stories and anecdotes, even though many are hypothetical ones about what would happen if . . . The room often breaks out into laughter, commiseration, or frustrated mutterings. Players become intensely engaged. In the Water Forum and the Growth Management Consensus Project the facilitator strode from side to side, occasionally climbing on the table, gesturing, dramatizing the issues, making jokes, shushing people or reminding them in colorful terms of players not in the room who would be outraged by the direction of discussion. Four hours flew past as the players' personalities and ideas emerged and developed, as they generated new ideas and all tried to absorb the simultaneous stimuli, impressions, and information, while also playing their multiple roles. Such drama engages players emotionally, and they come to understand what it is like to be in others' shoes. As a result players often come to care, not only about one another, but also about reaching a good ending. For example, the player who had a new idea about funding that would resolve the discussion over the habitat improvement plan in the Water Forum stood at the front of the room to explain his idea. The facilitator, who had introduced him in tones of anticipation and excitement, had written in big letters across the board, "BREAKTHROUGH!" Then awed silence reigned after he spoke, as each member in turn said, "I like the idea." "I can sell that to my board." The sense of relief and excitement was palpable. It was like the climax to a story, and all that came after was simply the denouement. Afterwards players said, "This process is amazing." "I do not know how this happened, but it is terrific."

All the players have roles simultaneously in other "games" besides the collaborative dialogue.[4] Their positions in their agencies may be harmed or enhanced by some strategy of the consensus building group. For example, a county transportation director told us he supported a regional transportation agency's scoring criteria for choosing projects, because by reducing his own discretion it saved him from pressures by mayors and other elected officials who wanted their local streets improved. Within the group a player may agree to a set of ideas, but fight similar ones in other arenas. For example, in the California Governance Consensus Project,[5] which worked with major state interests to develop better governance processes in the early 1990s, stakeholders simultaneously were agreeing on the importance of linking new revenues to government efficiency reforms and promoting unlinked new revenues or reforms in their own bills in the legislature. In the Water Forum, some stakeholders formally protested the actions of others at the State Water Board, while also working constructively with those same players in the Forum.

Although such contradictory actions understandably anger some within a group, on the whole participants accept that, as one facilitator often pointed out, they are "living in two worlds" and they have to "check their guns at the door." Until players are certain that the consensus building process is the most effective avenue for serving their constituencies' interests, they will continue to work in the parallel games, and perhaps contradict elsewhere the views they express in the consensus process. Generally participants tolerate the contradictions, because they recognize that in the other arenas they all have other roles.[6] They recognize that, whereas support for an idea within the consensus process depends on complementary things being included in a package, in outside activities they may have to pursue issues one by one. Inside the room they work cooperatively in part because of their role playing. They continue their outside roles as warriors and turf protectors until they are confident that the emergent agreements from collaborative dialogues will provide them a better option. This situation reflects the reality that very different institutional forms for public discourse and decision coexist uneasily today.

Creating new strategy through collective bricolage

How then does a dialogue move beyond storytelling and role playing to a breakthrough strategy that the group recognizes as meeting their interests? What is the process by which innovation emerges from dialogues? How does a coherent new strategy emerge? We contend, based on our research and experience, that when this happens it is through a collective form of bricolage. Bricolage (Levi-Strauss 1966: 16–33) is in sharp contrast to the instrumental model of seeking means to reach a given end because, on the one hand, the ends are not clearly known at the outset and on the other, the "reasoning" process does not use logical deduction, but is a creative design process. The bricoleur (there is no adequate English translation) is one who works on many diverse manual tasks: construction, repairs, artwork, etc., relying on whatever is at hand. The bricoleur has a heterogeneous store of materials and tools he has collected over time without necessarily any specific purpose. These include items developed in or left over from earlier projects, and ones collected simply because they might someday be useful. The items usually are not so specialized that only an expert can use them, nor are they limited to only one use. For example, a framed photo could serve as a manuscript stand for a typist, or a telephone could be used as a paperweight. An assemblage of leftover parts from other projects could be used to create a unique children's toy. Those of us who gather up policy ideas, concepts, and practices over time, to bring to bear in policy making are also bricoleurs.

The idea of bricolage has a kinship with the concept of the policy "garbage can" where unused or partially used policy ideas pile up until someone reaches in to find one or two that might be useful (Cohen, et al. 1972). For participatory, interactive decision making, the garbage can is not an adequate metaphor, because choices, problems, participants and solutions meet, interact and transform one another in such an exploratory process. The garbage can model falls short because it misses this interactive exploration and because it implies the choice from it is largely random.

Levi-Strauss describes the bricoleur as doing something much more sophisticated and creative than pulling at random from a "garbage can" and his idea is a powerful analogy for making sense of how innovation emerges in consensus building. A bricoleur engages in a *dialogue with a collection of materials,* to choose among them and to form a subset which in combination can be useful for managing a problem. The bricoleur "interrogates all the heterogeneous objects of which his treasury is composed to discover what each of them could 'signify' and so contribute to the definition of a set which has yet to materialize" (Levi-Strauss 1966: 18). The bricoleur does not have a clear end in sight, but rather a vaguely defined project or sketch of an idea. The project itself will take shape, and its characteristics will be determined by what is available and how it can be assembled. Moreover, the significance of the object in the end will depend on the role it plays in the total creation and, of course, on what that creation turns out to be. The process of moving from a collection of objects to a coherent and meaningful combination is one of dialogue. Swidler has argued similarly that people interrogate their culture for concepts and practices that will help them deal with change and new challenges. She shows how individuals and social groups interact with their culture to make new social strategies, but notes that in doing so they are limited to the tools and ideas in their respective repertoires (Swidler 1986).

Bricolage as a form of reasoning is, according to Levi-Strauss, fundamentally different from science or engineering, in which the end product determines what means should be used. In bricolage the end product is decided by the way the materials at hand can be assembled. So, in policy making, there is no one best way, but many different ways in which one might assemble heterogeneous and available concepts and policy ideas into a coherent and workable strategy. Bricolage is a nonlinear, holistic attack on a problem that results in a practical product. The decision about when the product is satisfactory is intuitive[7] as the group itself looks at it and stakeholders say "I can sell that."

In collaborative dialogues, players at the table have been picking up ideas, having experiences and learning different practices throughout their lives. During dialogue each has added to and modified his or her repertoire. Discussions may start with the obvious ideas that have already been proposed for the problem. But when the group comes to an impasse, the more creative participants look for analogies from the solutions to other problems, drawing on ideas that may not have been used for the issue at hand. They collaboratively contribute to piecing together a new strategy based on their collective repertoire. The many specifics in such discussions seldom fit neatly together nor are they opposites. In not fitting obviously into any scheme, they are like the bricoleur's heterogeneous materials. As the group members speak up and listen, some begin to see a pattern, or to develop a radically different approach that might not make some winners and others losers. When someone proposes "what if we tried this?" others play with the idea and extend the scenario to consider the dynamics of implementing it, rather than reacting directly or deciding whether they agree or not. No one knows whether to agree or not without first trying the idea out in her or his own frame of reference and seeing how it would fit in the whole context. Through scenarios, the idea evolves.

Group members sometimes become highly creative in this process, gaining energy from others' ideas to spin out more. Getting to this point takes time, however, and a high level of comfort among participants. It is risky to offer a new idea. It is testimony to how our norms stifle creativity that, in all the processes we studied, many participants expressed great hesitation, and often wondered aloud if their idea was sensible or apologized for raising a new idea when there was already so much on the table. The facilitator's encouragement was needed, even though participants knew that their ideas would not be ridiculed. Often the facilitator had to spot and articulate a new idea because the participant had not presented it as such. The ideas sometimes startled others, but in well-functioning processes they did not dismiss it out of hand. Once participants accepted that what they were doing was *playing* with ideas and *simulating* through their discussion the possible ramifications of a proposed policy, rather than advocating it or arguing against it, they were more comfortable.[8]

This idea of collective bricolage is similar to David Straus' view of problem-solving in his valuable guide to collaborative methods (Straus 2002). He defines a problem neutrally as a situation someone wants to change. As an architect he sees a design problem rather than something that can be accomplished in a linear or logical way. Problem-solving is like designing a house or a park, where there may be requirements for what it should be like, but there are also many ways to go about the task and many possible end products. In his architecture education he learned that finding a new way to look at a problem allowed him come up with new design ideas. He developed repertoires of design strategies hoping to codify them. He concluded, however, as did the pragmatists, that problem-solving is an educated trial and error process and that there is no failsafe way to be successful. It is not a process of checking out all options, which is time consuming and inefficient, but rather a heuristic approach where designers consult their repertoires, select one, try it out and if it does not produce the desired results select another. Straus identified 64 problem-solving strategies used in many fields, including brainstorming, listing ideas and stepping back to look at them, working forward or working backward, building up or eliminating, generalizing or exemplifying, and combining or separating. These heuristics can be useful in any context, but they are particularly pertinent in collaborative dialogue.

Creating a community of inquiry

While it is important to observe the principles laid out in Chapter 4 for authentic dialogue, there is more to achieving the kind of easy interaction needed for creative, cooperative interchange. It is good to begin with small talk, review what had been decided in the last meeting, update on events and activities since the previous meeting and plenty of opportunity for people to ask each other and staff questions. For example, in the Water Forum, a typical small group meeting began with banter and teasing of the facilitator regarding her recent illness and the presentation of a birthday cake to a stakeholder. This kind of interaction and personal recognition puts people at their ease and starts a comfortable communication that can carry through the meeting. This meeting moved on with the facilitator quickly reviewing the agenda, identifying the big issues for the evening, giving people a sense of priorities and things to anticipate and make time for. Often meals were provided for long meetings. Food not only keeps people from getting cranky, but meal time offers the opportunity for informal interaction and relationship building that can cut across stakeholder groups. For example, when the Water Forum first began, the members of the caucuses sat together and whispered to one another at meetings, but after a year on environmentalists became friendly with utility directors, talking about their families and their interests and working through differences in these meal breaks.

Both humor and conviviality are important elements of a creative collaborative process. Through humor, players can relate to others with whom they disagree and offer criticism gently and respectfully. Humor has rescued many meetings that could have broken down into rancor. In the Water Forum some older, white male participants dealt with a situation they found peculiar – being "managed" by a younger, attractive woman – at times by teasing her, and at other times by humorously acting out the roles of male adolescents with a teacher. When agreement was reached water providers jokingly told environmentalists they would now be out of a job, since their only function was to harass the providers. Environmentalists answered back in kind, amid general hilarity. Humor can acknowledge conflicts and uncomfortable power relations and make them emotionally manageable. An observer can measure the group's comfort level by the degree of shared humor in the room.

Dialogues can even be generated on the "undiscussable" topics with skilled assistance. In a public radio program for example (KQED Jan. 28, 2005), two experienced facilitators, one from the Public Conversations Project[9] and the other from the Search for Common Ground,[10] explained how they started dialogues on abortion. Just before the dialogue an abortion clinic in Boston had been attacked and someone was shot. The representative from Search from Common Ground invited people to come and let people "know your views." Questions to start a dialogue have to be well-honed to avoid the pitfalls of confrontation. They started off by asking,

> What is your history and how did you come to your views? It is not about giving your five point position. It is *why* you think the way you do. Not the headlines.

Then she noted that "once people get started you do not generally have to drag them back from argument. The idea is to help people clarify and understand. We let people ask questions, though we have to coach them on what kinds of questions."

The Public Conversations Project used three similar questions to launch the dialogue: What life experiences led you to your view? When thinking about abortion, what is the heart of the matter? Are you aware of dilemmas and inconsistencies or caveats in your views? They found that people have much more complex views than they have ever been able to express. They encouraged people to think of the views on a continuum and to place themselves on it. The facilitator said that in the process we discover cross-cutting shared issues. These included, for example, that even abortion rights advocates do not want abortion used as a birth control method and that everyone had concerns about what would become of children who did come to term. One of the radio guests summed up their goals.

> We hope that relationships that develop in dialogue will change what they do later. They can pick up the phone and work with someone they met at the dialogue . . . We hope that their behavior as advocates will change and that in future they can act without stereotyping and dehumanizing the other side.

This view echoes the ideas about a dialogue as functioning within a relationship, and as part of community of inquiry. Recognizing the individuality and human qualities of the participants is crucial to the change and transformation that can come from dialogue. The dialogues about abortion were emotional, as many dialogues are when they are on issues with deep meanings to participants. But the emotion was not anger directed at other participants, but emotion reflecting their own histories and the meaning of the issues in their lives. This kind of emotion can help to humanize the participants and allow them to put them in one another's place as part of community of inquiry.

Conclusion

We contend that dialogue, free ranging and exploratory, is at the heart of collaborative rationality, and that communities of inquiry are essential to the development of robust, informed and nuanced policy adapted to the unique conditions in particular times and places. This dialogue explores, challenges and changes frames; it makes creative use of metaphors; it proceeds to a considerable degree by role playing and storytelling; and it creates ways out of stalemate by a process of collective bricolage as participants draw on ideas from many sources to put together a new approach. This kind of dialogue however requires careful management to give participants a comfort level with one another as they set off and encouragement to challenge the status quo and find new ways of seeing issues and potential strategies. While these things can happen in small self-managing diverse groups, for larger ones skilled facilitators can make all the difference.

Notes

1   This draws on a 5 year study of MTC that Innes conducted with Judith Gruber, involving extensive observation of meetings, review of documents, and more than 100 interviews with participants and observers. The findings are detailed in a monograph (Innes and Gruber 2001) and an article highlights aspects of the story (Innes and Gruber 2005).
2   MTC had set up an advisory group which it called the Bay Area Partnership. This was made up of the heads of the many transit agencies in the region, directors of county transportation agencies, along with the Air Quality District.
3   Forester (1997) has explained that the transformational learning process that can occur in dialogue transforms identities. His account strongly evokes Turkle's (1995) account of young people engaged in Internet role playing.
4   Allison (1971) has described how we can see policy processes as games with stakes and players. His conception of game is simpler than the role playing discussed here, but it is in the same spirit.
5   Booher represented business and development stakeholders in this process. For some months Innes observed the dialogue.
6   This may partially account for why this study's research and observation suggest that consensus building groups work most effectively when each interest is represented at the table by a single type of player – e.g., agency staff, elected officials, lobbyists, or citizens, rather than a heterogeneous mixture of agency staff representing one interest and elected officials representing another. Whatever their role in relation to the stakeholder's interests, they can at least understand each others' professional situations empathetically.

7   Creating a new synthesis or perspective on the "whole" is a time-honored, political strategy. The politician tries to structure the environment and context so that others want to join him, or even to feel forced to join. Riker (McLean 2002) has coined the term "heresthetics" for this process. Heresthetics is similar to role-playing bricolage in that both are about policy, interactions, and structuring the events, practices, and available ideas. They are different, however, in an important sense: the former is about manipulation and the latter is about collaboration. In the former, the players may not know how they are being influenced. In the latter, the players themselves create the new scenarios and perceptions. See also Lao Tzu (1995).

8   A dilemma here is that employers may not be comfortable about sending their staff to "play a game." Playfulness, which is so essential to creativity, appears in contemporary United States culture to be irresponsible or irrelevant to accomplishing business. For role playing to be accepted, considerable change in public understanding will be required.

9   www.publicconversations.org/pcp/pcp.html (accessed Feb. 21, 2009).

10   www.sfcg.org (accessed Feb. 21, 2009).

Knowledge into action   6

The role of dialogue

How we make decisions in daily life

Information pervades our simplest decision processes, but much of it we scarcely notice. When a couple decides to go to a restaurant they rely on their previous experience with the restaurant, newspaper or friends' commentary, their own feelings about cooking that night, estimates of how long it will take to get there, how much dinner will cost, and perhaps a theory that getting out of the house would cheer them up after a hard day at work. They use their own and others' experience and their own feelings, along with objective data and theory. Moreover, they interpret this information within a frame, like reducing their stress or keeping their marriage interesting. They are likely to make the decision only after some dialogue in which they share their views with one another.

Similarly, if a city council is faced with a proposal for a new stop sign, members will probably consider statistics on the number and type of accidents at the intersection and traffic speeds, their personal experience driving through it and similar intersections, their assessment of the feelings of local residents and motorists based on personal interactions with their constituents, and testimony of city engineers and police about the causes of accidents and the probable consequences of placing the stop sign. They are likely to look at charts, listen to stories from pedestrians and motorists, and examine photos and diagrams. They will consider costs and imagine what the impacts will be on the traffic flow. Each brings his or her own values about risk and government responsibility. Each interprets the information within a frame, seeing the stop sign as a traffic calming device, a safety device, yet again another governmental expenditure, or a way of placating constituents. The quality of the information on each of these points can differ widely, and each council member will give more credence or importance to some of it than others will. Moreover, each listens to others' views and is to varying degrees influenced by these.

Challenges for building informed plans and policies

Informing decisions is at best a complex and messy process, as participants consider and sift data and arguments and discuss their implications for the issue at hand. All too often however decision makers shortcut this complexity, prematurely limiting the information they incorporate. They may follow a linear path rather than pursue a wide ranging exploratory effort to find the most useful knowledge and the most effective actions. They may be unable to identify, evaluate and sort through, much less integrate, the information of many types and from many sources that is needed to assure robust decisions and feasible actions. At worst they make decisions on the basis of limited, partial, and biased information and unfounded assumptions.

The city council process above represents the unusual situation where the decision makers have firsthand personal knowledge of the issues, the ability to place the arguments in their own frames, and the opportunity to discuss the matter with others in a reasonably informed way. Many significant public decisions are not like this, however. They involve decision makers who can at best know the situation second or third hand and see only certain parts of it, like the blind men and the elephant. They need others to help them frame issues and identify what is important and what it means. Decision makers in such a situation often search for certainty, looking for bottom line answers and simple fixes. In doing so they may get things exactly wrong or, at the very least, fail to incorporate key knowledge into their understanding – knowledge that would lead them to different choices.

One of the biggest obstacles to changing this situation is the myth around public decision making – a widely believed story that describes how policy making ought to work. The myth, referred to in Chapter 2, goes like this: policy makers and the public define issues and problems, establish goals and values. Analysts do research and identify and evaluate options. Policy makers compare these to their criteria and make a "rational" decision about what is best to do based on that information. In contrast to the collaborative model the tasks are linear, and the players have separate and distinct responsibilities. This story, built on positivist epistemology, emphasizes getting the "best" and most objective information about an issue and using deductive logic to move from goals to choices. It bemoans the situation when "politics" interferes with the "right" decision. This myth persists in considerable part because it maintains the status quo and serves all the players' needs, albeit in a somewhat perverse way.

Flaws in this myth make it increasingly dysfunctional for the twenty-first century. Very little of the reality of today's public action is captured in this story, and the literature documenting the discrepancy is increasingly hard to ignore. The idea of the rational decider utilizing research in an instrumental way to make policy choices from a position of power in government is gradually being replaced by the idea of an array of public and private players out there, linked together by networks in an evolving governance process, continuously learning and acting (Booher 2004; Healey 2007; Kickert, et al. 1997; Provan and Milward, 1995; Sørensen and Torfing 2007). Information may be available and presented to decision makers, but remain unused. Information in practice does not so much provide an "aha" experience or an answer to policy questions, as it becomes the taken for granted part of action (Innes 1998). Many public actions happen without formal decisions by official deciders, as informal action by both public and private actors becomes increasingly ubiquitous. We contend that knowledge built through a collective learning process builds the capacity of all players to make sounder choices (Innes and Booher 2003b). It changes them and changes the policy process and outcomes. It has often been said that planning is about linking knowledge and action (Friedmann 1987). Today it is time to examine how and when that linkage does and does not work.

Purpose of the chapter

In this chapter we will make the case that for knowledge to motivate action, it not only has to be tailor-made to particular times, places, and conditions, but also that dialogue has to be a crucial part of both developing and using it. Influential information has to be seen to "fit" the situation, and it has to be both understood and trusted by those who are to act on it. We make this case by first exploring findings on the ways social science research has and has not been used in policy and then move on to look at the types of knowledge that players in legislative, planning and regulatory arenas reach out for. We then look at examples that illustrate how dialogue has played a role in the effective development and use of information for controversial policy issues. We look at the difficulties of integrating science and lay knowledge and the challenges of disagreements among experts. Finally, we lay out, with examples, practices of joint fact finding in collaborative processes and examine how and why these work to embed information in public decisions making.

Exploding the myth

When policy makers do not use research

Evidence abounds that decision makers do not make much substantive use of the findings of the research social scientists and analysts provide for them. To the extent that they do, the use does not mirror the myth. This situation can be a source of frustration for planners, policy analysts and advocates, who often perceive it as a case of "politics" winning out over rational planning (Flyvbjerg 1998) or of willful trampling of important values. For decades social scientists puzzled over this issue, and produced a substantial literature about the relationship of research and action. Innes, in her work as a congressional staff member, found that she had access to practically any information she wanted to assist the Congressman in making his voting decisions. Any industry or advocacy group, any public agency or scholar would willingly provide the latest information. The Library of Congress was a vast resource at her fingertips and, when the Library did not have the information, their staff would conduct research and prepare a full report for the Congressman. Nonetheless he barely looked at the information, typically calling a colleague instead to get advice on how to vote. When Innes had her first planning internship, she discovered a similar pattern in the Boston Redevelopment Authority, where her supervisor discarded without analyzing it the raw housing survey data prepared for him by academic researchers. He did not see a need for the data, nor did he have the skills to make sense of it in a way useful in his job. These experiences led Innes to her career-long interest in how and when information influences public action. She could see it was not a simple matter of the quality or relevance of information. There was clearly much more at work.

Carol Weiss investigated how and when social science research could influence public policy. Her writings have made significant contributions that continue to offer important insights, even 30 years later (Weiss 1977, 1979; Weiss and Bucuvalas 1980). She identified fundamental reasons why use of such research for public decision making was so limited. Findings are inevitably narrowly focused, whereas practical policy issues are broad and complex. Social science rigor requires precisely defined variables and limited questions on one aspect of an issue. A study might show, for example, that people who live in housing near transit are less likely to use cars than others, but that research would not be enough to justify major public investment in transit-based housing, even if a causal relation could be established. A social science study can at best be one part of the picture to be weighed with other information, including studies of other factors affecting auto usage, costs and benefits of a variety of alternative policies to reduce auto usage, competing demands on public funds, social impacts in the neighborhood and concerns of neighbors, as well as political feasibility of this and the alternatives.

Moreover, formal research is normally designed in a way that does not mesh with the policy makers' frame of reference nor reflect policy makers' assumptions, values, concepts or priorities, but rather applies theories in the field. For example, a popular theory among economists is that if public services are paid for by their users, the investments will be used more efficiently than if provided by a general tax. Moreover, the theory argues that the user pays approach is the fairest way to finance these services, and transport finance experts accordingly argue for a gasoline tax. Policy makers in the U.S. typically believe that a gas tax is politically infeasible so the analysis is irrelevant. Moreover, the economists' theory involves a conception of fairness that politicians may not share. For example, politicians may think it is unfair to charge everyone the same regardless of their ability to pay. Policy makers may not even share the goal of efficiency. Even now that most take climate change findings seriously, they will not use them in their decisions if they believe doing so will force them into unpopular and expensive actions which advocates demand. In any case policy makers, whether they are agency heads, legislators, or other civic leaders, are busy people with information and advocacy coming at them from many directions. No one study is going to be decisive for them, no matter how open-minded they may be.

How policy makers do use research

Weiss has identified six categories of decision makers' use of research, but these are for the most part very different from the idealized model embodied in the myth. Based on her surveys of decision makers (Weiss 1979), she labels these "knowledge-driven," "problem-solving," "political," "tactical," "enlightenment," and "interactive." Her analysis goes on to explore each type from a normative and descriptive perspective and assess how each performs in terms of policy impact.

The knowledge-driven approach implies that research findings themselves should drive policy. New knowledge should create new action. To fill the gap between this knowledge and public action, proponents often resort to public relations campaigns to "sell" their findings to policy makers. This, which is often the strategy of social movements, think tanks, and even public agencies, according to Weiss, seldom leads to actual research use. Much more is needed to get public action than simply giving knowledge to policy makers.

The problem-solving approach may well be the one that is most consistent with the myth and most likely to fit the popular image of what policy research is for. This conception of research use is, however, not any more realistic than the first one. When policy makers have defined a problem and have a decision to make, they need data and analysis quickly. There is not normally time to gather new information, but existing data is, almost by definition, out of date, and is usually not geographically or otherwise targeted to the defined problem. The response may be to commission research by agency staff, consultants or special panels. History shows that even research commissioned specifically for a problem seldom has much impact. Weiss contends that "extraordinary concatenation of circumstances" is required for problem-solving research to directly influence a decision. There would have to be a

> well defined decision situation, a set of policy actors who have responsibility and jurisdiction for making a decision, an issue whose resolution to some extent depends on information, identification of the requisite informational need, research that provides the information in terms that match the circumstances within which choices will be made, research findings that are clearcut, unambiguous, firmly supported and powerful, that reach decision-makers at the same time that they are wrestling with the issues, that are comprehensible and understood and that do not run counter to strong political interests. Because chances are small that all these conditions will fall into line around any one issue, the problem-solving model of research use probably describes a relatively small number of cases.
>
> (Weiss 1979: 428)

Two of the other forms of research utilization are not directly about the substance of the findings. The political approach, for example, accepts that many players will have already staked out positions and ideological commitments, therefore political users strategically use research as ammunition. In the process of making a partisan case, they often take it out of context and eliminate the caveats and qualifications around its findings. Advocacy groups and social movements often use research this way, as do politicians. The political use of research gives participants confidence and provides them with an edge in debate. In this sense it has influence.

In the tactical approach what is relevant is the simple fact that research has been done. Public agencies may cite the research they are doing as evidence of their responsiveness or use the fact that they are doing it as a tactic to delay controversy until opponents have lost momentum. They may use it to avoid taking responsibility for unpopular policies, or just for enhancing the prestige of the agency and assuring that researchers will come to their defense if they are challenged. This use may not reflect the aspirations of researchers to shape policy, but it is an influential use.

Research findings probably enter the substantive policy arena most often through their potential to enlighten, according to Weiss. In the enlightenment model it is

> not the findings of a single study, nor even a body of related studies that directly affect policy. Rather it is the concepts and theoretical perspectives that social science research has engendered that permeate the policy-making process.
>
> (Weiss 1977: 429)

Weiss based her conclusion on a survey of decision makers in which she found that, of several criteria, challenge to the status quo was the single most important factor contributing to how they judged the usefulness of the research (Weiss 1977, 1979). Decision makers placed this "enlightenment" factor above research quality, conformity to their own expectations, or action orientation of the results. Respondents did not denigrate problem-solving studies, but placed a higher value on research that shook things up, even if its conclusions were not yet politically feasible. This is a counterintuitive finding for many professionals who try to tailor their information to be immediately practical, though this practicality seldom is enough to make it influential for reasons discussed.

The enlightenment strategy may be a good way to change how decision makers see the issues, but Weiss does not recommend it as a way to get research actually put to work. The diffusion of ideas takes time, and the findings can be conveyed in partial, oversimplified, or even incorrect, ways through media, popularizers, and word of mouth. Sensational research that is done with inadequate data and poorly supported arguments may take center stage because in this broad arena there is little way to screen out what is shoddy. Rather than enlighten, the findings may confuse or mislead. Moreover, by the time the ideas reach their policy audience, if they do at all, they may be out of date and long since contradicted by later research. Nonetheless there is little doubt that research findings from the academy find their way eventually into policy dialogues as participants search around for new ideas to address difficult issues.

Weiss contends, as we do, that the interactive approach is the most likely to lead directly to policy change. The interactive model is most akin to how information plays a part in the collaborative policy processes that we focus on in this book. This involves joint efforts among social scientists, administrators, practitioners, clients, interest groups, and so forth, working on a poorly defined policy issue, where knowledge is lacking or contradictory and ends are not well specified (Christensen 1985). The interactive approach is not linear; it is instead a messy effort going back and forth from goals to data to solutions in an iterative way. The participants engage in a joint process of making sense of a situation in consultation with one another, using one another's knowledge. Weiss recognized what few did at that time that, in the interactive model,

> the use of research is only one part of a complicated process that also uses experience, political insight, pressure, social technologies, and judgment. It has applicability not only to face to face settings, but also to the multiple ways in which intelligence is gathered through intermediaries and brought to bear.

Types of information used in policy making arenas

To understand how information can influence decision makers we start by identifying what information is actually used in practice and how, and by examining the practices and institutional arrangements we now have for the assessment and use of this information. We look at three public policy settings where information is important, the legislative arena, planning agencies, and regulatory/bureaucratic agencies, relying on our studies in the U.S. context. Each looks for different sorts of information from different sources.

The legislative arena

Lobbyists, legislative staff, and politicians recognize four kinds of knowledge as critical when legislation is under consideration.[1] Different players and consultants are recognized as experts in one or another type of knowledge, and savvy advocates make sure to have advisors for each of the four types. To influence decision makers it is first essential to provide substantive information about the issues. For example, if the problem is viewed as uncontrolled growth, substantive knowledge would provide data on where this is occurring and on what scale, along with an analysis of its causes and its consequences for such things as traffic, housing prices. It would include knowledge of what various jurisdictions have done about it and how these strategies worked. This is where academics and formal research play the biggest role, though it is often consultants and lobbyists who translate and distill this research for the policy makers.

The second necessary type of knowledge is about the process that will be used to put the legislation together. Are there several ideas in contention or just one? Will there be meetings or hearings? What committees will deal with this? What are the deadlines? What are the opportunities for influence along the way? These questions draw both on formal knowledge of how federal, state or local government works and informal knowledge about practices that may not be codified, as well as about special plans for addressing the particular issue. Long experience and inside knowledge are important.

The third type of knowledge is about the relationships among the likely players. Who can work with whom and who cannot? Who is supporting whom, and what alliances are there likely to be? Who can influence whom? Are there personal animosities that could be obstacles? Knowledge of this sort comes from direct experience, gossip, and long term professional and personal relationships in the policy arena. It is why lobbyists entertain, attend receptions, play golf, and hang around in state house corridors. Sometimes this knowledge is less about influencing an issue directly than it is about understanding the general lay of the land and building social capital on which the player can draw when needed.

The fourth type of knowledge is purely about politics. How is proposed legislation likely to play in the home districts of the legislators? How will the district reaction affect legislator attitudes, especially for those who do not have safe districts? What about the governor, mayor, or president? Will it be politically beneficial for him or her to sign the legislation into law? Who are the chief executives' most vocal constituents and how are they likely to weigh in on this? Are there power rivalries in the legislature that will affect the proposal?

It should be noted that none of this knowledge is a one-way process from lobbyist or staff to legislators. Instead it is a multiway process, where all the players work to influence one another through various forms of information. Because of the tightly networked nature of these players and their continuing relationships in any given legislative arena, they have to be both honest and accurate in the knowledge they provide. If, for example, an influence broker convinced a legislator that his constituents would be happy if he voted for a bill that in fact was contrary to their preferences, then not only would the broker be persona non grata in the legislator's office, but word of her unreliability would spread throughout the network, interfering with her credibility, effectiveness, and potential to get future lobbying jobs.

Planning agencies: multiple styles in conflict

Planning agencies and the players who try to influence them also use a range of knowledge to make plans, policies, and regulations. These types of information may not be easily reconciled in practice because they can represent differing epistemologies, methods, and purposes. Our study of the Metropolitan Transportation Commission (MTC) (Innes and Gruber 2005; Innes and Gruber 2001) identified four coexisting styles of planning and policy making in and around the agency, each of which used different kinds of information for different purposes, relying on a different implicit epistemology. As Weiss suggests, research reports about substantive policy questions did not play much of a role for any style. Some planners operated primarily in one style, but most moved from one style to another. We believe that the typology we found in this agency's work is relevant to other arenas where there is controversy, public involvement, and a high level of technical knowledge, as well as considerable funding to allocate.

One set of planners operated in a technical, bureaucratic style. Though their training had been in the rational planning mode, doing quantitative analyses of transportation problems, they did not have much opportunity to use these skills on substantive, policy-related research. They did not consider alternatives or evaluate them and make recommendations, as the textbooks suggest. Instead they used their skills primarily to provide information to justify projects that had already been decided on, to prepare the models and forecasts required by funding agencies, and to prove that proposed projects met funding agencies' criteria. They relied almost uniquely on quantitative, "objective" data and information they themselves produced or that was a product of another public agency. They did not trust information from anyone outside government. Their information largely involved approximations and averages extrapolated from government sources. They seldom had the resources or the time to gather their own data. Since such information would not be used to decide whether to take one or another course of action, there was no organizational motivation to gather it. There was motivation, however, to protect the agency from criticism about what they did do and to maximize their future funding. In some sense the data they produced was more protective armor than information to assist policy makers' decisions.

A political planning style was also at work at MTC, primarily practiced by the agency's executive staff, but also by some of the members of the Bay Area Partnership, which was made up of MTC constituent agencies and jurisdictions. The political approach was to work out a transportation plan that all the powerful players would buy into and that would maintain these players' loyalty to the leadership. Therefore the information they wanted was to know which powerful players wanted what and whether they had held up their end of previous agreements. This information was far from systematic. It was generally not quantitative, but qualitative and anecdotal. It was transferred by word of mouth and known primarily to insiders. The executive staff also wanted information on what it would take to sell their plan to the public. Because the plan was a packaging of what the powerful players wanted, rather than a strategy designed to solve transportation problems, it could not be sold in terms of what it would accomplish. Accordingly, with plan in hand, the MTC leadership commissioned marketing studies to see how it could be sold. Because they felt a lot would depend on people's confidence in the organization and on its visibility, they also commissioned research on how to "brand" their organization. They were not interested in the functioning of the regional transportation system, nor in the regional benefits of one policy versus another. They did however need the information produced by the technical bureaucratic planners to legitimize their packages of proposals.

The social movement planners – mostly members of advocacy groups – wanted information to help mobilize support and convince people that their vision of the region's transportation future was the right one. Stories and anecdotes were especially useful for these purposes, and they chose selectively among research findings those which supported their perspective. Information for them was a rallying cry and part of their advocacy strategy. For their confrontations with MTC, they used information strategically, combining qualitative testimonials with selected formal research. They did not trust agency information, which, they felt, was designed to promote the agency's agenda rather than necessarily the public's interest.

Partners and staff did collaborative planning for some tasks, especially right after the passage of The Intermodal Surface Transportation Efficiency Act of 1991 (ISTEA). Collaborative planners wanted information about each others' perspectives. The information that counted for them was what the participants agreed was true. They wanted, for example, to jointly develop their own performance measures and challenge and correct the data and methods used by the staff. They paid attention to stories and personal experience as much as to quantitative data and formal research. Planners in this style were the most likely to want information about how the transportation system was working and what interventions might be most effective. They did not so much use existing studies as seek out new information to answer questions that arose in their dialogue. They were the only planners who wanted information on values (as opposed to wants), and they got into battles with the technical planners over the use of such "subjective" information. They were interested in both problem-framing and problem-solving information as well as in information for monitoring and evaluation, unlike planners in other styles.

Regulatory agencies: informal knowledge and peer review

Agencies that promulgate rules and enforce regulations also need many different knowledges to help them do their job effectively. Some of it is informal insider knowledge about, for example, who the environmental violators are or experiential knowledge about the most effective ways to design or apply regulations. Such agencies also typically rely heavily on findings published in peer reviewed journals because they are the most scientifically acceptable. Because these are widely regarded as not biased by interests or flawed by inadequate methodology, they mesh well with the bureaucratic imperative for routinized, even-handed regulations. Even more importantly, agency bureaucrats see peer reviewed findings as the best protection from lawsuits. However peer reviewed science, as Weiss suggests, tends to be slow in emerging and far from timely in regard to real world events. It tends to make generalizations about categories of events, species, and pollutants based on large samples. Regulations, however, have to be applied in specific places at specific times, often on short notice. The places and problems are apt to be very unlike the average ones described by the science. Often local experts may be called upon in these situations – people who know a place well, perhaps through long years of experience and observation as well as through their own scientific or technical training. But their knowledge is based on a more interpretive epistemology than the positivist model that peer reviewed science typically reflects. These local experts, often consultants or perhaps employees of local agencies, employ a model of knowing akin to Dewey's as they learn through long observation, testing ideas against their experience and seeking to make practical judgments.[2] One of the strengths of CALFED was that its dialogue structure was inclusive of these knowledges, and it managed to get beyond this type of conflict.

How dialogue can make information influential

Here we will offer some examples to illustrate how and why dialogue can be critical to making information influential and how the lack of dialogue may condemn information to obscurity. We look particularly at examples of policy indicators, quantitative measures that have been developed ostensibly to provide guidance to policy makers.

U.S. unemployment indicator: a product of long term dialogue

One of the most influential domestic policy indicators in the U.S. has been the unemployment indicator. The story of how this came to be the case is instructive in showing how and why some information can be designed in a robust and widely acceptable way, while also influencing policy (de Neufville 1975; Innes 1990). It illustrates the importance of meshing information with policy makers' views and needs and demonstrates some of the ways dialogue played a part in designing a robust and useful measure. The design of the unemployment indicator and the methods for producing it were the subjects of years of public dialogue involving diverse players before it was accepted by stakeholders and Congress. Each stakeholder group started with its own unemployment indicator, designed for its own interests and policy objectives and then they engaged in dialogue in many venues from the 1920s well into the 1950s. These included conferences and committees of social scientists, user groups convened by the Bureau of Labor Statistics and the Census Bureau, meetings of the national business organization, the Conference Board, and of labor organizations. In addition, discussion took place in the media, including editorial pages of major newspapers as well as dozens of hearings in Congress, with thousands of pages of testimony from business and labor interests and social scientists. Other dialogues involved scientific and congressional inquiries into the adequacy of the random sampling method used for it, as it had just been developed in the 1930s and was still not widely trusted as accurate or reliable.

These dialogues simultaneously involved ongoing discussion over unemployment policy. Should the government provide support for the unemployed? If so which unemployed? Would the policy include everyone who did not have work? Or just people who had lost jobs? Who would be deserving of support and how could one tell if they actually wanted work and were not simply looking for a handout? Should there be an age limit? How much work would you have to do to be considered employed? What could the Treasury afford and how would the money be raised? What impact would such support have on the economy? It turned out that all these questions were closely connected to how the indicator would be designed. Agreement about the indicator could not be reached until Congress finally developed policies about these issues and created the Social Security and federal unemployment insurance in the late 1930s. The dialogues on indicator design were intrinsic to the development of these policies, as the focus on design forced reflection on policy issues that had been too controversial for discussion.

Eventually in the early 1940s the unemployment indicator was agreed upon and data gathering began at regular intervals. The indicator was reported in the media, and acknowledged by federal policy makers, who were required by law to tell the public what they would do about what the indicator showed. It became institutionalized in the sense that funding for it became a line item in the federal budget, and it was generally accepted as *the* measure of unemployment; a Council of Economic Advisors was set up that would have to prepare a public report on unemployment and other economic conditions; and labor and business organizations stopped producing their own unemployment indicators, instead using the government version. Moreover, economists and social scientists began to use the latter in their models and forecasts. When, during the Kennedy administration, conservatives tried to get rid of the indicator, leading spokespeople from all the interests and the academy defended it. It was much too integral to their work for them to lose it. By this time it had shared meaning and value to most players. It had been produced by a collaboratively rational process.

The unemployment case is a good example of what Tenenbaum and Wildavsky have provocatively argued – that policies control data rather than the other way around (Tenenbaum and Wildavsky 1984). It was only when there was a broad agreement on unemployment policy that there could be agreement on what data would be considered appropriate. Only when there was agreement on the policy could the data be turned into information. The raw numbers had to be constructed into an indicator with a meaning that would square with the decision makers' understandings and point in a policy direction they were willing to go.

Dialogue and research: mobilizing civic entrepreneurs

Dialogue can make the difference between unused and influential indicators and other information; it can resolve differences over data; and it can create shared meaning. The dialogue builds understanding, embeds the information in the context where it is to be used, and molds policy to information, as well as the information to the policy. The dialogue helps to motivate action because it can engage the players very directly. It can take raw data and turn it into information with implications for action. Dialogue over time around the information adapts it and refines it and helps to build broader and deeper shared knowledge on the topic.

The work of California's Collaborative Regional Initiatives (CRIs) illustrates the power of dialogue for linking knowledge and action. These networks of civic entrepreneurs initiated to address public issues that were not being solved by government[3] found that dialogue around research played a major role in their ability to mobilize regional action.[4]

The Sierra Business Council (SBC) joined research and dialogue in their highly successful regional indicator project *Sierra Wealth Index* (Innes and Sandoval 2004), which is now in its third edition.[5] SBC began by developing a set of indicators for the Sierra reflecting the state of the three forms of capital needed for a sustainable region – natural, financial, and social. The staff wanted the indicators to reflect and be grounded in the experience of the region so they used an advisory group, representing civic leaders with different perspectives, to discuss and help prepare the first report. SBC rolled it out at a series of well attended forums involving dialogues among a substantial cross-section of civic leaders about the meanings and implications of the indicators. It organized more dialogues at the annual conference and incorporated exploration of the indicators into their collaborative leadership training program. The *Index* became a widely read and influential document, helping leaders in various sectors throughout the region to see that the natural environment and the economy were linked and that they could not pursue one without protecting the other. SBC used a similar strategy with other reports, including *Planning for Prosperity,* which laid out exemplars of sustainable land use and became the basis for Placer Legacy,[6] a program which set aside thousands of acres for habitat and open space and prepared a long term plan for a sustainable county. In these processes regional leaders not only jointly learned about the nature of the issues and integrated the information into their understandings and knowledge, but they also became committed to action to improve the environment.

The San Diego Dialogue (SDD) similarly relied on communities of inquiry to decide what information they needed, what it meant and how it would become part of public decision making. This group, which was based in the University of California San Diego (UCSD), gathered powerful elites and leaders for dialogues about the issues facing the region. This CRI was grounded in the idea of generating and using information through dialogue. Members identified issues needing action, and staff commissioned studies by UCSD researchers on these. Staff brought the findings back for further dialogue among members. SDD used dialogue to help key players understand the implications of data and become motivated to act on it (Christensen and Rongerude 2004). While SDD itself was not empowered to take political action because it was part of a public university, its well-connected members were not bound this way, and some of them mobilized to get policy change. For example, the Dialogue began with a focus on the regional economy and how to keep it healthy. To address this question staff commissioned a study of people crossing the border into and out of Mexico and learned that many of them were frequent crossers. They then developed research that demonstrated that San Diego was a funda-mentally cross-border economy with the Tijuana region. These civic leaders began to build relationships with leaders across the border and were instrumental in getting the U.S. government to set up a special lane for frequent crossers. A similar lane was later set up at the Vancouver crossing into Canada.

Blending science and policy

Integrating scientific information into policy and management documents is a challenge due to the very different purposes and framing of scientific information and of man-agement information. Dialogue can help with this however. A case in point was in the collaborative San Francisco Estuary Project (Innes and Connick 1999), mentioned in

Chapter 5, where scientists and technical planners prepared the required status and trends report on conditions in the Estuary. The managers from the decision making agencies refused to publish the report unless it included appropriate management options. At first the scientists resisted this, saying these were policy issues and not their bailiwick. They wanted a pure science report, not tainted by politics and the pragmatics of management. The managers prevailed, and a collaborative committee including both scientists and managers spent another year preparing these management options. Managers did not want to document negative trends publicly without having a strategy prepared if action were demanded. Eventually it became clear to both that the meaning of the trends had to be understood in the light of possible actions and policies.

At MTC, however, such integration proved more elusive, almost certainly because the agency was not using much stakeholder dialogue. A big issue for public advocates in transportation planning, for example, is the reporting of performance measures. When they demanded that the agency report certain key indicators such as vehicle miles traveled (VMT), the agency balked. Like the managers in the Estuary project, staff said they did not want indicators published that referred to matters they could not control. Eventually, in response to continuing demands for performance measures, MTC hired a consultant to develop measures, but then only adopted those that fitted its agenda. In this they were like the congressmen who would not agree on an unemployment measure until they were prepared to accept its policy implications.

Developing community indicators with dialogue

The William and Flora Hewlett Foundation selected a troubled and poor minority neighborhood in Oakland California to receive more than $7 million over seven years to support a new Neighborhood Improvement Initiative (NII). Their stated objective was to empower the neighborhood to take charge and start addressing its own problems. The neighborhood residents decided on an elected NII board, and the Foundation selected the University of California Berkeley's Institute of Urban and Regional Development (IURD), under the direction of author Innes, as the technical assistance partner. Students and faculty helped the NII board prepare a neighborhood plan and began work with community members on possible projects. Part of the Institute's obligation was to develop indicators for the neighborhood. The Foundation offered no guidelines for this task, and this ambiguity was to lead to conflict. Innes interpreted the mandate as being about helping the people in the community to work through their own priorities and policies, and she applied her model of indicator development through dialogue embedded in the policy making process.

Trying to develop indicators for local decision making was a challenge because most community members had little experience with policy issues and little faith in the idea they could make a difference. Most struggled first and foremost to deal with the daily problems of families and making a living. The idea of indicators at best seemed to them irrelevant – at worst intimidating. Students and staff searched for data that was readily obtainable, that could be linked to the priorities the NII board had established, and that could be collected over time with limited resources. They then worked through community dialogues to select indicators that were meaningful to local people and pertinent to the priorities they had established in the plan. In the end a committee of local residents was able to agree on a set of simple, understandable indicators, including such things as asthma rates and high school graduation rates as compared to the rest of the city. The Institute prepared an illustrated book (7th St McClymonds Corridor Neighborhood Improvement Initiative, 2001), describing the indicators and their meaning.

This report made evident to community leaders that their neighborhood was suffering on many dimensions, from health to housing to education, at significantly higher rates than the rest of the city. These were problems for which the residents could not be blamed, and the indicators gave community members power and leverage they had not had before. These indicators had meaning in the neighborhood and accordingly had impacts. NII board members became angry as they learned about the indicators, especially the low high school graduation rates, and they publicized this indicator widely. This negative publicity pressured the high school principal to make some changes (though in the course of events she expressed her anger against Institute staff for giving the high school bad publicity). This new visibility for the high school's problems prompted both UC Berkeley's Chancellor and the Oakland School Board to give priority to improving this school. Two West Oakland artists seized on the indicators as part of their battle against gentrification of the neighborhood. They created an installation in their gallery with all the indicators in neon around the room, along with photos designed to show potential newcomers how undesirable the neighborhood was. The indicators helped neighborhood leaders to get a broad perspective on their own situation that in itself was empowering. Residents had tended to blame themselves for their problems, but the indicators demonstrated that the problems were systemic and lay in the institutions and in the way they were treated by the agencies, school district, and city. They could see they were not getting social or environmental justice and could accordingly more legitimately make demands on the system.[7]

The Hewlett Foundation was not interested in the empowering aspects of the indicators, oddly since the ostensible purpose of the project was self-managed neighborhood regeneration. Nor did it subscribe to the idea of indicators developed through dialogue. Instead, about three years into the seven-year project, without consultation, the Foundation decided IURD would have to gather data for standardized indicators designed by their consultant and used in their two other NII projects in the region. These indicators had little to do with what the West Oakland neighborhood was doing. They were one-size-fits-all or perhaps one-size-fits-no-one. This new demand was disempowering to the community, which already had the indicators it wanted – the ones that linked to their objectives and that had already helped to develop priorities for action. Foundation leadership apparently thought that their indicators would help maintain control over West Oakland activities and demonstrate outcomes for the Foundation board. The indicators they proposed were too broad, generic and area-based to offer insights about specific projects or policies, much less to manage the NII. Shortly after this directive the

Foundation abruptly discontinued the West Oakland NII, saving IURD from engaging in this futile task.[8]

Scientific conflicts

Many planning and policy debates revolve around scientific information that points in different directions. These conflicts can be highly disturbing to policy makers and the public, who often hope science will offer them certainty. The net effect can be a loss of public trust in science and a general skepticism about its value, as well as increasing difficulty in using scientific findings where they are most needed. If scientists cannot agree, the thinking goes, how can the layman know what to believe?

There are many reasons experts disagree, even if all are applying the highest standards of research (Ozawa and Susskind 1987; Ozawa 1991). Some disagreements are due to the design of research itself. Scientists use different hypotheses, focus on different variables, gather data in different ways from different sources, make different assumptions, or use different models of inference. No research can be designed without applying assumptions about what is important, about how to estimate unmeasured variables or future conditions, or about the dynamics of a particular situation. Experts apply frames to help them design research, and these too may differ. Their interpretations of findings may differ, even when all agree on the validity of the results. Uncertainty is an additional major factor in disagreements. Finally, translation of findings to humans is uncertain. Scientific testing of drugs or chemicals on animals cannot replicate the actual conditions humans face. Rigorous scientific research findings are of the form, "if these conditions apply, this action will produce this result" or "Does substance X induce cancer in laboratory animals and at what level of probability?" In the real world, however, the exact conditions seldom apply, and policy questions are of the form "Should substance x be banned from human consumption?" When scientists answer the latter question – which some do – they are stepping out of their research role into a political one.

This situation leaves plenty of room for scientists' personal policy preferences or institutional loyalties to play a part in their conclusions and advice to policy makers. It has created the phenomenon of advocacy science, as scientists may focus on findings that support their organization's interest. Scientists enter the fray representing environmental advocacy groups or regulatory agencies with environmental responsibilities, while others represent agencies with an interest in economic issues, and yet others may be consultants for housing developers or water purveyors. All are likely to come up with differing findings or differing interpretations of similar data. Scientists have plenty of blanks to fill in and plenty of discretionary decisions to make. When data are inconclusive, some scientists may express their allegiances by emphasizing the lack of evidence for an opposing view, rather than making clear for example that the inconclusiveness applies to all positions. They might choose measurements that emphasize the negative aspects of an issue, perhaps raising cancer concerns even when risk probabilities are small. The trouble with advocacy science is that it provides no way for policy makers to assess it, so it cannot advance a policy dialogue. The findings may be influenced by the tacit loyalties of the scientist, but that does not mean that the results are incorrect or that scientists falsify data or deliberately bias their findings. Policy decisions based on some science while ignoring competing science are unlikely to be robust or withstand legal and political challenges. It was for this reason that CALFED established an Independent Science Board to work through what was the soundest science they could identify about the many technical issues they faced in water management.

Institutional models for addressing scientific conflict

At least four institutional models are available to address scientific conflicts in the policy world.

Executive decision

The traditional approach has been to simply make an executive decision – to assert that the government's experts are right. President George W. Bush for example, in the face of competing evidence, sided with those who claimed Iraq had weapons of mass destruction. Similarly, he contended for a long time that there was inadequate evidence of climate change. This strategy of executive decision might have worked decades before globalization, improvements in communications, and the proliferation of sophisticated cadres of people around the world. In the twenty-first century, however, it was not long before both these assertions were widely challenged. Power in an interconnected world does not trump information. Challenges to inadequate information are made through the media and public opinion, through high profile experts, in the legislatures, and through lawsuits. The executive model of deciding on the adequacy of information is increasingly ineffective in democratized societies.

Adjudication

A fallback institution has been adversarial, where decisions about what is accurate are made through judicial or quasi-judicial administrative processes or in the court of public opinion. In formal courts, experts representing opposing interests and agencies present their findings, typically in a hearing-like setting, guided by attorneys. The process includes cross-examinations and formal depositions. Each side tries to discredit the other's expert witnesses, sometimes by finding errors in their scholarly articles or exposing who pays them, suggesting they are either careless or biased. Topics are strictly limited to what is pertinent to the case, and participants withhold information not helpful to their side. While some interaction and questions and answers may take place, it is far from the free ranging dialogue described in Chapter 5.

An example is the environmental impact review (EIR) process in California. All major development proposals must undergo this review, which lays out what kinds of impacts should be examined. A consultant typically prepares a draft EIR, and public agencies and stakeholders comment in public hearings and written statements on the predicted impacts and on the data and methods. At some point, perhaps months later, the agency formally responds to the comments, though there is no opportunity for those who made a comment to reply. There is no face to face, multiway dialogue. Sometimes the most politically significant issue with a proposed development is not covered by the official categories, and anyone who brings up the issue is declared out of order.

The advantage of such adversarial processes is that they do result in a decision and action. The disadvantages are that they may ignore relevant public concerns; they result in winners and losers; and they seldom offer the opportunity to achieve an agreement that benefits both sides. As a result the resolution may not be durable. Ill will may prevail as the losers bring further lawsuits challenging the decision or seize the next opportunity to challenge a choice. No agreed-upon body of knowledge emerges from such processes and no future working relationships among the participants. The knowledge itself in any case is verified only by the credibility of witnesses, rather than by peer review, an informed community of inquiry, or even a consensus among experts.

Blue ribbon panels

Another procedure is to set up a blue ribbon panel to seek consensus on the facts of the situation and provide reports and conclusions to policy makers. A blue ribbon panel may be diverse in the perspectives and disciplines it represents, though not always, as it is not a stakeholder group. It is made up of individuals who are respected and recognized and whose opinions should therefore carry weight. If these individuals can agree, as the theory goes, its conclusions can be viewed as accurate. This is the idea behind presidential commissions in the U.S., which have looked at such issues as poverty, housing, and intelligence failures. Sometimes panels of scientists like CALFED's Independent Science Board may be established. The Sierra Business Council set up a similar board of scientists to assist in the development of Placer Legacy's habitat conservation and open space strategies.

While such boards often produce high quality findings, the track record for implementing their recommendations has not been good. These may stir up public debate, but often the ideas fall by the wayside as public attention may have already turned to new issues during the one- or two-year inquiry. Such boards are not normally made up of stakeholders or people who can implement proposals or act on the information. Indeed the effectiveness of the panel is seen to depend on members' distance from the political fray. This can, however, be a recipe for inaction. These are not the engaged players who have a stake and a direct role in potential change. Moreover, they typically conduct their deliberations just among themselves, perhaps with formal presentations by the key actors about the issues and question and answer sessions with them. Thus such a board is not in a position to get the kind of widespread buy-in to the findings that was achieved in the unemployment indicator case with its long period of engagement with the key actors in the economy. The members of the National Commission on Terrorist Attacks,[9] recognizing this, went out personally to "sell" their conclusions to lawmakers and the public.

Joint fact finding

Joint fact finding is the label that has been given to collaborative ways of deciding on information (Karl, et al. 2007; Susskind, et al. 1999). It ranges from mediations among scientists to collaborative efforts including experts, stakeholders and perhaps decision makers. Reaching agreement in such forums has become an important part of resolving many policy disputes (Ozawa 1991). Federal regulatory agencies, particularly EPA, for example, have employed negotiations in the development of their regulations process (Susskind and MacMahon 1985). They do this recognizing that a regulation may depend for its effectiveness on fitting into the operation of the business. Moreover, it is likely to be more effective if it has the upfront acceptance of key industry and consumer organizations. It is also less likely to be challenged in the courts. Local and regional agencies also engage in informal negotiation over rules or permits. For example the Regional Water Quality Board in the San Francisco Bay Area has negotiated with localities over what their targets should be for reducing pollution going into the Bay and over their plans to make pollution reductions. Similarly, the Bay Conservation and Development Commission (BCDC), which regulates development on the San Francisco Bay shore, negotiates over permits with potential developers rather than applying rigid rules. This negotiation can result in the developer's improving the proposal from the perspective of BCDC criteria, while at the same time offering developers attractive alternatives. Such negotiations have forestalled lawsuits and public controversy over the agency's more than 40-year life.[10]

The term joint fact finding is in some respects a misnomer as it belies the full implications of this activity. It is far more than fact finding, or perhaps less. This term implies that the practice is built on scientific or positivist principles and that facts are objective things out there. In practice, joint fact finding is built on a social constructivist view of knowledge. The process weeds out dubious findings, uncovers assumptions, identifies biases, and dismisses unsupported claims. In the end truth is what the group decides it is. It is not just about "facts" but about relationships, causes, predictions. It is about "truth" deeply embedded in a context, a time and a place. Sometimes it involves reframing. Often competing information turns out not to be in conflict, but simply to have different emphasis, focus, or frame. Agreeing on information involves developing a shared frame. Both the Water Forum and CALFED engaged in significant joint fact finding over water supplies, impacts on fish and the effects of water flows.

Moreover, as the first part of this chapter suggests, the development of the information goes hand in hand with the development of the policy. Policy makers do not want to publish information that suggests problems unless they have a way to tackle the problems. Therefore the discussion with stakeholders is jointly about the data and its implications. Indeed the discussion of the data can often be a benign way to discuss contentious policy issues and resolve the differences over the information. An indicator design can be tantamount to reaching a policy conclusion. Systematic joint fact finding can also build many types of capacity for planning and policy decisions. They can build intellectual capacity in a community of players and create agreed on data bases as well as build social capital, networks, communication skills, and political capital. We offer several examples in the next sections to illustrate how joint fact finding can work.

Case examples of joint fact finding

Stakeholders and consultants do joint fact finding in the Water Forum

One approach to joint fact finding is the strategy exemplified in the Water Forum (Connick 2003). The stakeholders agreed on a set of technical consultants and gave them research tasks tailored to the group's mission. These individuals worked in an interactive way with stakeholders, checking in regularly. They gathered data, produced analyses and models, and reported with explanations of what they had done and why. Stakeholders, sometimes with the assistance of their own experts, asked questions about assumptions and parameters and elements of the analyses that could cause differences in estimates among experts. The experts often went back to the drawing board to revise their analyses or to answer new questions. Such experts need communication skills and respect for the stakeholders' views and concerns to do this work. Their job is not only to provide information, but also to learn from and with the stakeholders. In a sense they join in a community of inquiry with the stakeholders.

If such a process is properly conducted, the information is likely to be more robust than data that is produced simply through expert analysis. In the Water Forum, for example, the U.S. Bureau of Reclamation, using their experts and their models, predicted how much water would be available for the Lower American River. Stakeholders' experts discovered an error of 800,000 acre feet in Bureau estimates.[11] This was a massive discrepancy, and it threw the Forum into temporary chaos. The stakeholders demanded that Bureau analysts correct their estimates. At first Bureau analysts resisted, saying it was not a significant error − at least not on the scale they usually worked − but on the scale of the Water Forum it was very large. Eventually the Forum created a dialogue among the Bureau managers and experts and stakeholder experts, and the Bureau eventually changed its numbers.

High level scientific deliberations: the New York Bight[12]

In one of the earliest efforts to explicitly apply joint fact finding to highly science-intensive issues, the New York Bight Initiative sought to manage pollutants in "one of the most stressed marine ecosystems in the United States, the ocean region adjacent to New York Harbor" (McCreary 1999; Mandanaro 2005). The effort was sponsored by the New York Academy of Sciences, a nonpartisan and respected organization of scientists and took place from 1986 to 1988. It involved direct dialogue among a panel of scientists and a plenary negotiating group of 22 resource managers, users, and other stakeholders; a joint fact finding effort to review and present relevant technical information and evaluate the technical consequences of policy alternatives; and mediated negotiation of an 80-page single text document.

The group had to begin with the most basic questions, like whether or not the Bight was stressed, whether there was a need for a restoration and management strategy, and what issues should be addressed first. One of the first steps was to poll 100 resource users and managers, asking them to rank in order their top five issues from a list of 23 issues. In particular, they were asked to consider whether a given issue was pressing and characterized by scientific disagreement and whether it might be clarified or resolved through dialogue. It is telling that the original list was very long and that the issues ranged so widely across environmental and health concerns and identification of contaminants by source. This story shows how much potential controversy there can be just around the choice of focus and how infeasible it would be to address all the issues that stakeholders might have. It also shows how important it is to get agreement up front on the choices.

After lengthy discussion the group chose polychlorinated biphenyls (PCBs)[13] as their focus out of the many contaminants, and staff began to recruit scientists from those named by respondents to find those with necessary expertise. This task was made easier by the Academy's strong scientific reputation. Once the process got started, facilitators had a number of challenges, including assuring that the managers could make sense of and use the scientists' research findings. This would involve trying to bridge the cultural/epistemological gap between the two groups. Staff had to get the scientists to simplify their presentations for communication with a broad audience and avoid undermining their credibility by making the usual academic caveats about the certainty of their results. They had to get the scientists to think about implications for policy action rather than solely for more research. The many tasks included:

1   documenting and illustrating PCB movement through the ecosystem;
2   summarizing the existing regulatory framework;
3   dealing with which side has the burden of proof;
4   determining whether laboratory studies of biological effects are relevant to what is observed in the field;
5   clarifying and narrowing areas of disagreement; and
6   creating and ratifying an agreement.

After 2 years 18 of the 22 stakeholder experts agreed on recommendations, not including the Environmental Defense Fund and the chemical industry coalition at opposite ends of the spectrum. The compilation and synthesis of information they produced played a part in the acceptance of the New York Bight into the National Estuary Program, in which it would get federal attention. Many of the recommendations were pursued by various public agencies. The process model the group used informed later joint fact finding efforts as well as the practice of other negotiators and technical advisors. Last and far from least, the New York Bight process built personal and professional networks which continue to play a part in water management issues in the region. The New York Academy of Science has continued its institutional sponsorship of scientific dialogues pertaining to the estuary. This carefully planned and managed joint fact finding effort has resulted in social learning capacity building and the creation of social, intellectual and institutional capital.

Achieving scientific consensus through facilitation in the San Francisco Estuary Project (SFEP)[14]

The scientific consensus that was achieved in the San Francisco Estuary Project became the basis of the policy that emerged from the process in 1992 and remains a powerful component in statewide water management. It was remarkable because not only did the scientists represent competing agencies and interests, but the consensus that emerged was one that pointed toward a highly controversial policy of increasing water flows to the environment and away from other uses. This project, briefly described in Chapter 5, was a five-year collaborative effort under the auspices of the U.S. EPA, to develop a comprehensive conservation and management plan (CCMP) to protect biodiversity in the San Francisco Estuary. This estuary stretches from the Pacific Ocean back a hundred miles through a delta of islands, levees and wetlands to the city of Sacramento. It is central to the vast system of waterways that provide two-thirds of the state's water to farms, urban areas and fisheries. Its Management Committee was made up of diverse stakeholders, many of whom had long been bitter opponents on conservation and development issues. It included individuals from the major agencies with divergent, or even conflicting, responsibilities, ranging from the state Department of Water Resources, whose major constituency was farmers, to the federal Department of Fish and Wildlife, which concerned itself with the health of fish and endangered species. It also included representatives of activist environmental groups, realtors, and building interests, farmers, and local governments. Most of these had scientific advisors, many of whom served on the Technical Advisory Committee.

After years of dialogue no indicator species were identified that would provide a simple way to test the health of the estuary, as all reacted differently to pollutants and conditions. Some potential solutions would affect one set of stakeholders adversely and others would affect other interests. There was no simple answer, but the need to protect the fish species and the ecology remained. The estuary was a highly complex system with many interconnected parts and the CCMP would require a strategy that could deal with the systemic issues. The group needed to find a scientific consensus on how the Estuary could support biodiversity in ways that could be acceptable to all interests.

The SFEP organized two facilitated weekend dialogues among scientists representing the many different agencies and interests. The agencies sent off their scientists with instructions to reach an agreement. After two weekends almost all finally were able to agree that a measure of the salinity at a certain location in the Estuary would be the preferred indicator of its biodiversity potential. If this spot had an appropriate mix of saline and fresh water, they agreed it would provide the best conditions for maintenance of biodiversity in the Estuary as a whole.[15] This location of the salinity mix could be manipulated by increasing freshwater flows from the dams into the estuary instead of off to farms and homes. The only scientist who did not agree came from the state Department of Water Resources (DWR), which was resistant to releasing water into the Estuary that would otherwise go to farms, the principal constituency of DWR.

This consensus represented a reframing of the scientific question from the search for an indicator of a particular species or pollutant to the search for a measure of the system. It is difficult for anyone, including scientists, to give up allegiances and ways of seeing, but if the conditions of collaboratively rational dialogue are established, as they were in this case, and if scientists have a shared concern about a problem, they may be able to reach agreement through reframing. It is testimony to the power of scientific consensus that the federal government quickly adopted the salinity indicator, later known as X2, as its criterion for estuary health. Once this indicator was accepted by most stakeholders, federal agencies decided to apply it. In turn the state ended up having to release water into the estuary, despite a reluctant governor who was concerned about the powerful agricultural lobby which felt water was their entitlement. This policy represented a sea change in California water management and played a major part in both the Water Forum and CALFED.

Joint fact finding and adaptive management in CALFED

Many of the tasks CALFED worked on (see Chapter 3), ranging from ecosystem restoration to levee system integrity, engaged diverse stakeholders, staff, and experts in collaborative fact finding. Effective management of water operations is dependent on reliable, timely, and accepted information. Before CALFED began information in the water arena was often contested and operations proposals challenged in lawsuits. The operation of California's vast infrastructure of dams and channels, and the pumping operations and water releases from reservoirs is tightly linked with the protection of fish. Federal law makes it illegal for anyone to harm individual fish of a species listed as endangered, though some "incidental" take is permitted. Protecting these species is a complex task requiring adaptation to changing water and weather conditions and fishery health. The Winter Run Chinook Salmon, for example, migrates twice in its life cycle through the San Francisco Bay Delta, and the Delta smelt lives its life there. Both fish typically are entrained in considerable numbers at water pumping facilities at different times of year. Environmental agencies could, if they felt conditions warranted, at any time simply shut down the pumps that sent water to the farmers or to water districts. But at the same time the law requires the release of water to those with water rights. Moreover agriculture, one of California's most significant industries, requires predictability in its water supply. There is no simple solution.

CALFED established several interlinked task groups to manage water while minimizing the disruptions. The Operations Group (Ops) included representatives of the agencies that supply water and the agencies with the responsibility for protecting fish and wildlife, along with environmental stakeholders, water utilities, and representatives of EPA, among others. The group consolidated other collaborative efforts with the intention of making sure all agencies were working off the same information base. The idea was to permit the agencies to make real-time operational decisions for water supply and environmental protection rather than follow the slow and cumbersome regulatory procedures of the past, which had been subject to protest and conflict among players representing opposing interests. Decisions about water operations had seldom been timely and were often out of date by the time they were implemented.

Much of the joint fact finding was done by the Data Assessment Team (DAT) made up of staff from the agencies on Ops and stakeholders. This group analyzed data about endangered fish in the Delta, hydrology and project operations. It met weekly by conference call, involving people around the state. Sometimes the group used stakeholders' local knowledge about the depth of streams or location and size of fish kills. It sometimes arranged conference calls on a few hours' notice, if conditions seemed to demand urgent action. Then it made recommendations to Ops about proposed actions, which were normally ratified by the leadership and implemented by the agencies. This was a remarkably effective approach to water management as it meant decisions were timely, and there was little of the usual conflict. Interests knew their representatives had participated, shared knowledge, and jointly decided on a course of action.

The power of this joint fact finding approach was never clearer than on one occasion when the group made what turned out to be a bad decision. In fear of impending drought conditions, it recommended closure of the Cross Delta Channel to allow more water to flow into the Delta. It turned out that rain came shortly afterwards, and the channel closure had been premature. All the participants in the Ops group, however, including the powerful Los Angeles Metropolitan Water District, which was significantly harmed by the decision, testified that though the result was unsatisfactory, the process was right. Though it was a mistake in judgment, it was one in which they all shared. There was no blame to go around and divide CALFED players. If anything, the mistake seemed to strengthen CALFED as participants recognized their shared interest in collaboration around developing the facts and making the operations decisions.

Out of this operations management effort grew an innovative program known as the Environmental Water Account (EWA) (Brandt 2002) also heavily dependent on joint fact finding. This was a water banking program to provide water for the fish when needed, but which would also allow borrowing and lending water among users to provide more reliability in the water supply for all needs. The idea was to provide protection to endangered fish in the Bay Delta estuary while minimizing harm to those who contract for water. EWA works through a flexible account of water assets set aside for environmental purposes. The program acquires water or rights to water that are kept track of in the account. When management agencies modify the operations of the projects to protect the fish, they use EWA assets to compensate the projects for any reduction in the water. This "float" of water that does not have to be repaid immediately was what allowed EWA to increase the reliability of water supply.[16] Managing this system required timely inputs of data on water conditions and fishery health and much more. The EWA in 2002–03 had an annual budget of $50 million to buy water and storage from willing sellers. But the price depended on where the water was, how much it would cost to move, and how much to store it. To budget for EWA requires understanding of hydrology, water rights law, fish biology, engineering, and even the electricity market for hydroelectric power. It is clearly a case where multidisciplinary inquiry was needed. As agency staff and stakeholders tried to work out the practical aspects, they turned to modeling exercises and games, using data on hydrology, project operations, and fish populations from past years to experiment with different ways of managing the system and to test different interventions.

An independent review of the EWA outlined some of its benefits,[17] which went well beyond merely moving water around and perhaps saving some fish.[18] It involved substantial social learning and capacity building and changed the players themselves. The review said,

> The engineers and scientists who participated in the gaming developed an understanding of the water system as a whole that went well beyond the understanding each of them had brought to the process as individuals. The games showed them tangible examples of the interconnections between water supply activities and fish population. One participant . . . said "all of a sudden it made it seem more real to people. Because instead of talking about this list of assets that could mean nothing potentially, once you started plugging them into these models and looking at how that changed management in the system, then people started perking up, and people realized, OK we mean business here." [19]

The review concluded that EWA had done an effective job of assuring water supply reliability to the water contractors, while concomitantly providing an acceptable level of fish protection likely higher than could have been attained by fixed standards. Agencies and stakeholders who had feuded over how to protect endangered fish learned to work together to provide water for fish protection. Fishery management agencies came to better understand the perspectives and needs of operating agencies, while these agencies became more cognizant of fisheries' needs. Further, the relationships between water contractors, farmers, and environmental groups appeared to be improved. EWA had helped make timely, reasonable decisions in the presence of scientific uncertainty. It had advanced scientific knowledge, for example, in understanding Delta smelt ecology. This led to constructive scientific debate on alternative hypotheses on the smelt life cycle and on temporal and spatial variation in mortality rates. Salmon spawning estimates were improved. New insights were incorporated into alternative models, which in turn fueled further critical and creative thinking.

Expert vs. Collaborative problem-solving: reframing technical issues to reflect practical realities

In another example, a joint fact finding process including a variety of experts and stakeholders created a feasible strategy for cleaning up a hazardous waste site on environmentally fragile Cape Cod after an expert-based, instrumentally rational approach produced an infeasible and inappropriate solution (Scher 1999). The Cape is a low-lying hook of land and dunes curling around Massachusetts Bay, where 34 acres have been used as a major military reservation for over 50 years. This area was saturated with so many toxins that it became a Superfund site, a designation reserved for the very worst of the brownfields in the United States. Motor fuels, solvents, acids, chemicals and other waste had leached into the sandy soils and into the aquifer that provided drinking water for much of the Cape. In the late 1970s the municipal well in Falmouth began foaming like a dishwasher and private wells also became unusable. By 1986 the Department of Defense was conducting a full scale inquiry, identifying multiple sources of pollution and ultimately seven plumes of groundwater contamination.

The Department hired an engineering contractor to design a solution. The contractor focused on the contaminated plumes and took on the goal of total and simultaneous containment. Containment was something the contractors knew how to do. They developed a "pump and treat" plan that would pump the water out of wells, treat it, and re-inject the treated water. Many residents felt this committed the military to cleaning up the water, and the military felt this goal would ensure public support.

This design proposal, however, met with strong opposition. The strategy would involve pumping 27 million gallons of groundwater per day, more than the entire Cape pumped for its daily needs. Environmentalists contended it would threaten ecological disaster by drying up wetlands. Ponds popular for recreation would become mudflats. Salt water would intrude into the aquifer. The military had given an engineering firm a mandate to come up with a fix to the problem, so unsurprisingly the firm had defined both problem and solution narrowly. The military stopped work on the design, and there was agreement that the cure was worse than the disease.

In response to this crisis, in 1996 the Department of Defense, EPA, and the state Department of Environmental Protection established the Technical Review and Evaluation Team (TRET), a collaborative, multidisciplinary group. TRET represented a new project design approach in which stakeholders could "sort through complex, incomplete, and sometimes inconsistent information and find a technically and politically acceptable way forward. [It] served as an ad hoc think tank, an incubator for the formulation of new ideas and reformulation of old ones." Members of the team interacted with public representatives throughout their deliberative process. Their goal was a more complex and situated one than the one the original contractors took on: to provide "a viable plume containment project that meets [military] regulatory and community acceptance, without delaying the schedule. . ." and which would clean the plumes without "unacceptable impacts to the environment" (Scher 1999: 866). The goal in this case was framed in pragmatic terms rather than absolutes. The new process created an inclusive community of inquiry.

The TRET met day in and day out in their own separate building, where they could talk informally and hash out ideas. They were assisted by a team of facilitators and, as they talked, they began to understand their colleagues' points of view and to look for ways of addressing everyone's concerns. They met with representatives of the interests in the adjacent towns and engaged with them as well as with the broader public, using a kind of tiered approach to organizing communications. In this detailed set of dialogues they learned that each plume was different and would require different treatment. The final report recommended that each plume be dealt with singly, while recognizing the interconnections among plumes. The report advised working incrementally and learning as they went, very much in the spirit of Dewey's pragmatism.

Ironically it was this collaborative inquiry that built credibility for the military cleanup effort, in contrast to the rational, expert model which lost support and credibility, according to survey of participants. The joint fact finding and the unusually informal, inclusive dialogue helped assure that key issues were identified, multiple forms of knowledge came into play, and understanding of the technical, environmental, and community issues was shared.

Conclusion

We have contended here that simply conducting formal research on a problem and giving it to decision makers seldom influences them to do what the research seems to imply. The research may have a variety of functions, but informing decisions is not necessarily one of them. Our theory is that for knowledge to be influential in public action, it must be built and interpreted through inclusive dialogue so it meshes with understandings of the players. It can become influential in part because players learn and come to understand it and its implications, in part because it can come to have shared meaning and contextual relevance, and in part because learning about it can change the players themselves, what they want and how they think they can achieve it. The information must be collectively processed for it to become relevant and motivate action. Dialogue is critical because actionable information must be linked to a frame that is meaningful and salient to policy makers. Thus the city council member trying to decide on a new stop sign will pay selective attention to the information she has access to, depending on whether she regards it as a safety measure or a way of placating constituents. Some of the most intractable controversies in public policy are difficult to resolve exactly because people are using different frames (Schon and Rein 1994). Information must also be discussed among those with different perspectives or they will not accept it as accurate, meaningful or relevant, and they will not act on it. The time honored forms of fact finding and dealing with conflicting information have only had limited success in terms of resolving issues or practical results. Joint fact finding offers promise for dealing with complex and controversial issues, particularly where there is high technical content. Chapter 7 moves to the importance of inclusion and local knowledge in joint fact finding.

Notes

1   These observations are grounded in author Booher's 20 years of experiences as a lobbyist in California.

2   Goldstein's study of competing experts in habitat conservation planning in California illustrates well the conflict between agency scientists and local experts (Goldstein 2004). In this case they were unable to engage in authentic dialogue and the differences were never resolved.

3   See California Center for Regional Leadership (www.calregions.org) for an overview of these CRIs. Much of this section is built on our cross-cutting evaluation of the CRI program (Innes and Rongerude 2005).

4   BAASC was a CRI which did not use much dialogue and we attribute its failure to produce major outcomes to this fact.

5   www.sbcouncil.org/Publications/State-of-the-Sierra-Report-2007

6   www.sbcouncil.org/Projects/Placer-Legacy

7   This whole strategy for indicators emerged from the Oakland Indicators Project, a collaborative effort by the Pacific Institute, Urban Strategies Council and the Institute of Urban and Regional Development. Innes and Victor Rubin played key roles in developing the interactive dialogic model for designing the indicators. The strategy was also used by Innes' students to develop a widely used report on local environmental indicators to promote the cause of environmental justice.

8   The reasons for this abrupt end to the West Oakland and Hewlett's other two NII projects are too complex to explain here but they have much to do with a large cultural distance between the neighborhoods and the Foundation and a sense in the Foundation that they did not have the control they felt they should. A Hewlett report provides their analysis (www.hewlett.org/Archives/NII).

9   www.govinfo.library.unt.edu/911/report/index.htm

10   Speech by Will Travis, Executive Director of BCDC for the Delta Vision Assessment Team, Sacramento CA, October 2007.

11   The amount of water that would cover 800,000 acres to a one foot depth.

12   This account is taken primarily from McCreary (1999).

13   These are common pollutants found in many products in the past. While they are now banned in the U.S. because of the harm they do, PCBs are persistent in the environment and accumulate in animals over time.

14   Innes followed the last year of this process and did extensive interviews with participants (Innes 1994b). She and Sarah Connick prepared an updated and somewhat shorter version for the Consensus Building Handbook (Innes and Connick 1999).

15   There was disagreement about the exact location, but not about the idea that a mix of saline and fresh water was critical to the maintenance of biodiversity.

16   It should be noted that while observers appear to agree EWA was helpful in making the water supply more reliable for users, many believe it did not help the fish very much. The jury is out on this, but since not much funding or "environmental water" was provided, its ability to protect the fish was limited.

17   Review of the 2003–04 Environmental Water Account (EWA) submitted by the 2004 EWA Review Panel, 1/17/05.

18   At this writing it is too early to assess the impact of EWA on the fish as fish populations fluctuate widely over long periods and as other factors are currently decreasing a number of key species.

19   Page 47 of the review noted in endnote 17.

Using local knowledge for justice and resilience   7

The importance of local knowledge

In this chapter we make the case for seeking out and explicitly incorporating local and other lay knowledge into planning and public processes because inclusion of such knowledge is critical, not only to social and environmental justice, but also to resilience of our systems. Though such knowledge is more pervasive and, at times, more persuasive to decision makers than formal "scientific" knowledge, in both the scholarship and practice of planning and public policy, it is little noted and if noted, often not regarded as knowledge. Formal research however defines and narrows issues and takes us only part way to action (Weiss 1979). Information must be embedded in lay understandings if it is to be relevant, much less acted upon (Lindblom and Cohen 1979). Local knowledge fills gaps, provides information about context, and offers pragmatic, experience-based insights from those who know a situation firsthand. Local knowledge can challenge dominant professional discourses. Including lay voices, especially those of marginalized people who seldom have an impact on the decisions that affect their lives, is a matter of justice and authentic democracy.

The least educated and poorest are also entitled to participate in self-governance and public deliberation. Traditional governance and expert-based planning typically leave out these groups, who then suffer from environmental injustice and other forms of neglect and unfair treatment. Finally, inclusion and engagement of diverse voices and multiple knowledges, especially those that challenge the status quo, are critical to the achievement of collaborative rationality – that is, to identifying desirable strategies with strong chances of producing workable and societally desirable outcomes.

Beyond collaborative rationality, however, lies the potential for a resilient society capable of responding constructively and creatively to stresses, opportunities, internal learning, and interaction. We live in a complex and unpredictable world as technology and globalization continuously interact to constantly change our situation. The juxtaposition of differing cultures and values, environmental crises, wars and conflicts, and pressures on limited resources has results that constantly surprise. We cannot play out the fantasy of science fiction writers like Asimov (Asimov 1982) that someday man will be able to design the future. Indeed we cannot even predict the results of straight-forward policy interventions like introducing standardized testing in schools. Unanticipated "side effects" are not the exception, but the norm.

We contend that this complex world system is at the edge of chaos (Kauffman 1995), which means that it can adapt, learn, innovate, and move to new levels of performance. To achieve this requires enabling conditions for using distributed intelligence, where many diverse agents can take informed action in response to the information they receive from many sources. Engaging and encouraging the development and use of local knowledge is important to assuring feedback from agents who know firsthand about the evolving environment. Interaction among the various actors helps all to learn and make better decisions. Expertise plays only a small part in this process, though professionals can influence the effectiveness of the system by making sure there are diverse players, opportunities for interaction and feedback, as well as selection mechanisms to weed out ineffective approaches and to identify those that should be replicated (Axelrod and Cohen 2000). Resilience requires a full range of knowledges, including those that are seldom heard.

Multiple knowledges

Formal professional inquiry, including natural and social science and the research of professionals like planners and policy analysts, is but a small component of all the inquiry that goes into framing understandings, making decisions, and ultimately effecting change (Lindblom and Cohen 1979). Professional social inquiry (psi) has to interact with many other forms of knowledge to be useful. Lindblom makes the case that the vast majority of pertinent policy knowledge is lay inquiry – ordinary understanding, or even comparatively systematic inquiry by nonprofessionals (Lindblom 1990). He takes the view, as we do, that our reality is socially constructed. Therefore psi cannot be conducted in the neutral way that is the idealized approach for science. Nor does he believe social science can be the primary guide for public decisions. It is but one of many types of inquiry that at best work together to help both public and elites decide what actions to take. Dialogue among professionals and other knowledgeable players is therefore critical at all stages – problem framing, selecting information, developing a robust and integrated picture of the issues from multiple perspectives, and choosing strategy.

Lay knowledge "does not owe its origin, degree of verification, testing, truth status, or currency to distinctive . . . professional techniques, but rather to common sense, casual empiricism or thoughtful speculation" (Lindblom and Cohen 1979: 12). This knowledge could be grounded in a combination of media reports, firsthand experience, conversations with those with direct knowledge, conversations that help individuals make sense of what is happening and logic based on familiarity with comparable situations. Both a lawyer and a homeless person could have a layman's knowledge of how social service delivery systems work and do not work and of what the problems may be. The lawyer knows because of having tried many cases to get benefits clients are entitled to, as well because of his familiarity with newspaper accounts of horror stories, and his understanding of the pathologies of organizational behavior acquired from his practice. The homeless woman may know about the problems with service delivery because of her experiences trying to get services and from her conversations with homeless friends. Each has a picture of aspects of the system without having read scientific reports. They are apt to know things that do not show up in such reports, having, for example, real time awareness of how matters are evolving or of how political agendas may be affecting the quality or availability of service. They may have enough knowledge to develop their own coherent stories of the problem. Ultimately policy decisions are made by laymen like the city councilors we described in Chapter 6, using their lay knowledge, along with expert testimony.

Local knowledge is an important type of lay knowledge. Geertz defines it as "practical, collective and strongly rooted in a particular place" and contends local knowl- edge forms an "organized body of thought based on immediacy of experience" (Geertz 1983). It includes information about local settings as well as knowledge of specific characteristics, circumstances, events, and relationships. It includes understanding of the meaning and implications of these elements and how they work together. Such knowl- edge depends on different collection methods, standards of evidence, and analytic techniques than does professional inquiry. It may be acquired through experience and mediated through culture. It may involve intuition and oral storytelling. It may be built on knowledge handed down through generations of praxis. It can be systematic and data- based, though probably not according to rules of social science research. It is built on a holistic, interpretive understanding of many elements in a situation.

Local knowledge, when held by the disadvantaged or ethnic minorities, is even more likely to be ignored, not only by scientists, but also by planners and public administrators. There are many reasons for this, ranging from disadvantaged groups' unfamiliarity with professional terminology and practices, to experts' low expectations and prejudice with regard to such individuals. Disadvantaged groups are often frustrated and angry in ways they cannot articulate, but which come across as inappropriate in policy deliberation. They are apt to feel their lack of power more acutely than the mainstream layperson. They have had life experiences with which many professionals cannot readily empathize. They may have their own discourses and share little of the frames, language, and priorities of the experts. They may regard the experts' methods themselves as a source of their disempowerment.

At MTC, for instance, technical planners proposed a survey to get information on transportation needs for poor communities (Innes and Gruber 2001). When they consulted with representatives from the communities, the meeting became rancorous. These citizens did not like the questions, which they felt did not address their concerns, and they thoroughly mistrusted surveys, which they saw as an establishment method that can be biased and fail to tell their story. They wanted to talk to the technical planners and tell them about their problems. The idea made the technical planners uncomfortable because they did not know how to use open ended input. In public meetings, even com- paratively informal ones, staff declared questions out of order which raised issues not encompassed by the agency's mission statement or not on the agenda. Eventually the federal government withheld certification from MTC's planning process in great part because of the objections of disadvantaged groups. They felt disempowered because they believed that not only their interests, but their knowledge were not respected. They mobilized major opposition and in 2005 brought a lawsuit against MTC for discrimination in expenditure patterns against the poor and minority population.

Many public agencies see their role as finding out what the public's goals are so they can use them to prepare plans in the classic rational planning style. Citizens, especially the marginalized, are not apt to think in terms of goals but rather of daily life. Technical planners are so embedded in their own discourses that they typically do not recognize what citizens have to offer. One of the few ways planning and policy making can tap into the lifeworld, rather than relying solely on the world constructed by professional discourses and colonized by technology (such as the survey method with its closed ended questions), and by powerful state and private interests, is to hear these citizen voices and respect their knowledge and experience.

The planners and urban designers from Harvard MIT Joint Center, who were stationed in Caracas while planning Ciudad Guayana in Venezuela, recognized the importance of local views but they tried to learn by proxy applying their formal categories. They hired anthropologist Lisa Peattie to talk with the local people and find out about their needs. Her accounts (Peattie 1968,1987) explain how she lived in the squatter settlements with the workers. She shared the life of the residents and discovered their struggles to get child care or travel to work via a crowded bridge with little public transportation. The urban designers in Caracas were not interested. They wanted to know what the local population's interest was in "amenities," such as parks. The language of amenities was not one that meshed with the local people's framing. They needed the basics of life – shops and transportation. The designers were planning a city for their professionally constructed future middle class residents. What the lower income people experienced was not in their view relevant to that future. They missed the messy human reality of the lives of workers and their families that would have helped them develop an organic evolving city, instead of the sterile and barren place it was for years.

Anxieties

While this professional vision marginalized low income residents, we suspect that a number of anxieties were also involved in their rejection of local knowledge. We can identify at least three that interfere with many efforts to incorporate local knowledge into public decision making and as a result interfere with the resilience of natural and social systems. These involve epistemology, difference, and uncertainty. Epistemological anxiety has to do with the fact that experts and professionals are apt to have their identity and status wrapped up in their knowledge so they may not be prepared to entertain alternative knowledge claims. Public opinion expert Daniel Yankelovich pushed this explanation a step further, noting that even professionals whose status is secure often are uncomfortable and unwilling to take alternative knowledges into account (Yankelovich 1991). He attributes this to anxiety over accepting ideas or observations that rely on different ways of knowing than those accepted in the dominant culture. These dominant ways of knowing are ingrained in people in a given society starting from childhood. An individual, even an open minded one, may feel anxiety in stepping outside these norms, uncertain about what alternative standards to apply. In contemporary Western societies the positivist way of knowing with its emphasis on objective measurable variables and instrumental rationality remains dominant, despite the challenges that have been made to it.

Nowhere is epistemological anxiety more evident than in the medical establishment's resistance to alternative therapies, including those that have been used for centuries like acupuncture, or herbal remedies. Insurance may not cover such things, though it will cover more costly and invasive "medical" remedies. Doctors, in our experience, when asked about alternative medicine are apt to make claims to being scientists and note that there are no double blind studies to validate such "medicine." Ironically most medical doctors are not scientists at all, but clinicians. The best of them operate in a pragmatic, step by step, experimenting way to diagnose a patient and prescribe a remedy. They do not use generalizations from the literature as their primary guide – such "scientific" findings are but one component in their thinking. Moreover, much of what has been learned in medicine is from decades of trial and error in practice, passed along through internships. Much of their knowledge is intuitive. It is perhaps this tenuous foundation in science that encourages an epistemological anxiety that can emerge as contempt and disrespect for alternative medicine.[1]

Policy professionals and experts feel a parallel anxiety with respect to lay or local knowledge. Typically they know all too well some of the shaky underpinnings of their professional knowledge – the assumptions that went into it, the alternative theories they are not using, and the limitations of their data. Their own epistemological anxiety can be aggravated when confronted by local knowledge which uses different methods, focuses on different things and applies different warrants to determine what information is worth crediting.

A second and related type of anxiety is about difference. Difference in our societies is growing due to globalization and the emergence of new groups with differing cultural backgrounds. Not only may these groups not share the epistemology of professionals, but they may look different, speak differently, value different things, and come from different cultural backgrounds (Sandercock 2003). Difference is anxiety provoking. It is about the unknown. It means that tried and true ways of operating and interacting may not work. The problem grows along with increasing immigration from around the world, along with the growing gap of rich and poor. But resilience and collaborative rationality call for diversity and inclusiveness in public choice making. The anxiety over such inclusion and the difficulties of finding a language of mutual understanding are big obstacles. Should, for example, an effort to address the problem of gangs or of drug crime include gang members and drug addicts? If it does not, can the problem be solved? Yet anxiety over difference on all sides is apt to keep such stakeholders out of policy making.

A third type of anxiety that draws on the first two is about uncertainty. It is hard, especially in modern Western societies, for experts and professionals to cope with uncertainty. Positivist epistemology seeks certainty and objectivity, and modern Western culture encourages this largely futile search. The world is constantly evolving, and its complex interactions mean that there can be no certainty. What is needed to make such a world resilient is not efforts to create false certainties and precise predictions, but a mindset that embraces ambiguity and change and that allows experts, professionals, and citizens to live with multiple, shifting knowledges and realities and to adapt as needed.

Complexity theory offers a way to embrace uncertainty while still trying to improve the outcomes of our system. The insights of Frankfurt school critical theorists that the world is a place of contradictions and change are also important to developing an alternative mindset, but neither complexity theory nor critical theory has as yet become part of the standard paradigm of professionals. They are paid to reach definite conclusions and make specific recommendations, or at least that is what most presume. The ideas of drawing contingent conclusions or proposing experiments rather than actions with specified outcomes are not normally part of professional practice, despite the reality of deep uncertainty. There remain too many norms, practices and institutions that are built on the expectation of certainty.

This anxiety over uncertainty typically leads to a demand for control, as if control techniques could eliminate or reduce uncertainty. Policy professionals, regulators, and public administrators seek control through standardized bureaucratic procedures, carefully limited agendas, use of specialized discourses, carefully defined problem frames, and invitations for participation to individuals whose contributions are predictable. While these strategies do not eliminate uncertainty, they paper it over and allow decision makers to proceed as if there is certainty. These practices have implications that run counter to the creation of a resilient society. They tend to take the status quo for granted rather than challenge it; they rely on established discourses and standardized policy responses. They tend to exclude disaffected groups through their framing of the issues or access rules. They may simply operate by neglect, by pretending they believe that the poor would show up if they wanted to, rather than by making the proactive efforts to include them that are needed for people who have no reason to believe anyone will listen to them.

The risks of ignoring local knowledge

These anxieties and the concomitant professional practice of ignoring local knowledge has permitted major environmental and human disasters to occur. The desire to eliminate these anxieties has been built into standardized bureaucratic procedures, into professional norms and practices, and contributed to the institutionalization of the positivist knowledge paradigm. These structures and practices not only aggravate the problem, they can make it invisible. A few of the most famous examples illuminate how this dynamic works. We start with a joke that has circulated widely in recent years.

Counting sheep

Once upon a time there was a sheepherder tending his sheep at the edge of a country road in rural Wyoming. A brand new Jeep Grand Cherokee screeched to a halt next to him. The driver, a young man dressed in a Brioni suit, Ray Ban glasses, and a Rolex wristwatch jumped out and asked the herder "If I guess how many sheep you have, will you give me one of them?" The herder looked at the young man, then looked at the sprawling herd of grazing sheep and said "Okay." The young man parked the SUV, connected his notebook and wireless modem, entered a NASA site, scanned the ground using satellite imagery and a GPS, opened a database and 60 Excel tables filled with algorithms, then printed a 150-page report on his high-tech mini-printer. He turned to the herder and said "You have exactly 1,586 sheep here."

The herder answered "Say, you are right. Pick out a sheep." The young man took one of the animals and put it in the back of his vehicle. As he was preparing to drive away, the herder looked at him and asked "Now, if I guess your profession, will you pay me back in kind?"

The young man answered "Sure."

The herder said immediately "You are a consultant." "Exactly! How did you know?" asked the young man. "Very simple," replied the herder. "First you came here without being invited. Secondly, you charged me a fee to tell me something I already knew. Thirdly, you do not understand anything about my business, and I'd really like to have my dog back."

Cumbrian sheep farmers and caesium fallout: identity and blinders

A case from the U.K. illustrates how when scientists ignore local knowledge the results can be disastrous, not only because scientist may therefore offer inappropriate advice, but also because they can alienate the public in ways that are counterproductive for public action (Wynne 1982). Scientists can be ineffectual if they fail to recognize how the identity of local people can be wrapped up with their generations of praxis. In 1986 sheep farms in Cumbria were in the path of the radiation fallout from the Chernobyl nuclear meltdown. Scientists who arrived to assess the problem confidently asserted there would be no effect from the caesium fallout on the lambs. They did not consult local farmers about the soils nor about possible remedial actions. A few weeks later, on advice of scientists, the government imposed a complete ban on sheep movements and sales, while government officials assured the farmers that it would only be for three weeks. Three weeks would still allow farmers to sell their lamb crop. This sale was critical for their entire way of life because of the fragile and limited hill grazing land, which would be devastated if too many sheep were crowded in it for too long. In that case farmers would be ruined.

The scientists eventually recognized that the radiation was not dispersing as they had anticipated. They advised the government to continue the ban on sale indefinitely for a significant area of the region. Nonetheless they persisted in a wrong-headed conviction that caesium level would soon drop. The reason for this mistake was that they had transferred their knowledge of clay soils, where caesium is quickly locked up by chemical absorption and only contaminates the lambs on a one-time basis, to the acid, peaty soils of the Cumbrian hills which are very different. It took two years of persistent contamination for scientists recognize that in peaty soils the caesium remained chemically mobile and recycled continually back into the vegetation.

The scientists ignored other local knowledge that could have played productively into their advice to government. For example they ignored variation by farm. They ignored farmers' knowledge of their local environments, hill sheep characteristics, and hill farming management realities. Accordingly their advice to farmers and the government did not protect the farms' future, though this had been their purpose. They conducted experiments in which they spread bentonite on patches of land to absorb the caesium and tested fenced-in animals for how well they did in different conditions. Scientists ignored the farmers' critique that fenced animals would suffer wasting. Later scientists had to abandon the experiments for this very reason. All in all, the scientists' failure to be attentive to local knowledge led to flawed policy recommendations as well as to local perceptions that the scientists were arrogant and disrespectful. This in turn led to increasing hostilities and mistrust of the government among the locals.

Habitat conservation in California

A long running disagreement over habitat conservation in the Coachella Valley of California reflected anxieties over epistemology as well as uncertainty. In this case the differences were between regulatory agency scientists and local experts on the appropriate location and size of the habitat that should be conserved for the endangered fringe-toed lizard (Goldstein 2004). The groups came to an impasse in part because they did not respect each other's knowledge. The regulatory scientists trusted peer reviewed articles and findings of formal research, while the local experts trusted their own firsthand experience and observation. The regulatory scientists dismissed this as "anecdotal," though it was grounded in years of walking the area, making observations and sightings and making sense of the lizards' movement patterns. The local experts regarded the generalizations of peer reviewed science as of limited use in the specific time and place of Coachella Valley.

Then too there was anxiety over uncertainty. Agency scientists wanted to use peer reviewed findings because they were definite and would give them cover should there be a lawsuit. They recommended the largest possible area be protected to compensate for uncertainty, while the local experts argued that some of the area was not being used by the lizard. On the other hand the local experts wanted to err on the side of the potential future needs of the community and set aside less land. In this case dialogue did not resolve differences because ideal speech conditions were not established, interests were not revealed, and the differing kinds of knowledge were not reconciled, as they might have been in a professionally facilitated effort. There was, moreover, considerable rancor in the process. Both groups felt disrespected, as their identities and livelihoods were wrapped up in their understandings and ways of knowing.

Potato farming in the Andes: colonizing the lifeworld

As part of the Green revolution in Peru agricultural scientists tried to identify optimal potato seeds by testing them in the laboratory against standardized environmental conditions and matching seeds to types of plots. They then created averages for various types of plots to give a single value to be uniformly applied to each plot. This scientific "modernization" of agriculture meant more than just the use of a new seed type, but also demanded a new set of procedures, including specific irrigation requirements and defined quantities of fertilizer spread at particular times to duplicate the conditions applied in the original scientific experiments. The idea was that these practices, if followed carefully, would produce the optimal output (van der Ploeg 1993). The scientists imposed their positivist paradigm on a richly nuanced set of practices and situated knowledges that potato farmers had developed. Their knowledge of the variation in soils and climate in different parts of their region meant they used differentiated practices across the area, sharing their knowledge, and learning from one another. The scientists not only failed to take this contextual information into account, their method itself was intrinsically designed to ignore indigenous knowledge, as their goal was to build standardized practices. Moreover, to use these standardized practices farmers would be required to following a complex and unfamiliar program, which they often did not do.

The result of this imposition of an optimization concept (de Neufville and Christensen 1980) is to colonize the world of the farmers with a western approach and to try to impose certainty on a complex, contingent situation. Using this idea would be to ultimately remove human agency, which the scientists see as the source of the problem rather than what it is – the source of resilience. These farmers came to understand that this intervention was to benefit outsiders. In the process of trying to implement these "improvements" farmers would lose their indigenous knowledge and the wisdom that came with it. They had to follow the proposed practices to get international assistance, but in doing so they risked losing the ability to adapt when the practices did not work.

Love Canal: local knowledge and mobilization for environmental justice

Countless other examples can be found where local knowledge was crucial to public action, though it has often been a battle to get it accepted by experts or government. The case of Love Canal in Niagara Falls, New York, for example, highlighted the importance of local knowledge in identifying and mobilizing action on environmental hazards that had been ignored by government and industry (Fischer 2000; Gibbs and Levine 1982;

Schlosberg 1999). In this case it was no secret that a chemical company had dumped in and around the canal in the past, but no action was taken until residents began to be aware of high levels of disease among their children and community members began to report strange odors and substances surfacing in their yards. Love Canal Homeowner Association members worked with a biologist who helped them reinterpret government data, build capacity to develop additional information, and interpret it credibly. They gathered additional data through their own community investigations and surveys. In 1978 the media began to write articles about the situation. The U.S. Environmental Protection Agency (EPA) later reported a disturbingly high rate of miscarriages and birth defects and found that residents had high white blood cell counts, which could be a precursor to leukemia.

Finally in 1980 President Carter declared a state of emergency, and the government evacuated 800 families. This event became a major instigating factor in the passage of the so-called Superfund Act. The law provided for federal authority to cleanup major hazardous waste sites and protect nearby residents. Ultimately more than 1000 superfund sites were designated. A local resident, Lois Gibbs, who organized Love Canal community efforts, backed only by her high school education, went on to found the Citizens Clearinghouse for Hazardous Wastes to assist others across the country in their struggles and help them to develop their own community assessments. In the Love Canal case the residents' evidence got the media's attention and ultimately that of the federal government. Only after residents began to make their case, however, did the agencies do the research that they would trust. In the end, even without scientific certainty about the link of cause and effect, the endangered residents were evacuated. Locals brought not only timely and palpable experience to decision makers, but also the passion and commitment that kept this issue from being swept under the rug. Local research into the problem was a major factor in this story.

Environmental justice

Not long after the Love Canal case caught the nation's attention, a struggle over a proposed PCB landfill for an African American community in Warren County North Carolina in 1982 brought to public attention the question of whether there was a pattern of intentional placement of hazardous waste and polluting facilities in communities of color across the country. By the late 1980s a grassroots movement had emerged in the U.S., motivated by the conviction that there was an inequitable distribution of risk in the U.S. Poor people and people of color tended to live in areas that were more likely to be hazardous to their health. They suffered from asthma, birth defects, and cancers at greater rates than the general population. They were not, however, represented in the leadership of most mainstream environmental advocacy organizations, which accordingly did not address differential risk issues. These disadvantaged groups were not noticed or listened to by the government and business decision makers the way that more powerful groups like the Sierra Club were. They used different discourses and were concerned about different topics from mainstream environmental groups. They relied heavily on their own local knowledge and experience and lacked the resources larger groups had to gather and analyze data. They had all the problems of being heard that the Love Canal home-owners had and more because many of them were minorities or native peoples. They triggered anxiety over difference as well as epistemological anxiety. Groups, many of them small and focused on specific issues, proliferated and emerged as the loosely networked but vocal nationwide environmental justice movement introduced new discourses into local political arenas.

Environmental justice (EJ) is the idea that environmental hazards should not disproportionately affect some people, particularly those who have little or no power in society. Middle and high income people who live in well to do neighborhoods normally have the political savvy and clout to prevent noxious land uses from being sited near their homes. They also have many housing choices and are generally able to avoid moving into areas with known hazards or industry nearby. Thus the EJ movement has focused on the poor and people of color, as those most in need of organizing and advocacy. This move-ment has also emphasized the need for the assembling of local knowledge and data.

By the early 1990s public agencies had begun to incorporate environmental justice into their missions in response to growing visibility of the movement and the growing awareness of environmental hazards in developed areas. In 1992 the EPA created an office of Environmental Justice designed to integrate EJ concerns into EPA's programs and policies. A Presidential Executive Order in 1994[2] tasked each federal agency to make achieving environmental justice part of its mission. The agencies were to do this by iden-tifying and addressing disproportionately high and adverse human health or environmental effects of their programs, policies, and activities on minority populations and low-income populations. The executive order also required the agencies to prepare a strategy for integrating environmental justice into all agency activities.[3] As part of this effort, the US Department of Energy, one of the agencies whose activities are most often implicated in EJ, offered this definition.

> Environmental Justice is the fair treatment and meaningful involvement of all people – regardless of race, ethnicity, and income or education level – in environmental decision making. Environmental Justice programs promote the protection of human health and the environment, empowerment via public participation, and the dissemination of relevant information to inform and educate affected communities.

This framing, with its three point focus on fairness, involvement of all, and community education, falls short of meeting the federal order or addressing the basic challenge of EJ. First, it emphasizes equity rather than inequity. Second, it barely taps into the causes of environmental injustice. Third, it ignores local knowledge and experience. The focus on equity translated into creating new procedures for agencies to hear from affected groups. This strategy does not acknowledge that some groups have more difficulty par-ticipating due to income, language differences, or to their own, often well-founded, anxieties about not being treated respectfully. There is no suggestion that the agency might have to be proactive in encouraging and assisting those marginalized populations to participate meaningfully, nor any recognition that local knowledge would be useful. Finally, it does not acknowledge that the sources of environmental injustice lie more deeply in structural social and economic injustice, in physical planning practices, in corporatist and pluralist decision making, which barely recognize the existence of marginalized groups, and in the dominant neoliberal paradigm with its emphasis on economic growth and its hands off policies with regard to social justice.

Cities and regions in the U.S. are politically balkanized and de facto segregated by income and often by ethnicity, which means that marginalized and politically weak groups are clustered in areas where they can be vulnerable to the siting of hazardous waste or unable to protect themselves from ongoing hazards (Dreier, et al. 2004). Discourses like that of smart growth[4] or the new urbanism leave out the poor in their images of the cities' future and distract from discourse around social and environmental justice as we saw in the Bay Area Alliance case.

The U.S. Department of Environment (DOE) statement indicates that the agency anticipates "educating" the public about scientific knowledge of risks. There is no mention of listening or learning from local experience. The statement envisions a one way process, with the agency informing local people. It does not give any indication that local knowledge of a place could be helpful to the agency in its siting or regulatory decisions. Ironically the statement talks about empowerment, though it sounds as if the plan is to impose scientific views of risk on the local people. The environmental justice movement has established the legitimacy and importance of local participation in environmental decisions that affect local welfare. Public agencies today at least give it lip service. But participation that involves simply telling the public what the agency and its scientists think is hollow and another symptom of epistemological anxiety.

Strategies for incorporating local knowledge

In this section we will look at models and strategies for actually incorporating local knowledge into policy making and public action. We use examples where players have addressed the task in different ways. Each points up different challenges and each helps point a way toward harnessing local knowledge and energy for the benefit of society.

Watershed stewardship: local knowledge as a driver

A national movement in the U.S. has been promoting collaborative local watershed[5] management (Sabatier, et al. 2005). A driving idea for the movement is that local knowledge is necessary for managing water quality and flow in streams and rivers, but also that local knowledge, energy, and engagement are critical to monitoring and cleaning up. Many watersheds are small and only of significant interest to local residents who typically lack resources to bring in experts, other than those who volunteer their time. They are on their own to improvise, to take whatever actions they can alone, or to persuade local agencies to act.

In the San Francisco region's East Bay many creeks wend their way from the hills through a variety of urban neighborhoods. Parts of the creeks have been culverted and are invisible to local people, but parts are now being "daylighted" to allow freer flows, to provide access to these natural features of the urban landscape and to reduce the dangers of flooding. The so-called "flatlands" and filled land near the Bay tend to be inhabited by lower income people and ethnic minorities, unlike the hills. Low-lying areas near the Bay were originally largely industrial, and many of the sites became badly polluted by hazardous waste. Without citizens and advocacy groups, most of these creeks would have gotten little public action. City agencies do not have the staff or funding to do much, and the regional regulatory agencies pay little attention to such small streams. When they do take action, it may be at the instigation of a local nonprofit or citizen group.

Wardani (2008) conducted detailed case studies of local stewardship activities around two East Bay watersheds. This research showed that local engagement made a difference in the health of the creeks when the groups included participants from low income communities of color and private business. The research also illustrated the obstacles to effective stewardship that arise due to its informality.

Sausal Creek runs from the largely white, upper income areas in the Oakland Hills down through the largely Latino and Asian Fruitvale neighborhood to the Oakland Estuary. Concerned citizens formed Friends of Sausal Creek (FOSC) in 1997 with funding and coordination support from the county flood control district and a regional nonprofit watershed project. The city is an important partner in the effort and, working with the expert staff of the city's watershed program, the partnership mobilized a number of improvement projects in the middle watershed, where the creek was very visible as it ran through city and regional parks. FOSC identified six priority sites for biodiversity, and enlisted volunteers to remove trash and nonnative plants, monitored conditions, and mentored nearby residents on creating ecosystem habitat using native plants. FOSC also distributed flyers to explain how to protect Sausal Creek habitat.

The FOSC had the hardest time mobilizing people in the flatland Fruitvale neighborhood, partly because the stream there was largely culverted and not visible as a community resource and partly because of the lower socioeconomic status of the residents. Residents of Fruitvale not only had less time for meetings, but also had justified fears of going to night meetings in a neighborhood with considerable crime. A small vacant lot traversed by the creek had become notoriously unsafe and a dumping ground for trash. Neighbors did their best to remove the worst of it and to call the city for trash pickup, but it was not a winning battle. FOSC recognized that they would need engagement of all local groups if they were to protect this creek, but getting these folks engaged would be an uphill effort.

The second case was Rheem Creek in the largely low income and minority city of Richmond. Here the story was almost the reverse of Sausal Creek with regard to environmental justice because it was the people in the largely African American Parchester village at the mouth of the creek who led restoration efforts. One individual,

Whitney Dotson, followed in the footsteps of his father Reverend Dotson and became an activist leader and head of the Parchester Village Neighborhood Council. He had grown up in Parchester Village, accustomed to playing and swimming in Rheem creek and enjoying the open spaces of Breuner Marsh. His father's generation had staved off multiple threats to the marsh, including a municipal airport, a 1000-home development and a technology park. Working with environmental leaders and the Sierra Club they had been able to get an industrial site turned into Point Pinole Park.

Whitney Dotson built on that tradition of coalition building and networked relationships. Beginning in the mid-1990s, he and other North Richmond shoreline community leaders started the Community Health Initiative (CHI), an offspring of Contra Costa County's Center for Health set up in the community as part of toxic spill mitigation. CHI was made up of Richmond neighborhood partnerships seeking to address the injustices of toxic releases and air quality issues from Chevron and other dirty industries concentrated in the area, including a wastewater treatment plant and a waste transfer station sitting on a capped landfill. They, along with major environmental organizations, founded the Environmental Justice Coalition for Water, a regional and state technical and legal support organization. CHI, in partnership with regional nonprofits, obtained funding to assess the health of the creek, begin restoration efforts, and build community capacity through developing a community watershed vision. The local partners were crucial in the implementation of the grant and did most of the outreach, as they were known and trusted in the community. When the leaders took local residents on a field trip to high income Marin County to see a restored marsh, it was a revelation for them about injustices in their own community. It got them launched on their own vision for Rheem Creek. Once residents learned about alternatives, local energy, local knowledge of history and local vision were critical to the protection and improvement of this watershed.

In these small watersheds key knowledge was supplied through local energy, commitment, and place-based knowledge. For Sausal Creek watershed and flood control agencies provided regulatory and expert support to FOSC, while also conducting their own projects. In Richmond local initiative played a major role in getting things started. Local people used their networks and history of collaborative work to draw in environmental advocacy groups and nonprofits to assist with scientific knowledge, as well as with their networks and know-how for developing successful grant proposals. Both involved co-production of information and joint action among locals, public agencies, and nonprofits.

Action research in the Lower East Side of Manhattan: framing a market

A substantial part of the education of city and regional planners involves hands-on experiential learning for both students and faculty. Professor Ken Reardon led a team of planning students into the working class/immigrant Lower East Side of Manhattan to help the neighborhood plan for and protect a large and well known community market that was threatened with closure (Forester 1999: 119–21). The team came into the situation on the assumption that the market was an economic institution. It was a supermarket, the purpose of which, they believed, was to offer the lowest prices and allow the most efficient shopping experience. They originally saw their task as helping make this market more competitive with the big chains. Faculty met with local clients once or twice and then designed survey and interview instruments, before doing participant observation or getting to know the local people more informally. Not surprisingly the survey and interviews did not give them real insight because they had framed them within their own professional analyses of neighborhood economic development and their own experience as middle class grocery shoppers.

Once they did more informal, ethnographic style research, listening to the voices and perspectives of the local people, they realized they had been on the wrong track. This market was not simply a place to buy food. Rather it was a

> social institution that was about the preservation of certain traditional cultural values and an institution for sharing those understandings of different communities . . . The fact that they sold food was incidental to it . . . We had this theory that we were studying a mass volume supermarket in which the real factor was price, since it was an economic institution. In reality it was about a whole other set of values and experiences.
>
> (Forester 1999: 120)

While this university team was dedicated to serving the community and to incorporating local knowledge in their recommendations, their professional knowledge blinded them at first to what was needed. Only after they retreated from this could they genuinely hear the community and help them work toward what they wanted. It was an object lesson about local knowledge.

The People's Science Movement in Kerala (KSSP): building capacity while incorporating local knowledge

In the late 1980s an unusual innovation emerged in the state of Kerala India that engaged grassroots knowledge gathering in a fundamental way in the preparation of local and state plans. Several factors played into this development, according to Fischer (2000): a long term failure of state and local governments to meet a constitutional commitment to decentralize planning; perceptions of the government's inability to bring economic and social development to the majority of the population; the existence of a left wing political coalition with the goal of bringing people closer to their local governments; and a need to find new ways to deal with local economic development. Kerala's State Planning Board announced that 35 percent to 40 percent of planning activities would be initiated from below, and it allocated an equivalent share of funding to local governments. The Left Democratic Front initiated what it called the People's Planning Campaign and sought to mobilize and bring together local representatives, officials in line departments, governmental and nongovernmental experts, civic groups and the mass citizenry to cooperate in the project.

At the same time the People's Science Movement in Kerala (KSSP) was evolving into a social movement. This organization was established in 1962 by scientists and social activists in Kerala who were concerned that scientific information was inaccessible to the majority of people. It translated and published scientific works, relying on the volunteer efforts of its members. When, in 1972, the organization adopted the motto "Science for Social Revolution," the action opened the door for a mass movement with sixty thousand members. It shifted emphasis to active efforts to develop a "scientific" questioning attitude in the population, with the goal of empowerment and change. A successful challenge to the building of a hydroelectric dam on the grounds that it would harm biodiversity and a successful grassroots based literacy campaign in the city of Cochin brought the group credibility and the attention of mainstream science organizations, the Prime Minister, and the international community.

Of particular interest is the success of the group's efforts to integrate local knowledge with expert knowledge to prepare information for development planning. In an effort to counteract the tendency for local jurisdictions to use the funding they had been assigned on one-shot projects that had little lasting effect on development, KSSP instigated a participatory rural appraisal and resource mapping effort as a basis. This had been done elsewhere, but KSSP wanted it to be more scientific, while still participatory. They enlisted some of their members from the Center for Earth Science Studies and proposed to combine their scientific mapping with participatory mapping. They saw the process as a tool for communication among planning experts and local community members. There was a dearth of accurate information on such features as soils, slopes, streams, types of crops, and location of land under cultivation. Planners also needed to know where schools, roads and community facilities were. The Center designed the information gathering process and turned it over to KSSP, which identified volunteers and offered training on data gathering. Volunteers developed five overlay maps which were in turn used for developing the action plan, with the engagement of a newly informed citizenry capable of providing useful information. While this mapping practice, by the time of Fischer's research, had not spread to more than a minority of jurisdictions of the state, it provides a model for how science and local knowledge can be brought together.[6]

Environmental health in Brooklyn: cooperative data gathering and mutual learning

Jason Corburn in his book *Street Science* (Corburn 2005) tells of unusual fact finding collaborations between residents and technical professionals in the Greenpoint/ Williamsburg neighborhood in Brooklyn, NY. These efforts helped the professionals to "see" conditions otherwise invisible to them, while at the same time helped community residents to observe systematically and understand the environmental hazards around them. The efforts built working relationships between the community and public agencies, along with some degree of trust, while at the same time provided more robust and nuanced data for regulatory purposes. Residents provided information about varying conditions in different parts of the neighborhood, along with crucial insights about the practices of the different cultural groups, which included a mix of Latinos, Hasidic Jews, African Americans, Poles and Slavs. This collaboration helped to support policies that were adapted to the variations in the neighborhood and among the population.

This neighborhood was densely populated and poor, with much of its housing abutting industry. Less than half of adults had high school diplomas. It was afflicted with multiple kinds of air toxics and with lead hazards; asthma rates were high; and there were dietary risks from locally caught fish. The EPA chose this neighborhood to do its first community-based, cumulative exposure project because of the lack of local health studies, the disproportionate number of pollution sources and the concerns of neighborhood-based environmental groups. EPA was planning to use a standard model to predict the air dispersion of 148 toxics to estimate residents' exposure, but after requests from the New York City Department of Environmental Protection they agreed to discuss their methods first with the community activists. The local Watchperson Project, which monitored health hazards, developed a map showing hundreds of local polluters that did not appear in the database EPA was planning to use. This community group contended that EPA's methodology would just wash out these block-by-block differences. EPA scientists realized they could not use their model, which would require that they aggregate these sources.

Expert data collection methods typically involve taking random samples of the air or water in an area and then developing statistical models to predict risk levels for people over the whole area. Such data, which represent averages, inevitably miss pollution hot spots. They mask high risk levels for people who, for example, live near polluting businesses or brownfields. Using the method of generalizing about behavior across a population can also mask other risks, as populations do not have uniform habits. When the Watchperson Project organized high school volunteers to follow up on community complaints of odor, noise and air pollution, they discovered that half of the many dry cleaning establishments were located in residential buildings. Community members were trained to take air quality readings and found that indoor concentrations of dangerous pollutants in these buildings were more than a thousand times what they were in the street. This was a revelation to EPA analysts and provided information that was used for later policy.

When residents learned that EPA planned to estimate hazardous dietary exposures based on a standard urban diet, they objected. They pointed out there was no standard diet in this culturally diverse neighborhood. Eating contaminated fish caught locally was a particular issue. Given the diet, which included little fish, EPA had estimated little risk, but the Watchperson Project pointed out that some residents, especially in immigrant communities had diets heavily dependent on fish they caught locally. To include a measurement of angler risk the Project, jointly with EPA, developed a survey of fishermen and trained local people to conduct it. The language and cultural barriers made it likely that EPA officials would not get good responses if they conducted the survey. The results showed that some groups of local residents had a lifetime cancer risk of one in ten thousand, compared to EPA's acceptable level of one in one million.

This was a case where local knowledge had an impact because of the collaborative relationship between EPA and the community. EPA trained local community members to gather data they did not have the resources to gather. The community provided insights as well as access EPA did not have. The collaborative process identified phenomena unrecognized by the professionals and provided them with insights which allowed them to readjust their analysis to better account for the distributional characteristics of the environmental hazards and population practices. The process allowed integration of local and expert knowledges and led to more robust policy.

Fisheries management: complex systems and the need for resilience

The biggest challenge in fishery management is to develop information and practices that will assure a resilient fishery in a context where overfishing is the norm, natural variations in the fish populations are great, and where many factors interact to produce unpredictable change. Fisheries management is an arena where both local knowledge and local participation are widely accepted as necessary (McCay and Jentoft 1996). The local people are the fishers who are both part of the problem and part of the solution, unlike the local residents in Brooklyn, victimized by pollution not of their own making. The concept and practice of fisheries co-management has become increasingly widespread (Sen and Nielsen 1996) in response to the decline of fisheries worldwide and to a need for sustainable resource management. As Pomeroy contends, if a management regime is to be effective and legitimate, it needs to engage user groups along with government (Pomeroy 1995: 406).

While some small traditional subsistence fisheries have been able to self-manage sustainably, using their own knowledge and their own rules and monitoring, for the most part the conditions enabling such self-management no longer exist. Ostrom (1990) in her classic study, shows that unless one can limit appropriators (fishers), they will not buy into a system of self-regulation. Global demand for fish is high; new technologies allow massive catches by industrial fishing fleets; climate and water conditions are changing dramatically; and land-based activities such as dam building and diversion of fresh waters from rivers to agriculture and urban development affect spawning and biodiversity. All of these conditions in combination mean that fishers are unable to significantly affect the supply of fish by what they do or do not do.

In such a context governments have to play a role, but experience has demonstrated that, even with sophisticated science, government regulation of fish catches or other types of fishery management have not created a resilient fishery. Accordingly the idea of co-management is now in vogue (Pomeroy 1995; Wilson 1999). The idea is to link users and regulatory agencies together for management, but no effective institutional arrangements have been established as anxieties shape the experimental efforts at cooperation. A comparative study of fisheries around the world (Sen and Nielsen 1996) identifies five types of co-management, ranging from minimal opportunities for user input in government decisions, to some consultation, to cooperation as equal partners, to advisory groups that de facto make the decisions, to government delegation of authority to user groups.

In the U.S. in 1976 federal legislation established a form of fishery co-management by setting up eight Regional Fisheries Councils, each of which involved the National Marine Fisheries Service (NMFS), state fishery agencies, marine scientists, and representatives of both the recreational and commercial fishing industries.[7] The act, which was motivated principally by heavy foreign fishing, established exclusive offshore economic zones ranging from 3–200 miles. The Councils had the mandate to manage living marine resources in these zones and prepare a Fishery Management Plan (FMP) for the various stocks of fish. By 1993 however 40 percent of the fish stocks with known status were overfished, according to the U.S. National Oceanographic and Atmospheric Administration (NOAA). Some contended that NMFS and the industry had too cozy a relationship on these councils (Wilson 1999), so in 1996[8] the legislation was amended to also include public agency members and at large members on councils. The legislation required that FMPs must, among other things, specify "objective and measurable criteria for identifying when the fishery to which the plan applies is overfished . . . and contain conservation and management measures to prevent or end overfishing." This new legislation was to mean a more significant role for science, but it also created more opportunities for conflict with fishers over data and threshold criteria. Not only would these tasks be heavily knowledge-dependent, but they would also require buy-in from all members of the Council and the fishing community at large. Fishers operate with little oversight so the knowledge and the plan would have to be agreed upon if the recommendations were to be implemented.

The differences between the forms of scientific and local knowledge are not unlike the Andes potato farming case, but they are more complex because fisheries involve multiple kinds of scientists – stock assessment scientists, fishery biologists, other marine biologists, and industry scientists – as well as fishers. The stock assessment scientists tended to be modelers who predicted fish stocks based on observations. Fishery biologists looked at what was known about the behavior and needs of different fish. Fishers themselves paid attention to a myriad of data simultaneously, such as changing patterns of where fish could be found at different times of the day and year, the co-location of particular fish with other creatures, water temperatures, and the depth where particular fish could be found. Unlike many scientists, theirs was a nonlinear view of a constantly changing adaptive system.[9] They did not, however, have the larger view that the scientists had of a wider area and set of patterns, nor did they have the capacity to make predictions.

In this situation the players needed to work together to make coherent sense of what each knew and to understand how and why each interpreted the data they observed. This was difficult because of differing mental maps and multiple anxieties, as well as because of what each stakeholder had to win or lose. In the case of bluefish in the Northeast (Wilson), multiple committees were involved in assessing the stocks and preparing the FMP. This fish was popular with recreational anglers and, accordingly, considerable public attention was directed to this management effort, particularly at the state level, where the agencies tended to support sport fishermen. Differences arose in the dialogues about whether to label the stocks fully exploited or overexploited. The latter would trigger a legal requirement to reduce fishing effort. There was not disagreement about the data, but about whether the goal should be a sustainable fishery and whether the fishery could recover from its perceived decline. Even this was contentious, as some said the decline was a statistical artifact rather than an accurate reflection of the situation. The whole matter was particularly controversial because the label "overexploited" reduces recreational fishers' allowable takes.

Part of the source of differences was in unresolved problems of data gathering, measurement and analysis. The scientists sought "fishery independent" data. They selected spots for measurement according to a mathematically designed plan, where they used the same fishing gear each year at the same time to control for this factor (though of course fishers might select their gear according to conditions). They used models based on the ages of fish and traced cohorts through time. Fishers and some scientists contended that the methods of measuring age were inadequate and truncated the ages of bluefish at 6 years. Moreover, they challenged the methods of surveying, which involved trawling along the bottom of the sea, because not only did bluefish tend to swim much nearer the surface, they could readily outswim the trawl nets. This method would, fishers argued, underestimate the bluefish population. Finally the fishers were concerned that the scientists were not using the basic intuitive method they relied on to judge the health of the fishery, the amount of effort required to catch a particular quantity of fish.

Knowledge of the marginalized in collaborative stakeholder dialogues

So far we have shown that there can be at least moderately successful integration of science with local knowledge in participatory and collaborative research. What about the collaborative stakeholder dialogues that have been the primary focus of this book? Can local knowledge be integrated into these? In particular can the knowledge of the marginalized, vulnerable, and disadvantaged such as the homeless, migrant laborers, illegal immigrants, the inner city poor, children, the mentally ill, or gang members be included? A collaborative dialogue may well deal with issues affecting these groups. Without someone who can speak in an authentic way about their experiences, however, it may be difficult, if not impossible, to find a suitable course of action, much less one these groups might participate in.

Stakeholder dialogues work as effectively as they do because they involve representatives of interests who can speak for a constituency. Even when participants represent warring interests and get angry with one another, they usually can come to share a mutual understanding of what they are doing, a common way of expressing themselves, and similar views of what counts as knowledge. They are often professionals themselves or people accustomed to representing their interests on a volunteer basis, like many environmentalists or community activists. Therefore what some stakeholder dialogues have done is to seek out people who can represent the groups' interests. The state level Growth Management Consensus Project (GMCP) in California was a group of mainly lobbyists representing the major interests in growth management, such as environmentalists, developers, and business. To represent the disadvantaged, the group enlisted representatives of two advocacy groups for low income housing, along with representatives from the Mexican American Legal Defense Fund and the Latino Issues Forum (Innes, et al. 1994). While these individuals were well-versed in the issues and concerns of their constituencies, they were neither low-income renters nor impoverished Latinos with little English. One was a University of California professor and another was a lawyer.

Missing in this therefore, as in many stakeholder dialogues, were the actual voices of these disadvantaged groups and the opportunity for all stakeholders to directly experience the reality of their emotions and experience (Sandercock 2003). What was also missing was the opportunity for these players to react to ideas through their own lenses, or to participate in problem framing and agenda setting. There are no simple answers for this problem. By definition, the marginalized tend not to be organized into groups with spokespeople. Even when they are, like for example California's farm workers under Cesar Chavez, the other stakeholders may not be willing to sit and listen to people who are apt to go on with long speeches and anger, which is often the style such marginalized groups have had to develop. These players do not share the taken for granted background understandings of most of the other stakeholders. For example, a local community member Innes had worked with crashed a conference held on the UC Berkeley campus about community development and challenged the formal presentations in a long and contemptuous rant. She complained about a presentation that generalized about poverty on a national scale, wanting to know how this kind of data was going to help her and her neighbors. While her question was legitimate, we were frustrated by her interruption of the professional discourse and her discourteous treatment of our guest. She was using air time to vent and take away from the purpose of the seminar, which was primarily to share information among nonprofits and foundations.

It is also difficult to include voices of the poor in dialogues because they typically have more immediate priorities, like putting food on the table or dealing with health issues. The challenge of engaging migrant workers or the homeless is not only that they do not speak in the language of the other stakeholders, but also that there are practical obstacles to their participation. They may not have time or energy because they have to hold down multiple jobs or cannot get baby sitters. They may not be able to afford transportation. They may be anxious about how they will be treated or uncertain of what is appropriate to say. Even if funding can be found to support their attendance, they may not turn up, or when they do, they may not speak.

One effort we are familiar with worked particularly hard to overcome these obstacles. The Transportation and Air Quality Collaborative was a 100-person multi-stakeholder dialogue[10] addressed to the problems of congestion and air quality in the Sacramento region. The Center for Collaborative Policy (CCP) managed and facilitated this process, which was highly inclusionary. The disabled, the elderly, and poor under-served populations were represented by people who were not professionals and not familiar with stakeholder processes. CCP assigned someone full time to assist these people and help them learn how to speak effectively, how to think about their interests, and how to understand the information in play. Managing this effort involved huge transaction costs, but even with all the effort, problems remained. Some participants had what mainstream stakeholders would perceive as a chip on the shoulder, communicating in a belligerent style and fighting among themselves. Someone always seemed to be engaged in what Habermas would call dramaturgical action rather than communicative action.

This effort to help marginalized groups participate on an equal footing with powerful interests was laudable from the perspective of environmental justice, and it enabled new concerns to be heard. There was however a flip side. Some people complained that such training was condescending. They wanted to speak in their own voices. They wanted to be understood in their own terms. They argued that the other stake-holders should be trained to understand them. They were not comfortable expressing themselves if they had to frame everything in someone else's discourse and look at issues through someone else's lens. Indeed this story illuminates important contradictions. The groups can learn to speak in professional discourses, but then what they say no longer represents their authentic experience. They become colonized by these discourses and may no longer have the same touch with the lifeworld that they need to represent.

Strategies for integrating local with expert knowledge

It remains unclear how, or even whether, the voices, knowledge, and emotions of the marginalized groups can be integrated into collaborative dialogues without destroying the very features that make these dialogues valuable. While we believe facilitators and project managers should keep trying to accomplish this integration, in the meantime there are other approaches. These include: using participatory data gathering efforts to provide input to the dialogues; relying on spokespeople who are in close contact with disadvan-taged constituencies and can be eloquent in telling their stories and communicating their passion in a way that can be heard; keeping the local and disadvantaged people separated from the professionals and the scientists and brokering the information across the divide; or inviting marginalized people to address the group in their own way, without necessarily requiring them to stay and participate over time.[11]

Participatory mapping is one method that can be effective. Everyone can relate in some way to a map, from the least informed to the experts. A map can be an equalizer and can allow all to discuss the situation in common terms. Participants may have different information to put on the map, as they did in Kerala. Community members can be trained in what to look for and given monitoring equipment, as they were in Brooklyn, so they can provide the fine grained information that public agencies do not have the resources to gather. In the San Francisco Bay Area large scale public workshops were held, where many types of citizens with differing interests and knowledge sat at tables around density maps of their regions and worked through desired development patterns. British planner Tony Gibson (Forester 2008), wanting to get inclusion of more ordinary people who would not self-select for such processes, developed a game with houses and other pieces on a game board map of the community. He took this to laundromats, parks and other places where people gather. It was much easier to get engagement this way than in formal processes. He argued that often it is easier to communicate if you do it sideways while doing other things, rather than in the direct and more intimidating way that professionals are accustomed to.

Another approach is to bring in local people to tell their stories and communicate their feelings in the safe environment of a facilitated meeting. For example, Innes attended a working meeting on evaluating collaborative processes that included directors of nonprofits, academics, and scientists, along with representatives of foundations. Several speakers were invited to talk about what they were doing on the ground and how it worked. While some were accustomed to giving such presentations in more or less professional ways, one presenter was a Native American from a tribe in the Sierra which lived among the redwoods. For many generations this tribe had maintained the ecosystem, but there were new threats. The tribe was trying to get a proposal funded to help them address new issues of sustainability. This presenter told us in a moving and vivid way of the history of the tribe and their symbiotic relationship with the redwoods. He told us what the Sierra meant to him and his tribe. He spoke eloquently of things none us had experienced. He spoke of the values of his culture through his stories. We listened spellbound for the hour that he spoke. Then he told us how the funders wanted them to write a proposal a certain way, using the funders' categories and framework. He told us of submitting proposal after proposal and having it turned down. He could not understand this as he believed his tribe knew better than anyone how to manage the redwoods. We asked him a few questions and then he left. The experience changed me and I think the others at the table, though we could not quite say how. If he had come in with visual aids and distilled his message into seven points, it would have made far less impression.

Stories are critical to communication across lay and professional cultures, if professionals are willing to see them as more than just anecdotes. As sociologists and anthropologists have long noted, stories can capture the essence of a culture's value system whether factually true or not. Myths have a truth that goes beyond facts. The stories people tell are less about facts in any case than about making a point that cannot be made in a simple linear way. The stories convey more than an expert style statement of cause and effect. They express emotion and intensity of feeling and they say what is right and wrong (Forester 1999). They help to work through a problem. It is true that stakeholders in well run dialogues often tell stories and do role plays to illustrate their points (Innes and Booher 1999b), but they do so within a discourse and a controlled exchange. While it is possible that representatives like the Native American could participate in such a dialogue, it can make more sense to have them simply come and tell their stories and go back to their world and their praxis. Their world is about farming, living on the streets, or managing in the wilderness. It is not about negotiations and learning professional discourses.

Relationships of experts with local knowers

There are a number of models of what the relationship should be between science and local knowledge. Corburn (2003) identifies three basic ones. The most traditional, expert-based, view contends that locals have a deficit of the necessary technical knowledge. This view typically leads to decision makers and scientists discounting what locals say. A second view is that local knowledge can complement scientific knowledge. This knowledge could not contradict scientific findings, but it could enrich or add to them. A third view is that professionals and locals can co-produce the data and analyses, with each needing the other to get adequate information.

For the fishery world, Wilson articulates four models (Wilson 1999). The first is the deference model, which parallels Corburn's first model. This is based on the view that the most accurate picture comes from relying on scientists' judgment and using fishers only as assistants. Fishers may tag fish, keep log books, or carry observers on trips. Fishing industry advisors can help scientists in the identification of which research topics would be of most value.

The second and currently accepted approach, is the traditional ecological knowledge (TEK) model, built on the assumption that, not only is local knowledge necessary to get an adequate picture of fishery conditions, this knowledge is as valid as science. While fishers' insights may be described as anecdotal by scientists, they are the result of observations within the context of long term experience with what is and is not an important indicator of fishery health. Because fishers' knowledge is so local and contextual, it takes an effort for others to evaluate or use it, but part of the goal of TEK is to help fishers build their own knowledge base. This method has been used to monitor and understand stock change or judge the impact of dams on fish. The TEK approach has led to an understanding of how fishers and scientists tend to see things differently. Scientists have tended until recently to focus on fish population dynamics and statistical projections, using linear models with a limited set of variables, whereas fishers have a nonlinear view. They see the ocean as a textured and differentiated place, where small perturbations may have long term consequences and where fish stocks are not ultimately predictable. Some scientists however have begun producing models based on complexity thinking, demonstrating that small variations can result in large swings in stocks.

In the third model, players recognize that stakeholders construct the issues according to their institutional affiliations, experience, and interests. Fisheries science is framed within legal, political and economic agendas which lead scientists to ask certain questions and focus on certain issues. Government scientists are apt to construct a version of nature more amenable to bureaucratic management than it really is;

environmentalists, in order to mobilize their constituencies, construct a version where nature is more threatened than it really is; and fishers construct a version of nature that can support more fishing than it really can (Wilson 1999). This phenomenon is not unlike the conflict between regulatory and local experts in the habitat conservation case, where each responded to their organizational and political loyalties in their proposals for preservation of habitat.

The fourth model, which corresponds roughly to co-production in Corburn's typology, is "community science" in which collaborative fisheries science appears in the context of fisheries co-management. This approach will often both defer to the knowledge of professional scientists and respect TEK. It also takes into account the competing constructions of various stakeholder groups and is characterized by open dialogue about all the aspects of the problems.

All these models are challenging because of the fundamental difference in ways of knowing between scientists and local people. Scientists and experts operating in a positivist framing focus on quantifiable variables and seek simple numbers like averages or percentages, which allow them to do regression analyses or modeling based on aggregate behavior. Local knowers tend to focus on the variations, the richly differentiated tapestry of soils, changing weather and ocean conditions, localized air and water quality, and the range of ethnic groups and cultural practices in a community. While using averages or summary numbers is simple shorthand for regulators and it allows data to be manipulated through standard analytic and modeling procedures, it does not reflect lived experience.

Distributional information is critical for policy and planning issues, whether the dimensions are spatial, socioeconomic, or over time. Public agencies are apt however to look for simple measures to fulfill their mandates. It thus is likely that the interests of the poorest groups get short shrift because the data on poor neighborhoods are typically inadequate, with averages that conceal the severity of some problems. New modeling techniques based on complexity thinking, like agent based modeling, use the variations in the system instead of cancelling them out to make more nuanced projections and provide information about dynamics and variability in the system. Thus far these have been primarily used in public policy for predicting transportation behavior, but they have potential application in fishery management, water management and neighborhood change, to name a few possibilities.

Conclusion

To achieve collaborative rationality as well as social and environmental justice in public policy, the voices and experience of the local players closest to the situation, especially those who are normally marginalized, must be integrated into the dialogue. It is these voices that link public policy to the lifeworld, that make sure those robust and feasible conclusions can be reached. It is inclusion of their knowledge that is critical to a genuinely resilient system. It is inclusion of their views as members of disadvantaged and oppressed groups that most challenges the status quo and helps groups to move away from the comfortable self-reinforcing ideas in the dominant culture.

Genuine inclusion of lay and local knowledge, especially in processes that depend on science, is difficult. Anxieties over epistemology, uncertainty, and difference itself interfere with development of mutual respect and collaboration. The failure to integrate these knowledges has led to disastrous results around the world from Love Canal to Cumbria to the Andes. There are, however, emerging strategies that engage local people in knowledge production and local action. While these can be the basis for new initiatives, the biggest challenge remains creating workable settings in which face to face dialogues can include the truly disadvantaged in productive ways so their authentic voices can be taken seriously and local knowledge can be part of policy making.

Notes

1   It should be noted that increasingly doctors and medical practices are trying to incorporate multiple knowledges and multiple types of medicine to provide a holistic approach to the health of their clients.
2   The February 11, 1994, 12898, Federal Actions to Address Environmental Justice in Minority Populations and Low-income Populations.
3   From the DOE web site www.lm.doe.gov/spotlight/ej2.htm and www.lm doe.gov/env_justice/definition.htm
4   This is the idea that growth should be clustered, particularly around transit.
5   We refer here to a watershed as the geographical area drained by a river and its tributaries, conveyed to the same outlet.
6   An alternative perspective is that mapping and other visualization tools can themselves shape local knowledge and while bringing people closer to the planning process, can disconnect them from their local knowledge base (Van Herzele and van Woerkum 2008).
7   The Magnuson Fishery Conservation and Management Act of 1976.
8   The Magnuson Stevens Fishery Conservation and Management Act of 1996 and the Sustainable Fisheries Act.
9   Smith offers a vivid account of these differing perspectives (Smith 1995).
10 www.csus.edu/ccp/projects/recent.stm
11 Judith Allen (Allen and Allen 1997) writes of a group of tenants in London's Paddington neighborhood who presented their views in a short play acted out for the council. This had more impact on local housing policy than their efforts to engage in professional discourse.

Beyond collaboration 8

Democratic governance for a resilient society

> The overthrow of beliefs is not immediately followed by the overthrow of
> institutions; rather the new beliefs live for a long time in the now desolate and
> eerie house of their predecessors, which they themselves preserve, because
> of the housing shortage.
>
> Friedrich Nietzsche (Nietzsche and Lehmann 1986: 169)

As Neitzsche so eloquently reminds us, institutions resist change, even when our ideas
no longer mesh with them. We try to make do with the old ones because building new
institutions is so daunting. With this book we hope to move forward in an effort to develop
new forms of governance that mesh with the changing beliefs and emergent practices
we have outlined. These practices emerged outside and around traditional hierarchical
government with agencies separated into silos and applying inflexible procedures. They
emerged because of a felt need of those concerned to incorporate more voices and to
work in spaces among agencies on topics that would otherwise fall between the cracks.
These practices exist uneasily at best with traditional government and represent one of
many indications of a crisis of democratic governance – a widespread dissatisfaction,
at least in the U.S., with the performance of democracy. In this current era of rapid change
and uncertainty we need practices of decision making that can respond rapidly and allow
our societies to be resilient and adaptive. Thus we propose to move beyond collaboration
alone to creating resilient governance systems that build on the basic principles of collaborative rationality. We believe that experiences, ideas and practices now in existence
offer building blocks and vision to move toward such governance.

We begin this chapter with a discussion of what many scholars are calling the
"crisis in democracy," outlining some of the evidence for it and offering it as a context
in which new collaborative practices are emerging. We move on to explore the differing
mental models that guide those who operate within traditional government institutions
compared to those who function in a collaborative governance style, showing how
practices and mental models are linked. A further section lays out the ideal of a resilient
society and how we can move beyond collaboration to governance for resilience. In the
next section we offer key concepts and tools for resilient governance, including networks,

dialogues, feedback systems, and many of the other ideas we have touched on in this book. We look finally at the roles government and public officials have in a resilient governance system, where they would have more scope than today, but less control.

The crisis in democracy

Scholars have been arguing for more than 30 years that democratic nations face a crisis in governance (Agger, et al. 2008; Crozier, et al. 1975; de Sousa Briggs 2008; Hajer and Wagenaar 2003; Nye, et al. 1997; Patterson 2002; Pharr and Putnam 2000). One aspect of their assessment emerges from research on the effects of politics and government on society. They identify widespread democratic disengagement and apathy which appear to be generated by current practices and institutions of government such as partisan posturing and influence by special interests. Researchers found significant public distrust of elected and agency leaders.

The crisis is also manifested in pressures for change in democratic practices and institutions (Hajer and Wagenaar 2003). First, new spaces are emerging where governance activities take place, as they did in CRI projects like the Sierra Business Council or in the cases we outlined in Chapter 3. These exploratory efforts to address broad and complex cross-boundary problems coexist with and challenge traditional government agencies, each with its limited responsibility for certain policy issues and legislative bodies serving only defined geographic areas. In addition, government agencies are increasingly linked across scales and levels of government, often through informal networks like those in CALFED. Moreover, these traditional institutions are beginning to incorporate cooperation with nongovernmental organizations. Scholars call this phenomenon "network governance" (Kickert, et al. 1997; Sørensen and Torfing 2007)

The complexity and rapid change in contemporary society have also created an increasing awareness among policy leaders of the limits to hierarchical control by government agencies and to formal expertise in solving problems. This awareness leads to growing uncertainty about policy and a new focus on the need to manage uncertainty, rather than create programs and regulatory regimes that deny its existence. As society has become more culturally diverse, moreover, decision makers have to deal with an array of publics with different values, perspectives, cognitive styles, and worldviews. The complexity is also reflected in growing interdependence among government players, as agencies find they cannot be successful, even on their own limited agendas, if they continue to work unilaterally. Diversity poses challenges to communication and understanding, but interdependence creates the incentive to overcome these challenges. Finally, arising out of all of these is the changing dynamics of trust. Trust in traditional government originates in the legitimacy of constitutional institutions. In the context of new spaces, uncertainty, diversity, and interdependence this trust can no longer be assumed, but must be built through communication and joint action.

After an extensive study of democracy in Europe, North America, and Japan, Pharr and Putnam concluded the evidence was that decline in public trust is related to the performance of governments and politics rather than to social or cultural phenomena, heightened competition, or individualism (Pharr and Putnam 2000). Moreover, they found substantial evidence at the aggregate level of nations that confidence in government and social trust are strongly associated with one another. Nations where there is high confidence in political institutions tend to enjoy high levels of social trust generally.

Most of the cases in Chapter 3 came into being because of the perceived failure of government performance around an issue of importance. In each case groups created new spaces of deliberation to address the problem. In the Sacramento Water Forum public officials were explicit that the existing institutions of government were not resulting in effective water planning. Public agencies themselves created, financed, and enacted the agreement of the Water Forum to create a new space for water planning and management. In CALFED public officials and business leaders, in the face of a major threat to the state economy from stalemate on state water policy, created an informal water policy process that existed in a shadow space among powerful agencies. Like the Water Forum, CALFED was funded by government, and many of its leaders were top officials in state and federal agencies. New Jersey invented a process outside traditional planning practice to advance a growth management strategy by including both state and local agencies in a new kind of dialogue. In Cincinnati a court created a collaborative community-based process because the judge concluded that traditional litigation offered little prospect of adequately addressing the community-police conflict. Regional stake-holders in the San Francisco Bay Area created their own space in the BAASC to come up with a growth management strategy for the region, which they intended to implement by influencing traditional institutions such as the state legislature and city councils that had been unable to act. Finally, EBCRC began when a congressman sponsored legislation to create a pilot project and provide $5 million to a commission of public officials and area stakeholders to inform and improve the cumbersome process for military base conversions.

Many of the paradoxes and contradictions discussed in Chapter 4 emerge from the tensions between failures of government capacity and our need for those insti-tutions if we are to function at all. As Neitzsche said, we live in the desolate and eerie house of our ancestors because of the housing shortage. Stakeholders talk of living in two worlds – the world of collaboration and that of adversarial decision making. Collaboration can be beneficial for a stakeholder, but simultaneously harmful if it is an obstacle to adversarial strategies that might promise greater gain. Collaboration can both challenge existing institutions and protect them with ameliorative and non-threatening changes. Stakeholders must both choose options, and keep options open. They cannot regard problems as solved because agreements are often not permanent. New developments and information can lead to a need for changes in the agreement. Thus collaborative processes cannot fully eliminate conflict. Indeed doing so may not be a desirable goal as agonism generates much of the energy and creativity of collaboratively rational processes. The value of the processes lies in providing an alternative means of managing conflict and using them to develop productive results that represent a more inclusive set of voices than in standard government practices. Sometimes the value is mainly that the processes can provide a way forward when the traditional institutions are in gridlock and unable to address complex and controversial problems, or problems that are not central to their missions.

We suggest that the application of the principles of collaborative rationality offers a way to confront the declining trust in government institutions and practices. This is not to say all decisions need to be made through ideal versions of collaborative dialogue, but rather that ideas of inclusion, authentic dialogue, and working together across interests can substitute for many of the more hierarchical, rule-based methods of public agencies in the traditional mode, for the partisan wheeling and dealing of legislative bodies, and for the narrowly focused win/lose model of court decisions.

Mental models in traditional government and in collaborative governance

To develop new institutions we have to start by understanding the norms and practices now in use and, in particular, by understanding the mental models that guide both old and new practices. In the traditional model the tacit imagery is that a policy problem is like a machine which can be broken down into its components, analyzed, and fixed. There is a best solution, and the objective of inquiry is to find it. Organizations (both agencies and advocacy groups) develop remedies for the problems in their domain, typically with the aid of experts. Universities train students to become expert in finding solutions for policy and planning issues and in advocating for them. Agencies and advocacy groups, as well as legislators, proceed by announcing their remedies and defending them against those who disagree.[1] When this method is not convincing enough, they add another step in keeping with their conviction that they have the best solution – education. They do what some call outreach, but which others might call marketing, or even propaganda. The idea is to educate the public and other leaders about the correct way to understand the problem and solve it.[2] The institutions of pluralist democracy are compatible with this set of practices, as organizations and experts compete with each other to have their problem definitions and solutions adopted. The tacit assumption is that there is a market of ideas and that its invisible hand will assure that the best solution prevails.

In our research and practice we have found many manifestations of this dynamic, which we regard as one of the pathologies of the old institutions. For example, participants in the BAASC coalition operated from a traditional pluralist model of policy change. They came up with their solution for growth management and focused on getting it implemented by lobbying legislators. The strategy failed. Another example of the dynamic is the "not invented here" phenomenon. A major California state agency responsible for environmental protection refused to consider an approach developed in a consensus building process because the director decided the agency should develop its own solution. In another case, California legislative staff blocked proposed funding for a stakeholder consensus process to address a major fiscal issue, though the process had been requested unanimously by a bi-partisan commission. The staff decided they should develop the solution. We have found that agency leaders often turn down proposals for collaborative processes because they fear they will lose control or be criticized because they were unable to develop a solution themselves. After all, if they have to rely on stakeholders and the public, maybe they are not up to their job. All of this thinking is associated with the mental model of the older institutions.

This mindset is the basis of interaction heuristics in organizations that Argyris and Schon call "model I theory in use" (Argyris and Schon 1996). They found that this model dominates interactions in the vast majority of western organizations and is an obstacle to learning in those organizations. In this model the governing principles are:

1   define goals and try to achieve them;
2   minimize losing and maximize winning;
3   do not generate or express negative feelings; and
4   be rational.

Therefore participants seek to control others and the environment to ensure their solution and goals are adopted. To minimize negative feelings participants avoid testing their ideas publicly, preferring to work behind the scenes to get their views accepted and to discredit other views that conflict with their own. This was the approach Innes confronted in the EBCRC case when she raised a conflicting perspective in a meeting. The crucial double loop learning which allows getting beyond stalemate and repetition of failing strategies is not encouraged by such interaction behaviors. The Decide, Announce, Defend approach has little room for listening, much less adapting to new information or unanticipated change.

Collaborative rationality, by contrast, is in keeping with ideas from complexity science and pragmatism which see the world as inherently uncertain and decisions as necessarily contingent. In this view, planning and policy are not about finding the best solution – indeed there is no one best solution though there may be many better than the status quo. Collaboratively rational processes are about engaging with other members of a community to jointly learn and work out how to get better together in the face of conflict, complex changing conditions, and multiple conflicting sources of information. Such processes are not only about finding new ways to move forward, but they are ultimately about building community and governance capacity to be resilient in the face of the inevitable new challenges.

The mental model behind collaborative rationality, the model that could be a basis for new institutions of democracy and governance, is similar to what Argyris and Schon called model II theory in use (Argyris and Schon 1996). The heuristics of interaction in this model include:

1   obtain valid information;
2   make informed choices; and
3   assure internal commitment to the choices.

These are the same values that many facilitators of collaborative processes use (Schwarz 1994; Schuman 2005). Participants in a collaboratively rational dialogue bring their information into the process and suggest from their perspective what the information may imply. Other participants are free to challenge it and offer alternative data and inferences. Participants share power over the deliberations with anyone who has competence and relevance with regard to decisions about the problem. Participants recognize that all the information and inferences are contingent and subject to change if better information is forthcoming and if the consequences of preliminary actions suggest change is needed. The participants are free to make their choices without external pressure.

Use of this model can lead to double loop learning because through such interactions, the group not only may decide on a different approach, but may also learn that the problem is different from what they originally thought or decide to pursue an alternative goal. In the cases we studied that came closest to authentic dialogue, many of the participants revised their perspectives using mental model II. Double loop learning occurred, for example, when the Water Forum agreed that water planning required protecting both the environment and water supply, rather than making a trade off between these.

Ideas about traditional and collaborative governance

These two mental models are also manifested in different ideas about governance institutions and practices. In Table 8.1 we outline some of these differences, drawing on ideas about bureaucracy going back to Weber (1958) and on contrasting ideas from pragmatism and complexity science, as well as our own research and that of scholars who study network governance (Booher 2007; Kickert, et al. 1997).

Traditional governance relies on a concept of bureaucracy characterized by a top down hierarchy under central control. Agencies have closed boundaries in the sense that participation in decision making is only by those who have roles in that agency. This is a fair characterization of, for example, the California Department of Water Resources (DWR), one of the powerful agencies that became a part of CALFED. In collaborative governance by contrast a structure typically involves distributed control, open boundaries, and interdependent, nested network clusters of participants. Once the agency joined CALFED, agency representatives and stakeholders participated in several different groups that shared authority and made decisions in an informal process. These decisions were only then implemented by various responsible agencies including DWR (Innes, et al. 2007).

These forms of governance also imply different ideas about leadership and management. In traditional governance directive leadership may be called for, where the leader has a vision of what needs to be accomplished and marshals his or her team to this end. Collaborative governance instead implies generative leadership (Roberts 1997). In this approach leaders create conditions to bring teams together and help them build their collective capacity to learn about the problems they face and to create solutions. In traditional governance the role of the manager is an organization controller; the tasks are to plan and guide organizational processes: the activities are planning, designing, and leading. In collaborative governance the manager is a mediator and process manager. Her activities are guiding interactions and providing opportunities for team members to jointly inquire into problems and solutions. Her activities include selecting team members, providing resources, and influencing the conditions so that the inquiry can be productive.

Table 8.1 Ideas about traditional and collaborative governance

Governance dimension	Traditional governance	Collaborative governance
Structure	Top down hierarchy	Interdependent network clusters
Source of direction	Central control	Distributed control
Boundary condition	Closed	Open
Organizational context	Single authority	Divided authority
Leadership approach	Directive	Generative
Role of manager	Organization controller	Mediator, process manager
Managerial tasks	Planning and guiding organizational processes	Guiding interactions, providing opportunity
Managerial activities	Planning, designing, and leading	Selecting agents and resources, influencing conditions
Goals	Clear with defined problems	Various and changing
Criterion of success	Attainment of goals of formal policy	Realization of collective action and conditions for future collaboration
Nature of planning	Linear	Nonlinear
Public participation objective	Legal conformity, inform and educate, gain support of public for agency policies	Create conditions for social learning and problem-solving capacity
Democratic legitimacy	Representative democracy	Deliberative democracy
Source of system behavior	Determined by component participant roles	Determined by interactions of participants

For example, the agencies participating in CALFED internally followed the traditional approach to leadership and management. But the CALFED process as a whole was a form of collaborative governance, with its leaders' emphasis on managing the process, identifying and bringing in needed participants, facilitating and guiding the interactions in the committees and work groups, and providing resources and conditions for these groups. This dynamic was the source of some tensions as participants went back to their respective agencies and advocacy organizations with the decisions of the various work groups and presented them to bosses who were not involved directly in CALFED (Innes, et al. 2007). These participants were living in two worlds, the emergent institutions and the houses of their ancestors.

Traditional and collaborative governance also employ different ideas about goals, criteria for success, and the nature of the planning process. For traditional governance the assumption is that goals are relatively clear for well defined problems and that the criterion for success is attainment of the goals. Within the boundary of their authority and responsibility an agency's job is to find the best measures to fix a problem. It is a success if the measures are implemented. In this context planning is perceived as a stepwise linear process, from goals, to analysis and policy development, and then implementation. Collaborative governance, however, acknowledges goals that are sometimes in conflict, and in any case are likely to change during the course of deliberation. Hence the criterion for success is the realization of collective action and the capacity to adapt to change. This implies a nonlinear approach to planning where goals may be revisited as part of the analysis, policy development, or implementation and where exploratory implementation may occur throughout the process. It is not enough to produce a solution and implement it – success requires change in the problematic situation.

While CALFED agencies started with their own goals, the overall process had only the most generic of purposes, which developed and became more complex as the dialogue proceeded. CALFED started with a linear planning process following the steps laid out in environmental impact assessment law, but quickly evolved into the type of nonlinear process suggested by the collaborative governance model, without following a standard order and with many steps overlapping (Booher 2008; Innes, et al. 2007). Participants largely expressed satisfaction with the process. They did achieve some learning and collective action. Others outside the process, however, faulted it for not achieving specific goals; they approached it as if it were a hierarchical agency and evaluated it in that light.

Finally, traditional and collaborative governance suggest different ideas about public participation, democratic legitimacy, and the origins of system behavior. For traditional agencies the purposes of public participation are typically to comply with legal requirements, educate the public, and obtain public support for agency proposals (Innes and Booher 2005; King, et al. 1998). Legitimacy for actions is based in the theory and practice of representative democracy – that is, agency actions are legitimate because they flow from the direction of elected representative bodies, which in turn provide oversight. The way an observer tries to understand this policy system is by looking at the roles of the various agents and how they are fulfilling them.[3]

In collaborative governance the purpose of participation is to engage the public in joint learning and to build public capacity for problem-solving and adaptation. It is about listening and deliberating rather than announcing and defending. Collaborative governance is grounded in the belief that developing the most effective solutions requires informed public deliberation. The assumption is that many problems will require the public to at least support, if not play a part in, implementing, solutions, and therefore that social learning is a crucial part of planning and public policy (Booher 2008; Innes and Booher 2005; King, et al. 1998). Mutz argues that culture and political practices in the U.S. are, however, in conflict with the idea of deliberative public participation (Mutz 2006). The traditional norm is that citizens channel their participation through association with those who agree with them, in true pluralist style. They should avoid deliberating about political issues with those who do not agree because that will cause tension and conflict. This is, of course, contrary to collaborative governance, which, in the pragmatist tradition, depends on many forms of knowledge and to collaborative rationality which requires that very tension to get sound results.

Legitimacy for actions through collaborative governance flows from deliberative democratic theory. Thus actions are legitimate if all affected interests deliberated together about the issue in a noncoercive environment with valid information and reached agreement on those actions (Bohman 1996; Richardson 2002). To understand the behavior of this policy system we need to examine the interactions of the agents in the system rather than their roles. It is the cumulative effect of the interactions that determine how the system functions.[4]

Examples of this type of collaborative governance include CALFED's program to engage the public in forums across California's regions designed to build their capacity to develop and implement their own water management programs (Booher 2008; Innes, et al. 2006). For its 2005 State Water Plan, DWR, which was an active participant in CALFED, decided to adopt a collaborative governance approach. This was a departure from the normal expert-based process with public hearings. The collaborative version engaged water stakeholders and other members of the public in the plan making process. The result was

> a much more complex (and arguably more accurate) understanding of California's water challenges and opportunities. The 2005 process also appears to have hastened an evolution of DWR's institutional culture toward greater transparency and interagency cooperation, opened doors for previously marginalized stakeholder groups, and improved the agency's working relationships with the public.

Moreover, participants reported a greater gain in shared social and intellectual capital in the collaborative process than in the traditional processes (Ambruster 2008: 2).

The CALFED effort always struggled with legitimacy due to its informal nature, though as long as it was producing results and containing destructive conflict it was accepted. But as money and high level leadership deteriorated, the legislature began to argue for more formal oversight. Ultimately the creation of the California Bay Delta

Authority to provide legitimacy and control interfered with the collaborative process, illustrating the difficulty of collaborating within old style institutions.

Beyond collaboration: creating conditions for resilient governance

Sørensen and Torfing argue that the phenomenon of collaborative governance or what they call network governance is here to stay (Sørensen and Torfing 2007). They contend that

> policy, defined as the attempt to achieve a desired outcome, is a result of *governing* processes that are no longer fully controlled by the government, but subject to negotiations between a wide range of public, semi-public and private actors, whose interactions give rise to a relatively stable pattern of policy making that constitutes a specific form of regulation, or *mode of coordination.*
>
> (Sørensen and Torfing 2007: 3–4) (their emphasis).

The conditions that have led to wider experimentation with these new forms are only increasing the demand for alternative governance. In short the current conduct of American government remains a poor match for the problems it must address (Kettl 2005: 4).

Inquiring into the prospects for collaborative governance brings us back to the question of effective performance of government and the crisis of democracy. After all this is not an abstract debate about which form of government is better. Rather it is a question of how society can create institutions of governance that better address a multiplicity of needs in the face of constant change, complexity, and fragmentation. In recent years scholars who have been using complexity science to develop concepts for sustainable management of social-ecological systems have focused on the importance of resilience and adaptive co-management (Armitage, et al. 2007; Berkes, et al. 2003; Gunderson and Holling 2002; Röling and Wagemakers1998). The emerging findings from this research can help us better understand how democratic governance may need to evolve.

Resilience is a key concept that we can use for understanding how collaborative governance can work. A resilient system is one that can withstand shocks and surprises, absorb extreme stresses, and maintain its core functions, though perhaps in an altered form. Resilience refers to three main features, according to Berkes and colleagues (Berkes, et al. 2003):

- The amount of change a system can undergo and still retain the same controls on function and structure, or still be in the same state, within the same domain of attraction;
- The degree to which a system is capable of self-organization;
- The ability to build and increase the capacity for learning and adaptation in a system.

Research on resilience starts from two premises – first that change is normal and stability is what needs to be understood, rather than vice versa. The second premise is that sustainability should be understood as a dynamic process rather than an end product and accordingly that societies must have adaptive capacity (Armitage, et al. 2007; Berkes, et al. 2003; Holden 2008; Röling and Wagemakers 1998).

Research also suggests useful insights about the challenges in the search for resilient governance (Röling and Wagemakers 1998). First, the established ways of adapting to change rather than change itself cause problems in the performance of government. Second, responsiveness depends on individual and collective choices shaped by history, so our capacity to respond effectively to particular stresses is limited if there are no precedents. Third, in the contemporary context of rapid change, development and use of knowledge are primary tools for resilience. We need to perceive and interpret changing conditions collectively and to develop knowledge, expertise, and new organizational forms in response to what we learn. Adaptive learning is critical and must be continuous. Finally, elites who have a mandate to lead by virtue of their positions as elected officials, appointed agency directors, CEOs of large companies, or directors of major foundations are often insulated from direct experience of the changes. They can maintain their lifestyles and may see no problem with the current order of things. Witness the resistance to adaptation of the leading bankers and regulators in the face of the disastrous global recession of 2008–2009. As we argued in Chapter 7, local knowledge is critical to resilient systems and thus citizens and non-elites must be part of the policy process.

Resilience thinking shifts the purpose of governance from the questions "where do we want to be and how do we get there?" to "how do we move in a desirable direction in the face of uncertainty?" The latter question shifts the focus of decision making from debating alternative solutions to working together with our diverse knowledges to craft adaptive strategies that can help us move in a desired direction. Once we look at uncertainties we may even change our collective idea of the direction we wish to go. In this perspective governance processes are improved by making them flexible to deal with uncertainty and surprises and by building their capacity to co-evolve with change. Thus resilient governance means not only responding to change, but also creating and shaping it (Berkes, et al. 2003: 352).

Existing ways of doing things in government are typically firmly entrenched, however, so change toward a more fluid governance system will only occur slowly and incrementally. But that change is occurring today outside and alongside traditional government activities. In this book we have examined some of these emergent practices, experiments, and ideas, as these all offer insights for creating a resilient governance system. These will not replace formal government, but coexist with it for some time, perhaps as a shadow system, doing such things as allowing local governments to take actions they would not agree to if they were legally binding or public agencies to do things they are not yet formally empowered to do. The players can experiment and select what appears to work, combining ideas in various ways in pragmatic style. They may provide innovations and ideas that elected officials may take up. These experiments will provide new ways to get public input. In the process they will gradually change existing practices through the cumulative effect of evolving norms, expectations, and understandings as well as collective learning.

Planning and policy practices at all levels of government are central to the achievement of governance that contributes to societal resilience. Collaboratively rational practices of engagement around planning and policy issues by their nature allow for adaptive response to complex and uncertain situations as they include many players and forms of knowledge, and their results do not need to be enshrined in rigid rules or programs. These practices can implement broad strategies adaptively as they did in the Water Forum and CALFED. These processes however must be enabled by governing institutions that provide incentive structures for participation, technical knowledge, and legitimacy. Most of the processes we explored in this book were made possible by government policies and support. Supportive frameworks for collaboration include budgets, laws, regulations, and political and financial incentives for participation. To make resilience work public agencies need to alter the incentive structures of staff to reward them for participating in networks, experimenting and innovating, and helping produce societally beneficial outcomes that may not be strictly within the agency's mission. As institutional arrangements and policies can shape practices, these practices can in turn shape the institutions and policies.

In keeping with one of the themes of this chapter – that policy needs to move beyond debating alternative solutions – we do not propose a specific design for adaptive governance systems. We draw on the theory and case material in this book to tentatively offer ideas for evolving governance systems that can enable collaborative practices. The goal is to move beyond piecemeal collaborative efforts ultimately to a more fluid system of governance that can result in greater societal resilience and more responsive democracy.

Three features of adaptive governance

We contend that three key features are required for a governance system to be adaptive in the face of uncertainty:

1   diversity in its agents and components;
2   ample opportunity for interaction among the agents; and
3   effective methods for selection of appropriate actions.[5]

That is, the governance system first needs many types of agents, operating with different perspectives, knowledges, and interests. It needs to engage in many types of activities and to experiment. It needs to learn by doing and to spread this learning through feedback loops. It needs to engage multiple agencies at all scales from federal to local. It needs to incorporate business, environmental, and social equity players, as well as citizens of differing ethnicity, social and economic status, and locale. It also needs knowledgeable local players and experts from many fields. This diversity is crucial both to assure that a wide variety of information is at work and that there will be many options and many players with different capabilities to take a variety of actions. The idea is parallel to the rationale for maintaining biodiversity to ensure resilience in ecological systems.

Second, the system needs ample face to face interaction among its agents so that they can be informed about one another's activities, learn from these, and can make more informed choices about their own actions. The face to face aspect assures the building of social capital and the development of shared understanding as well as allowing for collaborative rationality with its requirement of key speech conditions of accuracy, legitimacy, comprehensibility and sincerity. Such interaction can create transformations in beliefs and perspectives, as our cases illustrate. The agents need to be networked among themselves to share and discuss information and experiments, to develop common understandings, and to adapt their activities on short notice as events and information demand. These interactions need to cross sectors, scales, and jurisdictional boundaries, as well as public and private sectors. This interaction needs to be collaborative to assure that listening and mutual learning take place. Some of the forums where these interactions can occur include citizen workshops, interagency collaborations, stakeholder dialogues, partner relationships among public agencies and nonprofits, and networks. These interactions cannot be orchestrated in detail from a central authority if this is to be an adaptive system. They have to be self-organizing and evolving like the larger system itself.

Finally, governance systems need informed and effective selection mechanisms. For a system to be productively adaptive it must include a way to eliminate ineffective strategies and agents and to encourage those with more valued outcomes. In nature, individual organisms or even entire species may die off if they use unproductive strategies and cannot adapt. If a system is characterized by high biodiversity, then others can replace these and the dynamics may change. The system takes new shape, but it remains living and evolving. By the same token, in adaptive governance some practices catch on as agents learn about them from one another. Others fail to thrive as the first few efforts do not seem productive. Unfortunately government often interferes with the natural selection process, as it continues to fund approaches that are ineffective because powerful politicians want them or simply because of inertia. Government can similarly fail to support potentially promising practices for fear these might not work. A fluid governance system can allow experimentation and innovation to occur before programs are legislatively designed and institutionalized. The informality of the system makes it easier to drop failing efforts. All of this selection process depends on effective feedback and functioning networks through which performance information can flow.

Networks: the core of adaptive governance

At its heart, adaptive governance is about harnessing the power of networks – networks that connect people, ideas, and knowledge in changing combinations across organizations and public problems. These fluid linkages have emerged to address many problems where traditional structures of government have failed. Such problems often involve place making, like efforts to develop integrated regional governance (Hajer 2003a) or do strategic spatial planning (Healey 2007). The existence of interdependence among players and the inability of a single actor or organization to make progress working alone is a critical factor in drawing actors together in networks (Aldrich 1979). Although in one sense, governance networks are not new – actors concerned with solving public problems have always been linked, if loosely, across an array of institutions and organizations – the perception of increasing interdependence and complexity has piqued interest in how network approaches can improve the governing of society (Kettl 2005).

Networks may primarily improve information-sharing or they may serve as forums for public policy deliberation, decision making, and implementation (Klijn and Koppenjan 2000). By connecting diverse actors around specific problems or geographic areas, networks build sensitivity to local realities that centralized government often cannot achieve (Hajer and Wagenaar 2003). They also increase coordination across many bound-aries such as those between government agencies, levels of government, experts from different fields, and opposing ideological camps (Schneider, et al. 2003).

It is through these capacities that governance networks can improve resilience of complex systems. Resilience grows as networks strengthen linkages in the system. These linkages facilitate the self-organization of nodes of interaction, dialogue, and collaboration to address emerging problems or crises. Networks do not get rid of conflict. Rather, by bringing together interdependent actors with different interests, perspectives, and resources, network nodes can serve as sites of creative energy for finding mutually beneficial ways to move forward (Klijn and Koppenjan 2000: 140). After actors have crafted a plan, each can draw on his or her own external linkages to access and mobilize a larger range of resources and people (De Rynck and Voets 2006). Finally, networks, as well as their component agents, can learn and adapt through experimentation, monitoring, and responding to feedback.

Components for resilient governance

The examples of emergent practices contain within them components that can be assembled in a variety of ways to create governance for resilience. No one component is sufficient by itself; many or most of these will exist in combination in a resilient gov-ernance system. These components include:

Diversity and interdependence

Diverse and interdependent players can be assembled to jointly do tasks in which all have a stake. Diversity provides the many faceted perspectives, and interdependence creates the opportunity for the invention of options for mutual gain, moving beyond the zero sum negotiations that typify conflicts today.

Collaborative dialogues

Multiway dialogues in which all are heard and respected are important. These can not only do joint visioning and tasks, but they can also build social capital among previously competing parties. They can create linkages among these players, along with shared understandings of the issues. Such dialogues can allow shared purpose to emerge and can channel conflict into constructive strategy making. They can be the opportunity, not only for problem solving, but also for the development of innovative strategies to address seemingly intractable issues.

Collaborative development of knowledge

Collaborative development and use of knowledge is crucial because no single source or type of information is adequate to encompass the many issues that must be considered. Moreover, different participants see through different lenses, each of which offers valuable information. Finally, such jointly developed information is essential to assuring trust among diverse players.

Networks

Networks of players can be built. They can be a natural outgrowth of collaborations or created and nurtured by public agencies to deliver services or link public and private sectors for joint tasks.

Boundary spanning

Cross-sector, cross-jurisdictional, and cross-scale activities are critical, as are linkages and joint activities between the public and private sector, including nonprofits. Boundary spanning activities not only allow the sharing of information and the building of under-standing of differing agendas and competencies, they also create the potential for discovering mutually beneficial actions. Most of all, they enable resilience by creating new flows of information and by developing shared meaning among the actors on the issues.

Monitoring and feedback

Resilience requires monitoring, feedback systems, and ways of responding in real time to what is learned (Innes and Booher 2000). Indicators should be developed for key changes in, for example, traffic patterns, educational achievement, and mortgage foreclosures. Moreover, there need to be ways of jointly analyzing these data and selecting appropriate responses.

Small, diverse working groups

A central technique for working in a complex and uncertain context is the use of small, diverse groups to work through specific tasks. This has been a major component in CALFED, the Water Forum, and many other effective collaborative processes. Such groups can build trust and joint learning as well as produce feasible and innovative proposals.

Roles of government

These governance practices suggest new roles for federal, state, and local governments, as well as citizens, interest groups, scientists, and the private sector. Governing for resilience requires government to play an active role, though one that differs in key respects from current practice. A focus on adaptive governance rather than government shifts the role of government away from single-handedly developing and implementing plans and programs and instead to steering or metagovernance (Bogason and Musso 2006). Metagovernance refers to "the management of complexity and plurality" (Jessop 1998: 42). Government can do this by enabling and encouraging self-organization and by building capacity in a variety of ways. The public sector has access to resources – budgets, personnel, and democratic legitimacy – that are essential to creating a resilient system. Government can offer incentives for cooperation among players; it can create forums for dialogue around joint actions to be taken by agencies and private players; and it can set targets and direction (Klijn and Koppenjan 2000).

Elected officials

There are at least four ways in which political officials can engage in metagovernance (Sørensen 2006). First, they can establish political, organizational, and financial means for action, for example by crafting laws and incentive structures that foster cooperation and learning. Creating forums for dialogue with statutory legitimacy may give hesitant actors the motivation to engage (Schneider, et al. 2003). Second, elected officials can articulate visions of the future and shape public perceptions of the issues and solution through story, metaphor, and imagery. This can inspire actors or reframe issues from intractable ones to manageable ones. Third, elected officials can engage as neutral facilitators or mediators of processes. Fourth, they can engage as active participants in negotiation of collective solutions.

In Delaware in 2001, for example, Governor Ruth Ann Minner responded to a high state incidence of cancer by forming a stakeholder collaborative task force to advise her on methods for reducing incidence and mortality. Many citizens living with the effects of cancer were included in brainstorming, and subcommittees addressed specific goals. Actions were quickly implemented, including cancer screenings, increased preventive procedures and coordination, linking patients with medical care and services. By 2006 the reduction in cancer mortality was double that of the rest of the country. Governor Minner set in motion dialogues and networks, which in turn produced innovative strategies and motivated prompt action and change.[6]

Governance for resilience entails adaptation of the standard roles of elected officials. They may less often prepare detailed policies and programs and more often establish frameworks and mobilize players. In our view these new roles can ultimately give them more scope and power than they now have. Instead of limiting citizens' capabilities to participate in the remaking of institutions and practices, they can enhance citizen capabilities (Hayward 2000). Elected officials will continue to be leaders, but more as visionaries, enablers, regulators of process, and decision makers of final resorts than they are today. They will be the ones to establish the tasks, set the priorities, create incentive structures, and remove obstacles to cooperation.

Leaders of public agencies

Agency leaders will need to develop skills at building organizations that can learn and work across boundaries (Wondolleck and Yaffee 2000) as they do in the private sector. The task may require changing reward structures, providing training and resources, and recruiting people with skills in community outreach and conflict management. It will include creating jobs with new responsibilities and descriptions such as for network facilitators and liaisons. Leaders can also make changes to organizational structures and processes like budgeting to promote cross-boundary cooperation and build responsiveness and flexibility.

For example, a Superintendent of Yosemite National Park elevated community engagement and outreach to a more prominent and valued position in park management. He also modeled an ethic of collaboration by engaging personally with community members and spearheaded community-building dialogues outside of formal planning processes. These actions alleviated long-running tensions between the park and surrounding communities and built capacity for addressing emerging issues more proactively and collaboratively (Lever, et al. 2008). In a second example, the Chief of Police in San Jose California invented a process to get the police and community members talking to each other. As a result the community began to trust the police and the police began to realize the community wanted good policing. Demands for a police review board dissipated, a community police partnership began, and today the city has one of the lowest large city crime rates in the U.S.[7]

Civil servants

The focus on resilience shifts the role of civil servants from following rules and procedures, achieving performance targets, or developing plans to building and participating
in networks that improve functioning of complex systems (Stoker 2006: 44). As process
managers, civil servants can motivate other actors, build shared perception of problems,
create organizational arrangements for collaboration, and provide conflict management
assistance (Klijn and Koppenjan 2000). They can identify missing stakeholders and provide
logistical and staff support to collaboration.

Limits on government roles

There are limits to government roles in collaborative processes in part because these
government roles are not always compatible (Klijn and Koppenjan 2000). For instance, an
agency tasked with environmental protection cannot be a neutral facilitator for decision
making in a project with potentially negative impacts on the environment. The use of
networks, moreover, carries risks, such as the emergence of groupthink, lack of trans-
parency in decision making, insularity, and exclusion of the disempowered (Klijn and
Koppenjan 2000). These are problems that government can guard against by such
methods as assuring fully diverse participation and insistence on public access to decision
processes. In addition, collaborative governance is time- and resource-intensive, and many
issues are not sufficiently critical to attract and maintain participants' commitment
(Scharpf 1978). Finally, collaborative governance approaches are not a panacea. There
will continue to be many policy problems that cannot be solved with a stakeholder
collaborative process and must be referred to courts or legislatures for resolution.

Government has to address many problems where it is impractical to work
with key outside stakeholders, in foreign policy for example, but public agencies can still
make use of collaborative rationality to improve the outcomes of their decisions. They
can assure that a diversity of perspectives and knowledges is involved in their deliberations and can create the conditions of authentic dialogue among participants. A case
in point is the decision making leading up to the Vietnam War. We know from many
of the accounts that numerous officials in U.S. foreign policy agencies had important
knowledge about the dangers and misconceptions that were leading to an all out war.
They were concerned and tried to engage in the decision making. Some were frozen
out and not invited to meetings, ridiculed, and even removed from their positions for
their views. Others kept silent to avoid being excluded (Goldstein 2008; Halberstam
1968; Sheehan 1988). We can only imagine how this tragedy might have been averted
if collaborative rationality had been the norm.

Government has the opportunity to help actors recognize their interdependence and to organize themselves to address key tasks in ways that are accountable to
the public. For example, local governments in the U.S. are protective of their autonomy,
particularly in land use decision making, but they have no power over other jurisdictions'

land use decisions that affect them and little power over regional infrastructure decisions that shape their options. A new, more collaborative approach mandated by a state government could compensate for perceived loss of autonomy by empowering localities to influence each other's choices. What a state can do is create forums that join players across a region, as New Jersey did in its state planning process, with its incentives to cooperate to address growth and development issues. What state level players cannot do in the context of adaptive governance is micromanage such forums or unduly constrain them with rules and targets. Rather, they can establish the metagovernance framework and the incentives and let the players with local power and knowledge work through the most effective strategy.

Concluding thoughts

Change will not come quickly, but there is much that can be done through leadership and creativity, as we found in many examples we have recounted here. Policy professionals, planners, and public administrators have potentially significant roles in moving societies toward resilient governance systems through their agenda setting activities, their problem framing efforts, and their ability to focus public and political leaders' attention on emergent ideas and practices. They can do much to begin incorporating principles of collaborative rationality in their daily practices, engaging stakeholders and citizens in authentic participatory dialogues that they in turn use for making recommendations and getting public support for change. They can search out local knowledge and learn from it. They can set up processes to resolve conflict among scientists and among scientists and laymen. They can model collaborative practice and demonstrate its value to doubters through successful deliberations on topics where past efforts have led only to stalemate. Many elected and appointed officials will continue to demand control of decisions, regardless of the value of ideas generated through collaborative processes. We see evidence, however, that these norms are changing as many types of pressure build on the old institutions and new beliefs become stronger. The shadow system of collaboration and networks continues to grow. Eventually traditional government leaders may discover new opportunities for leadership by playing a part in metagovernance. Whatever the path, we feel certain this change is underway and hope that this volume will provide help and insight to those engaged in remodeling the institutions of democracy.

Notes

1   This phenomenon is so widely recognized that it has an acronym: DAD, decide, announce, and defend.
2   This practice has spawned a new acronym, DEAD.
3   Graham Allison used a version of this approach in Model II in his classic book *The Essence of Decision* which developed three alternative ways of understanding policy outcomes (Allison 1971).

4   This approach has some kinship with Allison's Model III, which examines policy as the result of a series of games played by the individuals in the policy arena, Ibid. While our framing is influenced by complexity science, Allison's perspective antedated much of complexity thinking.

5   These are drawn from Axelrod and Cohen's application of complexity thinking to social systems (Axelrod and Cohen 2000).

6   www.policyconsensus.org/casestudies/docs/DE_cancer.pdf www.policyconsensus.org/publications/news/PCI_Newsletter_Dec_08.html
     Video – www.policyconsensus.org/tools/videos/de_cancercollaborative.html

7   Joseph D. McNamara, "Sudden Death in Oakland" *San Francisco Chronicle* Friday, April 3, 2009.

References

7th St McClymonds Corridor Neighborhood Improvement Initiative (2001), West Oakland Snapshots: 2001 Report. Berkeley, CA, Institute of Urban and Regional Development, University of California.

Agger, A., Sørenson, E. and Torfing, J. (2008), It takes two to tango, in Yang, K. and Bergrud, E. (eds.) *Civic Engagement in a Network Society,* Charlotte, NC: Information Age Publishing.

Aldrich, H. (1979), *Organizations and Environments,* Englewood Cliffs, NJ: Prentice Hall.

Allen, J. and Allen, P. M. (1997), *Our Town: Foucault and Knowledge-based Politics in London,* Amsterdam: Gordon & Breach Science Publishers.

Allen, P. (2001), A complex systems approach to learning in adaptive networks, *International Journal of Innovation Management* 5, 149–80.

Allison, G. T. (1971), *The Essence of Decision: Explaining the Cuban Missile Crisis,* Boston, MA: Little Brown.

Ambruster, A. (2008), Collaborative versus technocratic policy making: California's statewide water plan, Sacramento, CA: Center for Collaborative Policy, California State University. http://www.csus.edu/ccp/publications/collab.vs.techno_abstract.stm.

Amy, D. (1987), *The Politics of Environmental Mediation,* New York: Columbia University Press.

Argyris, C. (1993), *Knowledge for Action: A Guide to Overcoming Barriers to Institutional Change,* San Francisco, CA: Jossey-Bass.

Argyris, C. and Schon, D. (1996), *Organizational Learning II: Theory, Method, and Practice,* Reading, MA: Addison Wesley Publishing.

Armitage, D., Berkes, F. and Doubleday, N. (2007), *Adaptive Co-Management: Collaboration, Learning, and Multi-Level Governance,* Vancouver: UBC Press.

Arrow, K. J. (1963), *Social Choice and Individual Values,* New Haven, CT: Yale University Press.

Asimov, I. (1982), *The Foundation Trilogy: Three Classics of Science Fiction,* Garden City, NY: Doubleday.

Axelrod, R. (1984), *The Evolution of Cooperation,* New York: Basic Books.

Axelrod, R. M. and Cohen, M. D. (2000), *Harnessing Complexity: Organizational Implications of a Scientific Frontier,* New York: Basic Books.

Barbour, E. and Teitz, M. (2006), Blueprint planning in California: forging consensus on metropolitan growth and development. *Occasional papers.* San Francisco, CA: The Public Policy Institute of California.

Bardach, E. (1998), *Getting Agencies to Work Together: The Practice and Theory of Managerial Craftsmanship,* Washington, DC: Brookings Institution Press.

Bar-Yam, Y., Ramalingam, C., Burlingame, L. and Ogata, C. (2004), *Making Things Work: Solving Complex Problems in a Complex World,* Brookline MA: Knowledge Press.

Bay Area Alliance for Sustainable Communities (2004), State of the Bay Area: A Regional Report. Pathways to Results, Measuring Progress toward Sustainability, San Francisco, CA: Bay Area Alliance for Sustainable Communities.

Berger, P. L. and Luckmann, T. (1967), *The Social Construction of Reality: A Treatise in the Sociology of Knowledge,* Garden City, NJ: Anchor Books.

Berkes, F., Colding, J. and Folke, E. (2003), *Navigating Social-Ecological Systems: Building Resilience for Complexity and Change,* Cambridge: Cambridge University Press.

Bernstein, R. J. (1971), *Praxis and Action: Contemporary Philosophies of Human Activity,* Philadelphia, PA: University of Pennsylvania Press.

Bernstein, R. J. (1976), *The Restructuring of Social and Political Theory,* Philadelphia, PA: University of Pennsylvania Press.

Bierbaum, M. (2007), State plan and smart growth implementation: the New Jersey case, in Knaap, G., Haccou, H., Clifton, K. and Frece, J. (eds.) *Incentives, Regulations, and Plans,* Cheltenham, UK: Edward Elgar.

Bogason, P. and Musso, J. A. (2006), The democratic prospects of network governance, *The American Review of Public Administration* 36: 3–18.

Bohm, D. (1996), *On Dialogue,* London: Routledge.

Bohman, J. (1996), *Public Deliberation: Pluralism, Complexity and Democracy,* Cambridge, MA: MIT Press.

Booher, D. (2004), Collaborative governance practices and democracy, *National Civic Review* 93: 32–46.

Booher, D. E. (2007), Collaborative governance, in Rabin, J. (ed.) *Encyclopedia of Public Administration and Public Policy,* London: Taylor & Francis.

Booher, D. E. (2008), Civic engagement as collaborative complex adaptive networks, in Yang, K. and Bergrud, E. (eds.) *Civic Engagement in a Network Society,* Charlotte, NC: Information Age Publishing.

Booher, D. E. and Innes, J. (2002), Network power in collaborative planning, *Journal of Planning Education and Research* 21: 221–36.

Brandt, A. W. (2002), An environmental water account: the California experience, *University of Denver Water Law Review* 5: 426–56.

Brinkman, P. A. (2004), Explaining the suspect behaviour of travel demand forecasters, in *Urban Transport X: Urban Transport in the 21st Century,* Southampton: WIT Press.

Brown, S. L. and Eisenhardt, K. M. (1998), *Competing on the Edge: Strategy as Structured Chaos,* Boston, MA: Harvard Business School Press.

Brunner, R. D., Colburn, C. H., Cromley, C. C., Klein, R. A. and Olson, E. A. (2002), *Finding Common Ground: Governance and Natural Resources in the American West,* New Haven, CT: Yale University Press.

Bryson, J. (2004), *Strategic Planning for Public and Nonprofit Organizations: A Guide To Strengthening and Sustaining Organizational Achievement,* San Francisco, CA: Jossey-Bass Publishers.

Bryson, J. and Crosby, B. (1992), *Leadership for the Common Good: Tackling Public Problems in a Shared Power World,* San Francisco, CA: Jossey-Bass Publishers.

Bryson, J. and Crosby, B. (1993), Policy planning and the design and use of forums, arenas and courts, *Environment and Planning B: Planning and Design* 20: 175–94.

Buber, M. (1958), *I and Thou,* New York: Scribner.

Capra, F. (1996), *The Web of Life: A New Scientific Understanding of Living Systems,* New York: Anchor Books.

Carpenter, S. L. and Kennedy, W. J. D. (1991), *Managing Public Disputes: A Practical Guide to Handling Conflict and Reaching Agreements,* San Francisco, CA: Jossey-Bass Publishers.

Carpenter, S. L. and Kennedy, W. J. D. (2001), *Managing Public Disputes: A Practical Guide for Government, Business and Citizens' Groups,* San Francisco, CA: Jossey-Bass Publishers.

Castells, M. (1997), *The Power of Identity,* Malden, MA: Blackwell Publishing.

Center for Collaborative Policy (Undated), Conditions needed to sustain a collaborative policy process. Sacramento, CA: Center for Collaborative Policy California State University. http://www.csus.edu/ccp/collaborative/sustain.stm

Chisholm, D. (1989), *Coordination Without Hierarchy: Informal Structures in Multiorganisational Systems,* Berkeley, CA: University of California Press.

Chiva-Gomez, R. (2004), Repercussions of complex adaptive systems on product design management, *Technovation* 24, 707–11.

Chrislip, D. D. (2002), *The Collaborative Leadership Fieldbook: A Guide for Citizens and Leaders,* San Francisco, CA: Jossey-Bass Publishers.

Chrislip, D. D. and Larson, C. E. (1994), *Collaborative Leadership: How Citizens and Civic Leaders can Make a Difference,* San Francisco, CA: Jossey-Bass Publishers.

Christensen, K. (1985), Coping with uncertainty in planning, *Journal of the American Planning Association* 51: 63–73.

Christensen, K. and Rongerude J. (2004), San Diego dialogue: reshaping the San Diego region. Berkeley, CA: Institute of Urban and Regional Development, University of California.

Cilliers, P. (2005), Knowing complex systems, in Richardson, K. A. (ed.) *Managing Organizational Complexity: Philosophy, Theory, and Application,* Greenwich, CT: Information Age Publishing.

Cohen, M., March, J. and Olsen, J. (1972), A garbage can model of organizational choice, *Administrative Science Quarterly* 1–25.

Connick, S. (2003), The use of collaborative processes in the making of California water policy. Dissertation, Environmental Sciences, Policy and Management, University of California, Berkeley.

Connick, S. (2006), The Sacramento Area Water Forum. Working paper, Berkeley CA: Institute of Urban and Regional Development, University of California.

Connick, S. and Innes, J. (2003), Outcomes of collaborative water policy making: applying complexity thinking to evaluation, *Journal of Environmental Planning and Management* 46: 177–97.

Corburn, J. (2003), Bringing local knowledge into environmental decision-making: improving urban planning for communities at risk, *Journal of Planning Education and Research* 22: 422–33.

Corburn, J. (2005), *Street Science,* Cambridge, MA: MIT Press.

Corburn, J. (2009), *Toward the Healthy City: People, Places, and the Politics of Planning,* Cambridge, MA: MIT Press.

Crozier, M., Huntington, S. and Watanuki, J. (1975), *The Crisis of Democracy: Report on the Governability of Democracies to the Trilateral Commission,* New York: New York University Press.

Crump, L. and Susskind, L. (eds.) (2008), *Multiparty Negotiation,* Los Angeles, CA: Sage Publications.

de Neufville, J. (1983), Planning theory and practice: bridging the gap, *Journal of Planning Education and Research* 3: 35–45.

de Neufville, J. and Barton, S. (1987), Myths and the definition of policy problems: an exploration of homeownership and public-private partnerships, *Policy Sciences* 20: 181–206.

de Neufville, J. and Christensen, K. (1980), Is optimizing really best? Symposium on optimizing, implementing and evaluating public policy, *Policy Studies Journal* 3: 1053–60.

de Neufville, J. I. (1975), *Social Indicators and Public Policy: Interactive Processes of Design and Use,* Amsterdam: Elsevier Publishing.

De Rynck, F. and Voets, J. (2006), Democracy in area-based policy networks: the case of Ghent, *The American Review of Public Administration* 36: 58–78.

De Sousa Briggs, X. (1998), Doing democracy up-close: culture, power, and communication in community building, *Journal of Planning Education and Research* 18: 1–13.

De Sousa Briggs, X. (2008), *Democracy as Problem Solving: Civic Capacity in Communities Across the Globe,* Cambridge, MA: MIT Press.

Dewey, J. (1927), *The Public and its Problems,* New York: H. Halt.

Doyle, A. C. (1922), The problem of Thor Bridge. http://sherlock-holmes.classic-literaturc.co.uk/the-problem-of-thor-bridge/

Dreier, P., Mollenkopf, J. and Swanstrom, T. (2004), *Place Matters: Metropolitics for the 21st Century,* Lawrence, KS: University Press of Kansas.

Dryzek, J. (1990), *Discursive Democracy: Politics, Policy and Political Science,* Cambridge: Cambridge University Press.

Durant, R., Fiorino, D. and O'Leary, R. (eds.) (2004), *Environmental Governance Reconsidered: Challenges, Choices, and Opportunities,* Cambridge, MA: MIT Press.

Eisenhardt, K. and Tabrizi, B. (1995), Accelerating adaptive processes: product innovation in the global computer industry, *Administrative Science Quarterly* 40: 84–110.

Epstein, J. and Axtell, R. (1996), *Growing Artificial Societies: Social Science from the Bottom-Up,* Cambridge, MA: MIT Press.

Fainstein, S. S. (2000), New directions in planning theory, *Urban Affairs Review* 35: 451–78.

Fischer, F. (2000), *Citizens, Experts, and the Environment: The Politics of Local Knowledge,* Durham, NC: Duke University Press.

Fischer, F. (2003), *Reframing Public Policy: Discursive Politics and Deliberative Practice,* Oxford: Oxford University Press.

Fischer, F. and Forester, J. (Eds.) (1993), *The Argumentative Turn in Policy Analysis and Planning,* Durham, NC: Duke University Press.

Fisher, R. and Ury, W. (1981), *Getting to Yes: Negotiating Agreement without Giving In,* Boston, MA: Houghton Mifflin.

Fisher, R. and Ury, W. and Patton, B. (1991), *Getting To Yes: Negotiating Agreement without Giving In,* New York: Penguin Books.

Fitzgorald, F. (1986), *Cities on a Hill: A Journey through Contemporary American Cultures,* New York: Simon and Schuster.

Flyvbjerg, B. (1998), *Rationality and Power: Democracy in Practice,* Chicago, IL: University of Chicago Press.

Forester, J. (1980), Critical theory and planning practice, *Journal of the American Planning Association* 46: 275–86.

Forester, J. (1982), Planning in the face of power, *Journal of the American Planning Association* 48: 67–80.

Forester, J. (1989), *Planning in the Face of Power,* Berkeley, CA: University of California Press

Forester, J. (1993) Learning from practice stories: the priority of practical judgment, in Fischer, F. and Forester, J. (eds.) *The Argumentative Turn in Policy Analysis and Planning,* Durham, NC: Duke University Press.

Forester, J. (1997), Beyond dialogue to transformative learning, in Borri, D., Khakee, A.and Lacignola, C. (eds.) *Evaluating Theory-Practice and Urban Rural Interplay in Planning,* Berlin: Springer.

Forester, J. (1999), *The Deliberative Practitioner: Encouraging Participatory Planning Processes,* Cambridge, MA: MIT Press.

Forester, J. (2006), Making participation work when interests conflict: moving from facilitating dialogue and moderating debate to mediating negotiations, *Journal of the American Planning Association* 72: 447–56.

Forester, J. (2008), Participatory planning and the roots of planning for real: a profile of Tony Gibson, *Planning Theory and Practice* 9: 102–118.

Forester, J. (2009), *Dealing with Differences: Dramas of Mediating Public Disputes,* Oxford: Oxford University Press.

Freeman, J. (1997), Collaborative governance in the administrative state, *UCLA Law Review* 45: 1–98.

Friedmann, J. (1987), *Planning in the Public Domain: From Knowledge to Action,* Princeton, NJ: Princeton University Press.

Fung, A. and Wright, E. O. (2001), Deepening democracy: empowered participatory governance, *Politics and Society* 29: 5–41.

Gans, H. (1962), *The Urban Villagers: Group and Class in the Life of Italian Americans,* Glencoe, NJ: The Free Press.

Gastil, J. and Levine, P. (eds.) (2005), *The Deliberative Democracy Handbook: Strategies for Effective Civic Engagement in the Twenty-First Century,* San Francisco, CA: Jossey-Bass Publisher.

Geertz, C. (1983), *Local Knowledge: Further Essays in Interpretive Anthropology,* New York: Basic Books.

Gibbs, L. and Levine, M. (1982), *Love Canal: My Story,* New York: State University of New York Press.

Giddens, A. (1984), *The Constitution of Society: Outline of the Theory of Structuration,* Berkeley, CA: University of California Press.

Gleick, J. (1987), *Chaos: Making a New Science,* New York: Penguin Books.

Goldstein, B. E. (2004), War between social worlds: scientific deadlock during preparation of an endangered species habitat conservation plan (HCP) and the co-production of scientific knowledge and the social order. Dissertation Department of City and Regional Planning, University of California, Berkeley.

Goldstein, G. M. (2008), *Lessons in Disaster: McGeorge Bundy and the Path to War in Vietnam,* New York: Times Books.

Gray, B. (2003), Framing of environmental disputes, in Lewicki, R. J., Gray, B. and Elliott, M. (eds.) *Making Sense of Intractable Environmental Conflicts: Concepts and Cases,* Washington, DC: Island Press.

Green, S. A. and Jerome, R. B. (2008), City of Cincinnati Independent Monitor's Final Report. Cincinnati, Ohio.

Gruber, J. (1994), Coordinating growth management through consensus-building: incentives and the generation of social, intellectual, and political capital, Berkeley, CA: Institute of Urban and Regional Development, University of California. http://iurd.berkeley_edu/catalog/Working_Paper_Titles/Coordinating_Growth_Management_through_Consensus_Building_Incentives.

Gruber, J. E. and Neuman, M. (1994), San Diego regional growth management strategy, in Innes, J., Gruber, R., Neuman, M. and Thompson, R. (eds.) *Coordinating Growth and Environmental Management through Consensus Building,* Berkeley, CA: California Policy Seminar (California Policy Center), University of California. http://iurd.berkeley.edu/catalog/Other/Coordinating_Growth_and_Environmental_Management_Through_Consensus_Building_Vol_1

Gualini, E. (2001), *Planning and the Intelligence of Institutions: Interactive Approaches to Territorial Policy-Making between Institutional Design and Institution-Building,* Aldershot, UK: Ashgate Publishing.

Gunderson, L. H. and Holling, C. S. (2002), *Panarchy: Understanding Transformations in Human and Natural Systems,* Washington, DC: Island Press.

Habermas, J. (1981), *The Theory of Communicative Action: Reason and the Rationalization of Society,* Boston, MA: Beacon Press.

Hajer, M. (1995), *The Politics of Environmental Discourse: Ecological Modernization and the Policy Process,* Oxford: Clarendon Press.

Hajer, M. (2003a), A frame in the fields: policymaking and the reinvention of politics, in Hajer, M. and Wagenaar, H. (eds.) *Deliberative Policy Analysis: Understanding Governance in the Network Society,* Cambridge: Cambridge University Press.

Hajer, M. (2003b), Policy without polity? Policy analysis and the institutional void, *Policy Sciences* 36: 175–95.

Hajer, M. and Wagenaar, H. (eds.) (2003), *Deliberative Policy Analysis: Understanding Governance in the Network Society,* Cambridge: Cambridge University Press.

Halberstam, D. (1968), *The Best and the Brightest,* Greenwich, CT: Fawcett Publications.

Hardin, G. (1968), The tragedy of the commons, *Science* 162: 1243–48.

Harrison, C. (2007), Taking a bite out of home rule: New Jersey's state plan gets some teeth, *Planning* 73: 28.

Hayward, C. R. (2000), *De-facing power,* Cambridge: Cambridge University Press.

Healey, P. (1992a), A planner's day: knowledge and action in a communicative perspective, *Journal of the American Planning Association* 58: 9–20.

Healey, P. (1992b), Planning through debate: the communicative turn in planning theory, *Town Planning Review* 63: 143–162.

Healey, P. (1996), The communicative work of development plans, in Mandelbaum, S., Mazza, L. and Burchell. R. (eds.) *Explorations in Planning Theory,* New Brunswick, NJ: Center for Urban Policy Research, Rutgers the State University of New Jersey.

Healey, P. (1997), *Collaborative Planning: Shaping Places in Fragmented Societies,* (2nd Ed.), London: Macmillan Press.

Healey, P. (1999), Institutionalist analysis, communicative planning, shaping places, *Journal of Planning Education and Research,* 19: 111–21.

Healey, P. (2006), *Collaborative Planning: Shaping Places in Fragmented Societies,* London: Macmillan Press.

Healey, P. (2007) *Urban Complexity and Spatial Strategies: Towards a Relational Planning for Our Times,* New York: Routledge.

Healey, P. (2009), The pragmatic tradition in planning thought, *Journal of Planning Education and Research* 28: 277–92.

Healey, P. (forthcoming), The idea of 'communicative planning': practices, concepts and rhetorics, in Vale, L. and Sanyal, B. (eds.) *History of Planning Ideas.*

Healey, P., De Magalhaes, C., Madanipour, A. and Pendlebury, J. (2003), Place, identity, and local politics: analyzing partnership initiatives, in Hajer, M. and Wagenaar, H. (eds.) *Deliberative Policy Analysis: Governance in the Network Society.* Cambridge: Cambridge University Press.

Heikkila, T. and Gerlak, A. (2005), The formation of large-scale collaborative resource management institutions: clarifying the roles of stakeholders, science, and institutions, *Policy Studies Journal* 33: 583–612.

Hillier, J. (2002), *Shadows of Power: An Allegory of Prudence in Land Use Planning,* London: Routledge.

Hillier, J. (2003), Agonizing over consensus: why Habermasian ideals cannot be real, *Planning Theory* 2: 37–59.

Hindmarsh, R. and Matthews, C. (2008), Deliberative speak at the turbine face: community engagement, wind farms, and renewable energy transitions, in Australia, *Journal of Environmental Policy & Planning* I0: 217–32.

Hoare, C. H. (1994), Psychosocial identity development in United States society: its role in fostering exclusion of other cultures, in Salett, E. P. and Koslow, D. R. (eds.) *Race, Ethnicity and Self: Identity in Multicultural Perspective,* Washington, DC: National Multicultural Institute

Hobbes, T. (2009), *The Leviathan,* Washington, DC: Regnery Publishing.

Hoch, C. (1984a) Doing good and being right: the pragmatic connection in planning theory, *Journal of the American Planning Association* 50: 335–45.

Hoch, C. (1984b), Pragmatism, planning, and power, *Journal of Planning Education and Research* 4: 86–95.

Hoch, C. (1992), The paradox of power in planning practice, *Journal of Planning Education and Research* 11: 206–15.

Hoch, C. (1996), Book review of *Postmodern Public Administration: Toward Discourse, Journal of Planning Education and Research* 15: 251–52.

Hoch, C. (2002), Evaluating plans pragmatically, *Planning Theory* 1: 53–75.

Hoch, C. (2007), Pragmatic communicative action theory, *Journal of Planning Education and Research* 26: 272–83.

Holden, M. (2008), The tough-minded and the tender-minded: a pragmatic turn for sustainable development planning and policy, *Planning Theory and Practice* 9: 475–96.

Holland, J. (1995), *Hidden Order: How Adaptation Builds Complexity,* Reading, MA: Addison-Wesley.

Hong, L. and Page, S. (2001), Problem solving by heterogeneous agents, *Journal of Economic Theory* 97: 123–63.

Innes, J. (1990), *Knowledge and Public Policy: The Search for Meaningful Indicators,* New Brunswick, NJ: Transaction Books.

Innes, J. (1992a) Group processes and the social construction of growth management: Florida, Vermont and New Jersey, *Journal of the American Planning Association* 58: 440–53.

Innes, J. (I992b), Implementing state growth management in the U.S.: strategies for coordination, in Stein, J. (ed.) *Growth Management: The Planning Challenge of the 1990's,* Newbury Park, CA: Sage Publications, pp. 18–43.

Innes, J. (l994a), Growth management consensus project, in Innes, J., Gruber, J., Neuman, M. and Thompson, R. *Coordinating Growth and Environmental Management Through Consensus Building,* Berkeley, CA: California Policy Seminar (California Policy Research Center), University of California. http://iurd.berkeley.edu/catalog/other/Coordinating_Growth_and_Environmental_Management_Through_Consensus_Building_Vol_1

Innes, J. (l994b), San Francisco Estuary Project, in Innes, J., Gruber, J., Neuman, M. and Thompson, R. *Coordinating Growth and Environmental Management Through Consensus Building,* Berkeley, CA: California Policy Seminar (California Policy Research Center), University of California. http://iurd.berkeley.edu/catalog/other/Coordinating_Growth_and_Environmental_Management_Through_Consensus_Building_Vol_1

Innes, J. (1995) Planning theory's emerging paradigm: communicative action and interactive practice, *Journal of Planning Education and Research* 14: 183–89.

Innes, J. (1998), Information in communicative planning, *Journal of the American Planning Association,* 64: 52–63.

Innes, J. (2004), Taking the three E's seriously: the Bay Area Alliance for Sustainable Communities, Berkeley, CA: Institute of Urban and Regional Development, University of California. http://repositories.cdlib.org/cgi/viewcontent.cgi?article=1040&context=iurd

Innes, J. and Booher, D. E. (1999a), Consensus building and complex adaptive systems: a framework for evaluating collaborative planning, *Journal of the American Planning Association* 65: 412–23.

Innes, J. and Booher, D. E. (1999b), Consensus building as role playing and bricolage: toward a theory of collaborative planning, *Journal of the American Planning Association* 65: 9–26.

Innes, J. and Booher, D. E. (1999c) Metropolitan development as a complex system: a new approach to sustainability, *Economic Development Quarterly* 13: 141–56.

Innes, J. and Booher, D. E. (2000), Indicators for sustainable communities: a strategy building on complexity theory and distributed intelligence, *Planning Theory and Practice* 1: 173–86.

Innes, J. and Booher, D. E. (2003a), Collaborative policy making: governance through dialogue, in Hajer, M. and Wagenaar, H. (eds.) *Deliberative Policy Analysis: Governance in the Network Society,* Cambridge: Cambridge University Press.

Innes, J. and Booher, D. E. (2003b), The impact of collaborative planning on governance capacity, working paper, Berkeley, CA: Institute of Urban and Regional Development, University of California, Berkeley. http://iurd.berkeley.edu/catalog/Working_Paper_Titles/Impact_Collaborative_Planning_Governance_Capacity

Innes, J. and Booher, D. E. (2005), Reframing public participation: strategies for the 21st century, *Planning Theory and Practice* 5: 419–36.

Innes, J. and Connick, S. (1999) San Francisco Estuary Project, Case 5 in Susskind, L., McKearnon, S. and Thomas Larmer, J. (eds.) *The Consensus Building Handbook: A Comprehensive Guide to Reaching Agreement,* Thousand Oaks, CA: Sage Publications, pp. 801–27.

Innes, J. and Gruber, J. (2001), *Bay Area Transportation Decision Making in the Wake of ISTEA: Planning Styles in Conflict at the Metropolitan Transportation Commission,* Berkeley, CA: University of California Transportation Center. http://www.uctc.net/papers/514.pdf

Innes, J. and Gruber, J. (2005), Planning styles in conflict: the Metropolitan Planning Commission, *Journal of the American Planning Association* 71: 177–88.

Innes, J. and Rongerude, J. (2005), Collaborative regional initiatives: civic entrepreneurs work to fill the governance gap. *Insight.* San Francisco: James Irvine Foundation.

Innes, J. and Rongerude, J. (2006), Collaborative regional initiatives: civic entrepreneurs work to fill the governance gap. Berkeley, CA: Institute of Urban and Regional Development, University of California. http://iurd.berkeley.edu/catalog/Working_Paper_Titles/Collaborative_Regional_Initiatives_ Civic_Entrepreneurs_Work_Fill

Innes, J. and Sandoval, G. (2004) Turning businesspeople into environmentalists: The Sierra Business Council, Berkeley, CA: Institute of Urban and Regional Development, University of California. http://iurd.berkeley.edu/catalog/Working_Paper_Titles/Turning_Businesspeople_Environmentalists_Sierra_Business_ Council

Innes, J., Connick, S. and Booher, D. E. (2007) Informality as a planning strategy: collaborative water management in the CALFED Bay-Delta Program, *Journal of the American Planning Association* 73: 195–210.

Innes, J., Connick, S., Kaplan, L. and Booher, D. E. (2006), Collaborative governance in the CALFED Program: adaptive policy making for California water, Berkeley, CA: Institute of Urban and Regional Development, University of California. http://iurd.berkeley.edu/ catalog/Working_Paper_Titles/Collaborative_Governance_ CALFED_Program_Adaptive_ Policy_Making

Innes, J., Gruber, J., Neuman, M. and Thompson, R. (1994), Coordinating growth and environmental management through consensus building, Berkeley, CA: California Policy Seminar (California Policy Center), University of California. http://iurd.berkeley.edu/ catalog/Other/ Coordinating_Growth_and_Environmental_Management_Through_Consensus_Building_ Vol_I

Isaacs, W. (1999a), *Dialogue and the Art of Thinking Together,* New York: Doubleday.

Isaacs, W. N. (l999b), Dialogic leadership, *Systems Thinker* 10: 1–5.

Jessop, B. (1998), The rise of governance and the risks of failure: the case of economic development, *International Social Science Journal* 50: 29–45.

Johnson, D. W. and Johnson, F. P. (1997), *Joining Together: Group Theory and Group Skills,* Boston, MA: Allyn and Bacon.

Kaner, S. and Lind, L. (2007), *Facilitator's Guide to Participatory Decision-Making,* San Francisco, CA: Jossey-Bass Publishers.

Karl, H., Susskind, L. and Wallace, K. (2007), A dialogue, not a diatribe: effective integration of science and policy through joint fact finding. *Environment* 49: 20.

Kauffman, S. (1995), *At Home in the Universe: The Search for the Laws of Complexity,* London: Viking.

Kelly, K. (1994), *Out of Control: The Rise of the Neobiological Civilization,* Reading, MA: Addison-Wesley.

Kernick, D. P. (2005), Facilitating resource decision making in public organizations drawing upon insights from complexity theory, *Emergence: Complexity and Organization* 7: 175–94.

Kettl, D. F. (2005), The next government of the United States: challenges for performance in the 21st century. IBM Center for the Business of Government, Washington DC.

Kickert, W. J. M., Klijn, E. H. and Koppenjan, J. F. M. (1997), *Managing Complex Networks: Strategies for the Public Sector,* London: Sage Publications.

King, C. S., Feltey, K. M. and Susel, B. O. N. (1998), The question of participation: toward authentic participation in public administration, *Public Administration Review* 58: 317–26.

Kingdon, J. W. (2003), *Agendas, Alternatives, and Public Policies,* New York: Longman.

Kirp, D., Dwyer, J. P. and Rosenthal, L. (1995), *Our Town: Race, Housing, and the Soul of Suburbia,* New Brunswick, NJ: Rutgers University Press.

Klijn, E. H. and Koppenjan, J. F. M. (2000), Public management and policy networks: foundations of a network approach to governance, *Public Management* 2: 135–58.

Koontz, T. (2004), *Collaborative Environmental Management: What Roles for Government?,* Washington, DC: Resources for the Future.

Kovick, D. (2005), The Hewlett Foundation's conflict resolution program: twenty years of field building, Menlo Park, CA: The William and Flora Hewlett Foundation.

Lakoff, G. and Johnson, M. (1980), *Metaphors We Live By,* Chicago, IL: University of Chicago Press.

Lave, C. A. and March, J. G. (1993), *An Introduction to Models in the Social Sciences,* Lanham, MD: University Press of America.

Lever, C. C., Di Vittorio, S. B. and Gilless, K. J. (2007), Stepping outside the boundary: organizational change and community building at Yosemite National Park, dissertation, Environmental Science, Policy and Management, Berkeley CA: University of California.

Levi-Strauss, E. (1966), *The Savage Mind,* Chicago, IL: University of Chicago Press.

Lewicki, R. J., Gray, B. and Elliott, M. (eds.) (2003), *Making Sense of Environmental Conflicts: Concepts and Cases,* Washington, DC: Island Press.

Lindblom, C. E. (1990), *Inquiry and Change: The Troubled Attempt to Understand and Shape*

Society. New Haven, CT and New York: Yale University Press and Russell Sage Foundation.

Lindblom, C. E. and Cohen, D. K. (1979), *Usable Knowledge: Social Science and Social Problem Solving,* New Haven, CT: Yale University Press.

Lorenz, E. (1993), *The Essence of Chaos,* Seattle, WA: University of Washington Press.

Mandanaro, L. (2005), Evaluating collaborative environmental planning outputs and outcomes: restoring and protecting habitat and the New York New Jersey Harbor Estuary Program, *Journal of Planning Education and Research* 27: 456–68.

Mandelbaum, S. J., Mazza, L., Burchell, R. (eds) (1996), *Explorations in Planning Theory,* Rutgers, NJ: CUPR Press.

Margerum, R. (1999), Integrated environmental management: the foundations for successful practice, *Environmental Management* 24: 151–66.

Margerum, R. D. (2008), A typology of collaboration efforts in environmental management, *Environmental Management* 41: 487–500.

McCay, B. and Jentoft, S. (1996), From the bottom up: participatory issues in fisheries management, *Society and Natural Resources* 9: 237–50.

McCreary, S. (1999), Resolving science-intensive public policy disputes: reflections on the New York Bight Initiative, Case 6 in Susskind, L., McKearnon, S. and Thomas-Larmer, J. (eds.) *The Consensus Building Handbook: A Comprehensive Guide to Reaching Agreement,* Thousand Oaks, CA: Sage Publications, pp. 829–58.

McKelvey, B. (2001), Energising order-creating networks of distributed intelligence: improving the corporate brain, *International Journal of Knowledge Management* 5: 181–212.

McLean, T. (2002), William H. Riker and the invention of heresthetic(s), *British Journal of Political Science* 32: 535–58.

Menand, L. (2001), *The Metaphysical Club: A Story of Ideas in America,* New York: Farrar, Straus & Giroux.

Merriam-Webster (2003), *Collegiate Dictionary,* 11th edn (CD version), Springfield, MA: Merriam-Webster Inc.

Mitroff, I. I. (1974), *The Subjective Side of Science*: *A Philosophical Inquiry into the Psychology of the Apollo Moon Scientists,* Amsterdam, New York: Elsevier Scientific.

Moffitt, M. L. and Bordone, R. C. (eds.) (2005), *The Handbook of Dispute Resolution,* San Francisco: Jossey-Bass Publisher.

Moobela, C. (2005), From worst slum to best example of regeneration: complexity in the regeneration of Hulme-Manchester, *Emergence: Complexity and Organization* 7: 185–208.

Murphy, J. P. and Rorty, R. (1990), *Pragmatism: from Peirce to Davidson,* Boulder, CO: Westview Press.

Mutz, D. C. (2006), *Hearing the Other Side: Deliberative Versus Participatory Democracy,* Cambridge: Cambridge University Press.

New Jersey State Planning Commission (1988), Communities of Place: a legacy for the next generation, the preliminary state development and redevelopment plan for the state of New Jersey. New Jersey State Planning Commission.

New Jersey State Planning Commission (1990), Regional design: a report of the regional design system state planning advisory committee. New Jersey State Planning Commission.

New Jersey State Planning Commission (1991), Communities of place: the interim state development and redevelopment plan for the state of New Jersey. New Jersey State Planning Commission.

Nietzsche, F. and Lehmann, S. (1986) *Human, All Too Human: A Book for Free Spirits,* Lincoln, NE: University of Nebraska Press.

Nye, J. S. J., Zelikow, P. D. and King, D. C. (eds.) (1997), *Why People Don't Trust Government,* Cambridge, MA: Harvard University Press.

O'Leary, R. and Bingham, L. B. (eds.) (2003), *The Promise and Performance of Environmental Conflict Resolution,* Washington, DC: Resources for the Future.

Olson, M. (1965), *The Logic of Collective Action: Public Goods and the Theory of Groups,* Cambridge, MA: Harvard University Press.

Ostrom, E. (1990), *Governing the Commons: The Evolution of Institutions for Collective Action,* Cambridge, MA: Cambridge University Press.

Owen, A., Jankowski, P., Willlams, B. and Wulfhorst, J. D. (2008), Improving public participation in resource protection: case studies in North-Central Idaho, *Journal of Environmental Policy and Planning* 10: 255–69.

Ozawa, C. (1991) *Recasting Science: Consensual Procedures in Public Policy Making,* Boulder, CO: Westview Press.

Ozawa, C. and Susskind, L. (1987), Mediating science-intensive policy disputes, *Evaluation Studies Review Annual 1987,* 2–24.

Patterson, T. E. (2002), *The Vanishing Voter: Public Involvement in an Age of Uncertainty,* New York: Alfred A. Knopf.

Peattie, L. (1987), *Planning: Rethinking Ciudad Guayana,* Ann Arbor, MI: University of Michigan Press.

Peattie, L. R. (1968), *The View From The Barrio,* Ann Arbor, MI: University of Michigan Press.

Pharr, S. J. and Putnam, R. D. (eds.) (2000), *Disaffected Democracies: What's Troubling the Trilateral Countries,* Princeton, NJ: Princeton University Press.

Pomeroy, R. (1995), Community-based and co-management institutions for sustainable coastal fisheries management in Southeast Asia, *Ocean and Coastal Management* 27: 143–62.

Popper, K. R. (1966), *The Open Society and its Enemies,* London: Routledge and Kegan Paul.

Portugali, J. (2008), Learning from paradoxes about prediction and planning in self organizing cities, *Planning Theory* 7: 248–62.

Prigogine, I. and Stenger, I. (1984), *Order out of Chaos,* New York: Bantam.

Provan, K. G. and Milward, H. B. (1995), A preliminary theory of interorganizational network effectiveness: a comparative study of four community Mental Health Systems, *Administrative Science Quarterly* 40: 1–33.

Putnam, R. and Feldstein, L. (2003), *Better Together: Restoring the American Community,* New York: Simon and Schuster.

Putnam, R. D. (1993), *Making Democracy Work: Civic Traditions in Modern Italy,* Princeton, NJ: Princeton University Press.

Reike, E. A. (1996), The Bay-Delta Accord: a stride toward sustainability, *University of Colorado Law Review* 67: 341–69.

Rein, M. and White, S. (1977), Policy research: belief and doubt, *Policy Analysis* 3: 239–71.

Richardson, H. S. (2002), *Democratic Autonomy: Public Reasoning about the Ends of Policy,* New York: Oxford University Press.

Ridgeway, G., Schell, T., Gifford, B., Saunders, J., Turner, S., Riley, K. J. and Dixon, T. (2009), Police-community relations in Cincinnati. Los Angeles CA: RAND Corporation.

Ridgeway, G., Schell. T., Riley, K. J., Turner, S. and Dixon, T. (2006), Police-community relations in Cincinnati: year two evaluation report. Los Angeles CA: RAND Corporation.

Riley, K. J., Turner, S., Macdonald, J., Ridgeway, G., Schell, T., Wilson, J., Dixon, T., Fain, T., Barnes-Proby, D. and Fulton, B. (2005), Police-community relations in Cincinnati. Los Angeles CA: RAND Corporation.

Rittel, H. W. J. and Webber, M. (1973), Dilemmas in a general theory of planning, *Policy Sciences* 4: 155–69.

Roberts, N. (1997), Public deliberation: an alternative approach to crafting policy and setting direction, *Public Administration Review* 57: 124–32.

Rogers, E. (1962), *The Diffusion of Innovation,* New York: Free Press.

Röling, N. G. and Wagemakers, M. A. E. (eds.) (1998), *Facilitating Sustainable Agriculture: Participatory Learning and Adaptive Management in Times of Environmental Uncertainty,* Cambridge: Cambridge University Press.

Rose-Anderssen, C., Allen, P., Tsinopoulos, C. and McCarthy, I. (2005), Innovation in manufacturing as an evolutionary complex system, *Technovation* 25: 1093–105.

Rosell, S., Gantwerk, H. and Furth, I. (2005), Listening to Californians: bridging the disconnect. Executive Summary. La Jolla, CA: Viewpoint Learning.

Rothman, J. (1997), *Resolving Identity-Based Conflict in Nations, Organizations, and Communities,* San Francisco, CA: Jossey-Bass Publishers.

Rothman, J. (2006), Identity and conflict: collaboratively addressing police-community conflict in Cincinnati, Ohio, *Ohio State Journal on Dispute Resolution* 22: 105–32.

Sabatier, P. A., Focht, W., Lubell, M., Trachtenberg, Z., Vedlitz, A. and Matlock, M. (eds.) (2005), *Swimming Upstream: Collaborative Approaches to Watershed Management,* Cambridge, MA: MIT Press.

Sandercock, L. (1998), *Towards Cosmopolis,* Chichester: John Wiley.

Sandercock, L. (2003), *Cosmopolis II: Mongrel Cities in the 21st Century,* New York: Continuum.

Sarkissian, W., Hofer, N., Shore, Y., Vajda, S. and Wilkinson, C. (2009), *Kitchen Table Sustainability: Practical Recipes for Community Engagement with Sustainability,* London: Earthscan.

Saunders, H. H. (2001), *A Public Peace Process: Sustained Dialogue to Transform Racial and Ethnic Conflicts,* New York: Palgrave.

Saxenian, A. (1994), *Regional Advantage: Culture and Competition in Silicon Valley and Route 128,* Cambridge, MA: Harvard University Press.

Scharpf, F. W. (1978), *Interorganizational Policy Studies: Issues, Concepts and Perspectives,* London: Sage Publications.

Schell, T., Ridgeway, G., Dixon, T., Turner, S. and Riley, K. J. (2007), Police-community relations in Cincinnati: year three evaluation report, Los Angeles CA: RAND Corporation.

Schelling, T. C. (1978), *Micromotives and Macrobehavior,* New York: W.W. Norton.

Scher, E. (1999), Negotiating superfund cleanup at the Massachusetts Military Reservation, Case 7 in Susskind, L., McKearnan, S. and Thomas-Larmer, J. (eds.) *The Consensus Building Handbook: A Comprehensive Guide to Reaching Agreement,* Thousand Oaks, CA: Sage Publications, pp. 859–78.

Schlosberg, D. (1999), *Environmental Justice and the New Pluralism: The Challenge of Difference for Environmentalism,* Oxford: Oxford University Press.

Schneider, M., Scholz, J., Lubell, M., Mindruta, D. and Edwardsen, M. (2003), Building consensual institutions: networks and the national estuary program, *American Journal of Political Science* 47: 143–58.

Scholz, J. T. and Stiftel, B. (eds.) (2005), *Adaptive Governance and Water Conflict: New Institutions for Collaborative Planning,* Washington, DC: Resources for the Future.

Schon, D. A. (1979), Generative metaphor: a perspective on problem-setting in social policy, in Ortony, E. (ed.) *Metaphor and Thought,* Cambridge: Cambridge University Press.

Schon, D. A. (1983), *The Reflective Practitioner: How Professionals Think in Action,* New York: Basic Books.

Schon, D. A. and Rein, M. (1994), *Frame Reflection: Toward the Resolution of Intractable Policy Controversies,* New York: Basic Books.

Schuman, S. (ed.) (2005), *The IAF Handbook of Group Facilitation: Best Practices from the Leading Organization in Facilitation,* San Francisco, CA: Jossey-Bass Publishers.

Schuman, S. (ed.) (2006), *Creating a Culture of Collaboration: The International Association of Facilitators Handbook,* San Francisco, CA: Jossey-Bass Publishers.

Schwarz, R. M. (1994), *The Skilled Facilitator: Practical Wisdom for Developing Effective Groups,* San Francisco, CA: Jossey-Bass Publishers.

Sen, S. and Nielsen, J. R. (1996), Fisheries co-management: a comparative analysis, *Marine Policy* 20: 405–18.

Sheehan, N. (1988), *A Bright Shining Lie: John Paul Vann and America in Vietnam,* New York: Random House.

Shellenberger, M. and Nordhaus, T. (2005), The death of environmentalism, *Grist Magazine.* http://oracle.cas.muohio.edu/ies/students2005/DeathofEnvironmentalism.pdf

Shields, P. (2003), The community of inquiry: classical pragmatism and public administration, *Administration and Society* 35: 510–38.

Shields, P. (2004), Classical pragmatism: engaging practitioner experience, *Administration and Society* 36: 351–61.

Smith, A. (1776), An inquiry into the nature and causes of the wealth of nations, Dublin: Whitestone.

Smith, M. E. (1995), Chaos, consensus, and common sense, *The Ecologist* 25: 80–86.

Society of Professionals in Dispute Resolution (1997), Best practices for government agencies:

guidelines for using collaborative agreement-seeking processes, Washington, DC: Society of Professionals in Dispute Resolution.

Sørensen, E. (2006), Metagovernance: the changing role of politicians in processes of democratic governance, *The American Review of Public Administration* 36: 98–114.

Sørensen, E. and Torfing, J. (2007), *Theories of Democratic Network Governance,* Basingstoke and New York: Palgrave Macmillan.

Stacey, R. (2001), *Complex Responsive Processes in Organization: Learning and Knowledge Creation,* London: Routledge.

Stacey, R. D. (1996), *Complexity and Creativity in Organizations,* San Francisco, CA: Berrett-Koehler Publishers.

Stoker, G. (2006), Public value management: a new narrative for networked governance? *The American Review of Public Administration* 36: 41–57.

Straus, D. (2002), *How to Make Collaboration Work: Powerful Ways to Build Consensus, Solve Problems, and Make Decisions,* San Francisco, CA: Berret-Koehler Publishers.

Susskind, L. (1981), Citizen participation and consensus building in land use planning: a case study, in de Neufville, J. I. (ed.) *The Land Use Policy Debate in the United States,* New York: Plenum Press.

Susskind, L. (1999), A short guide to consensus building. An alternative to Robert's Rules of Order for groups, organizations, and ad hoc assemblies that want to operate by consensus, in Susskind, L., McKearnan, S. and Thomas-Larmer, J. (eds.) *The Consensus Building Handbook: A Comprehensive Guide to Reaching Agreement,* Thousand Oaks, CA: Sage Publications, pp. 3–57.

Susskind, L. and Cruikshank, J. (1987), *Breaking the Impasse: Consensual Approaches to Resolving Public Disputes,* New York: Basic Books.

Susskind, L. and MacMahon, G. (1985), Theory and practice of negotiated rulemaking, *Yale Journal on Regulation* 3: 133–65.

Susskind, L. and Thomas-Larmer, J. (1999), Conducting a conflict assessment, Chapter 2 in Susskind, L., McKearnan, S. and Thomas-Larmer, J. (eds.) *The Consensus Building Handbook: A Comprehensive Guide to Reaching Agreement,* Thousand Oaks, CA: Sage Publications, pp. 99–136.

Susskind, L., McKearnan, S. and Thomas-Larmer, J. (eds.) (1999), *The Consensus Building Handbook: A Comprehensive Guide to Reaching Agreement,* Thousand Oaks, CA: Sage Publications.

Swidler, A. (1986), Culture in action: symbols and strategies, *American Sociological Review* 51: 273–86.

Tenenbaum, E. and Wildavsky, A. (1984), Why policies control data and data cannot determine policies, *Scandinavian Journal of Management Studies* 1: 83–100.

Thomas, C. W. (2003), *Bureaucratic Landscapes: Interagency Cooperation and the Preservation of Biodiversity,* Cambridge, MA: MIT Press,

Thompson, R. (1997), Ever since Eden: cognitive models can teach us about environmental disputes. Dissertation, Berkeley CA: Department of City and Regional Planning, University of California.

Throgmorton, J. A. (1996), *Planning as Persuasive Storytelling: The Rhetorical Construction of Chicago's Electric Future,* Chicago, IL: University of Chicago Press.

Toffler, A. (1984), *The Adaptive Corporation,* New York: McGraw Hill.

Tsoukas, H. (2005), *Complex Knowledge: Studies in Organizational Epistemology,* Oxford: Oxford University Press.

Turkle, S. (1995), *Life on the Screen: Identity in the Age of the Internet,* New York: Simon and Schuster.

Tzu, L. (1995), *The Tao Te Ching,* New York: St Martin's Griffin.

Van Der Ploeg, J. D. (1993), Potatoes and knowledge, in Hobart, M. (ed.) *An Anthropological Critique of Development: The Growth of Ignorance,* London: Routledge.

Van Eijnatten, F. and Van Galen, M. (2005), Provoking chaordic change in a Dutch manufacturing firm, in Richardson, K. A. (ed.) *Managing Organizational Complexity: Philosophy, Theory and Application,* Greenwich, CT: Information Age Publishing.

Van Herzele, A. and van Woerkum, C. M. J. (2008), Local knowledge in visually mediated practice, *Journal of Planning Education and Research* 27: 444–55.

Waldrop, M. M. (1992), *Complexity: The Emerging Science at the Edge of Chaos,* New York: Simon and Schuster.

Wardani, J. (2008), Stewardship stories for watershed justice. Masters Thesis, Departments of City and Regional Planning and Landscape Architecture and Envrionmental Planning, University of California, Berkeley.

Weber, M. (1958), Bureaucracy, in Gerth, H. H. and Mills, C. W. (eds.) *From Max Weber,* New York; Oxford University Press.

Weiss, C. H. (1977), Research for policy's sake: the enlightenment function of social research, *Policy Analysis* 3: 531–45.

Weiss, C. H. (1979), The many meanings of research utilization, *Public Administration Review,* 426– 31.

Weiss, C. H. and Bucuvalas, M. J. (1980), *Social Science Research and Decision-Making,* New York: Columbia University Press.

Wenger, E. (1998) *Communities of Practice: Learning, Meaning. and Identity,* Cambridge: Cambridge University Press.

Wilson, D. C. (undated) Bluefish Science in the Northeast Region: a case study. Hirtshals, Denmark: Institute for Fisheries Management and Coastal Community Development.

Wilson, D. C. (1999), Fisheries science collaborations: the critical role of community. Hirtshals, Denmark: Institute for Fisheries Management and Coastal Community Development.

Wondolleck, J. M. and Yaffee, S. L. (2000), *Making Collaboration Work: Lessons from Innovation in Natural Resource Management,* Washington, DC: Island Press.

Wynne, B. (1982), *Rationality and Ritual: The Windscale Inquiry and Nuclear Decisions,* Chalfont St Giles, Bucks, UK: British Society for the History of Science.

Yankelovich, D. (1991), *Coming to Public Judgment,* Syracuse, NY: Syracuse University Press.

Yankelovich, D. (1999), *The Magic of Dialogue: Transforming Conflict into Cooperation,* New York: Simon and Schuster.

Yanow, D. (2000), *Conducting Interpretive Policy Analysis,* Thousand Oaks, CA: Sage Publications.

Index